To Doctor Lorenz
from
Ella W. Wallace

for who enjoys travelling

A MONKEY'S TALE

The Epic True Story of a Man, a Monkey and 32,000 Miles of Uncharted Adventure

Thillman Wallace

With Mary Katzke

Chugiak, Alaska

Cover art by Mary Katzke
Interior book design by Lizzie Newell
Published by Mary Katzke

ISBN-13: 978-1930222212

Acknowledgments

This book would not have been finished without the assistance of Ella Wallace, Stephanie LeProwse, Mike Wallace, Troy Henkels, Mary Wasche, Noland Powell, Christie DeMolina, Tessa Dennis, Aaron Dennis and Rozina Thompson, and the Chugach Writers Group.

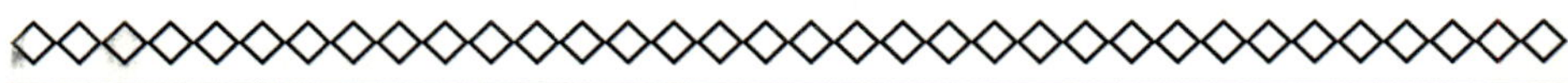
ARCTIC SEA
GREENLAND
BAFFIN BAY
BERING SEA
HUDSON BAY
CANADA
NORTH PACIFIC OCEAN
NORTH ATLANTIC OCEAN
UNITED STATES
MEXICO
GULF OF MEXICO
BRAZIL
SOUTH PACIFIC OCEAN
SOUTH ATLANTIC OCEAN

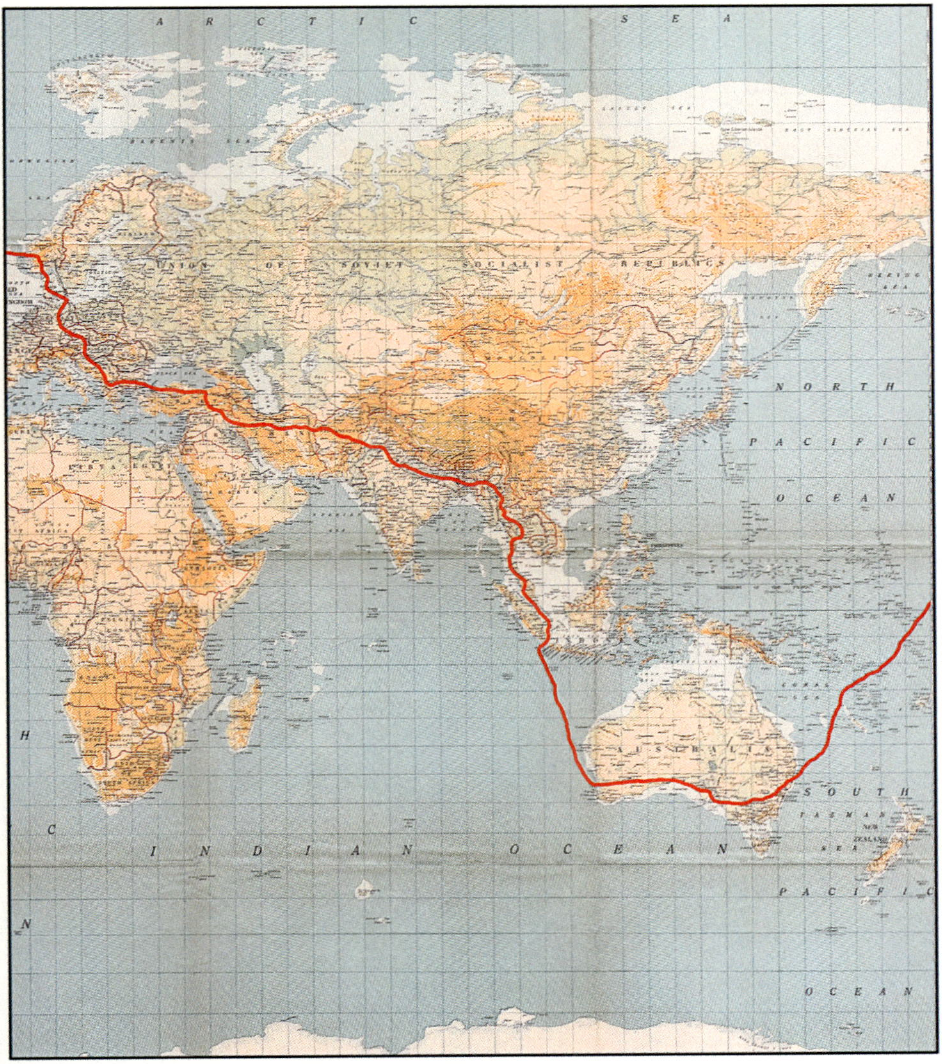

Thillman's travels to Alaska around the world the long way, 32,000 miles.

Contents

"This book is dedicated to all those people of conflicting nations who helped me along my journey. It's not the masses that create turmoil; it's a few at the top who keep things messed up."

Thillman Wallace

An Introduction
by Co-Author Mary Katzke

TO GET TO Thillman Wallace's home in January 2015, one must drive up a harrowing road named Packhorse Trail carved out of the side of a mountain in the small, scattered rural town of Chugiak, Alaska. Up past Klondike Concrete, a business started by the Wallace Brothers, the road is freshly snow-covered and icy, composed of sharp switchbacks knifing their shoulder-less, jagged way along the edge of a steep drop off into birch trees clinging to the side of the earth. Along the way we see relics of times past: beautiful wagon wheels, wooden mining cars with a history of their own, a sleigh once pulled by horses, and the "Funferall" a Chris Craft that belonged to Howard Hughes himself still awaiting restoration. Clutching the wheel, we continue on past hand carved totem poles weathered to Alaskan perfection and a deserted saw mill.

In 1960, Thillman, his wife, Ella and his brother, Mike Wallace, homesteaded three hundred twenty acres in Alaska up past what is now called Skyline Drive in Eagle River. The mountain, currently known as Wallace Mountain, sits at the entrance to Chugach State Park and Mount Baldy's Trailhead hiking area high above the community. After three unsuccessful attempts to live above the clouds (vandals, arson and bears) they decided to build at a lower elevation. In 1965, Thillman purchased land in Chugiak where their solid log home has been perched ever since completion in 1970.

The front entrance to this perch looks out over the vast Knik Arm tidal flats and the grand, majestic "Mount McKinley" also commonly known as "Denali", the highest mountain peak in North America. One hundred and fifty miles of the spectacular Alaska Range sprawl out in the distance with all its splendid glory. The walkway approaching the front door is adorned with an accumulation of treasures that speak of a long life of adventures, including rustic tools from years of hard work and the bicycle once ridden from Vancouver to Anchorage over the gravel "Alcan Highway" also known as the "Alaska Highway" by wife, Ella.

Thillman's daughter, Stephanie, 45, a fit, outdoorsy mother of four, answers the door. Her love and dedication to the man who raised her is apparent in every move she makes, a reflection of his character and own depth of kindness. She grew up on this land, a viable player in many of her father's manic visions. Entering the Wallace home is like stepping out of the 21st century and back into time when Alaska was a land of hardy pioneers. The giant log beams supporting the structure are magnificent and imposing, each hand peeled by the Wallaces. A fireplace of monumental proportion captures our focus, created of red brick and-made by the Wallace brothers' and now timeworn from years of hearty fires. Large windows from either side reveal the spectacular vista. Alaskan artwork hangs from the walls, each piece with personal meaning. A walrus painting, once a wedding gift, stands out amidst family heirlooms and small treasures from around the world, framed by a vast collection of family photos.

Ella works quietly in another room, respectfully giving us privacy to speak freely of times preceding their union. Brother Mike listens thoughtfully while parakeets chirp in the background, two dogs wag their tails full of excitement and a domesticated duck takes a swim in the guest bathroom's large porcelain tub.

Yet, of all the iconic symbols of a full and interesting life, one battered machete (see photo 1) and a raggedy jacket with tears of monkey claws on the right shoulder are the emblems he has brought forward to set the stage to begin sharing the story he so passionately wishes to tell: one man, one monkey, facing challenges usually found only in fiction, all crisply immortalized through journals and recalled with a sense of detail that most can only dream of having at any age, never mind 82.

Now this burning tale is barely whispered between sips of water. He is hobbled with a mysterious disease robbing him of the use of his limbs, his blue eyes are watery, almost filmy- but his determination to tell this remarkable story from his bedside remains strong enough to carry him through the telling of his tale.

Using tools not even imagined during his epic journey, we lean in expectantly, captivated, and bearing with honor this privilege and enormous responsibility. Fingers ready at the keyboard,

iPhone set to record, digital camera softly clicking away…we are

…ready to go back in time, to the very beginning of his epic saga.

Chapter 1:

Growing Toward My Journey

BEFORE I GET STARTED on my saga of how I came to travel over 32,000 miles with my pet monkey Chin, I want you to know I consider myself one lucky person from the get go. Our brick two-story home in Upstate New York, with an old mill built in 1812, stood on a peaceful three and a half-acre plot of land with a creek, pond and waterfall, and was filled with loving parents and my two brothers, Art and Mike. I rode my bicycle to school where I was a decent student in a class of thirty-two. No genius, but I managed to be in school plays, and even become senior class president. I raised a bit of hell, once putting a fox head in my teacher's desk and scaring the bejeesus out of her. But I wasn't mean.

My father, the son of an immigrant from Germany who came over in 1876, was the Branch Manager of a machine shop. He was always well-dressed, even when he towed us around on our toboggan. Dad would bring a briefcase home every night with his "homework". We had a car, even when I was real young and no one else did. We took road trips. We weren't rich but felt like we were. Mom was an excellent cook and made us picnics outside during the summer. My parents taught us to be strong but gentle; to be a bully was forbidden. The advertising slogan of Kleenex at the time was "tough, but oh so gentle." The ad showed a big square-jawed man almost looking like a bulldog- using a tissue. Never in my lifetime did I hear my father say an unkind word to my mother. That impressed me. None of us imagined that in a few short years, I'd be hungry, sick and scrabbling for life in a Malaysian ditch.

THE KIDS I hung around with weren't perfect. They stole grapes and shot birds which bothered me. One even shoplifted a candy bar. The worst thing I ever did as a kid was to throw a bottle through the window of an abandoned house. It got stuck in the screen and that image has always stayed with me. I felt any time I was reprimanded, I deserved it. Today I see so many screwed up families; the children don't stand a chance.

I read a lot and three books stayed imprinted on my mind: "*Barefoot Abe*", shown with an axe outside a log home he'd made with his own hands; "*They Were Strong and Good*" about one family's journey through American history; and "*Ferdinand the Bull*" where the strongest bull was the meanest. The hero, a younger bull sat under a tree, ate flowers and pranced around the ring still winning in the end, spending the rest of his days eating flowers and grass. The lesson was: be tough, but oh, so gentle. If you've got it, you don't have to show it. My parents raised us with that philosophy.

We weren't into sports- and proud of it. We *worked* after school. We worked on farms baling hay and other chores, worked on estates, did gardening, and cut grass. My older brother, Art, was the entrepreneur in the family and raised 3,000 chickens, while I raised pigs, 100 ducks, sheep and dogs. He had the first lemonade stand and we started a bait shop together called Mill Pond Bait and Tackle. We made little dams out of concrete on the creek and raised our own minnows. We sold shiners, chubs, and night crawlers. We let people try out their rods and reels on our pond before they bought them. Those were happy days and perhaps not predictably likely to spawn the bold adventure I embarked upon.

The day that changed the course of my otherwise storybook life was December 7, 1941. I had been playing in the yard, hungrily awaiting the Sunday dinner bell when I was called in to find my parents in the kitchen, embracing and weeping. I had rarely seen my mother emotional, and to see my father crying was deeply troubling. We learned that the "Japs" had invaded Pearl Harbor. My brother Mike ran outside with his BB gun and started firing at the sky. From that moment forward, we would do anything to stand up for our country, not to mention soothe our distraught parents. I resolved to fight- and die, if necessary- for my country. I couldn't wait to finish high school so I could enlist and fight those Commies. Instead, I felt compelled to honor my parents' desire that I attend college for at least one year.

During the summer after high school, I had my first experience living away from home where I worked as a "pond monkey" at my uncle's saw mill in Idaho. My job was to straddle and jockey logs in the river to sort and direct them. It was a taste of the life I would come to love seeing new places, taking on new challenges, and glimpsing just how much the world varied and offered.

College was the worst time of my life. I wanted to be over in Korea. Doing the right thing: getting killed for my country. I was that gung-ho.

Right after school got out the following June, I went to join up. A social studies and history teacher of ours, Noland Powell, had come back from the war (WWII). He had jumped into France with the paratroopers and made it back and he spoke well of his experiences. I remember going to the enlistment center in Buffalo to sign up for the army in June 1952. I wanted to go to Korea so bad I virtually begged. Guys who didn't want to go were being sent. Special Forces was just being organized while I was in my sixteen weeks of basic training.

Basic training at Fort Dix sometimes meant eighteen-mile marches in very humid, hot, sandy conditions. Many fellow officers would just pass out from carrying their backpacks and rifles. On one trip, I carried seven M1s weighing 9.4 pounds each for six other guys and myself, two on each shoulder, two across my back, and one in my arms. That's how good my physical condition was because I was straight from working on farms and landscaping. The sergeants would often use me as the first one to go through an obstacle course to show how it's done. 'Gold Brick' was someone who didn't carry his own load. A Polish guy in our unit could do everything fancy, spit'n polish, but when it came time to hit the dirt, he would kneel down, and then lay down. I was proud that I could do the hard work, and was no gold brick.

During that time we learned SF (Special Forces) was a branch of the OSS (Office of Strategic Services). Spy work. That really intrigued me. It would be on par with the rangers. I'd already volunteered for jump school, so I signed up for the 10th SF Group Airborne under Colonel Aaron Bank, founder of the US Army Special Forces later known as the "Green Berets". When I was in his office being interviewed for that position, on the wall behind him was a puzzling black and white photograph of him leading a platoon of goose-stepping Germans, and yet he was an American. Years later during his retirement years, Bank played a quiet but critical role in warning the nation about the risks of terrorism and modern technology and he was largely responsible for the high level of security at U.S. nuclear power plants since the early 1970s.

Accepted quickly into SF, I was assigned to HQ Company. My immediate superior was Colonel Ewald who had been responsible for getting a whole division of German soldiers to surrender. The way it was explained, you could either go to Korea and fight man to man, one on one, or in SF you could have a much broader impact by destroying a bunch of planes. As a kid when we played hide and seek, everyone else went in a straight line but I would go way around, fooling the others. This was the most challenging thing I had ever faced, and I was smitten.

In jump school, we had to have five jumps in three weeks of training to qualify as a paratrooper. (see photo 2) It's often six months later before you have your next jump. When I exited the plane on my 6th jump, I jumped too far, with a bad body position. Because I leapt so far out, the propeller blast blew me into my chute, dissecting it into two smaller chutes making it look like a brassiere. I was one of the last men out and one of the first men down. As I was going down (we were jumping at about 1,000 feet) in a twenty-mile an hour wind, I saw this jeep with a big red cross on it racing towards me. The drop zone officer in charge spotted me and yelled with a bullhorn "Hey, you got a Mae West" (Mae West: early movie star with great big boobs). I hollered back "Yeah, I know it." He hollered, "Pull your reserve!" and I yanked. It popped open just as I hit the ground. When I hit, I whacked my head and the wind dragged me away. The sand in the chute release strap had made it hard to manage. Once I got up, I helped another guy out of his chute and went back to chow. Shortly after, I started to not feel so good, started seeing double. I went outside and was waiting for a car to pass, but it turned out the car wasn't moving. After a four-day hospital stay, I was diagnosed with a 'delayed concussion'. I was still able to make eleven additional jumps before completing training. By the time I got shipped to Germany, I was focused and ready, trained and determined.

We were sent to radio school with an interesting outfit of 800 physically fit, intelligent men. We were stationed in Bavaria at a camp that was like a castle, where Hitler had trained his SS troops. In his office, Colonel Banks showed us a civilian suitcase that was actually a hidden military radio. Compact and adaptable to many types of power supplies, this would be a clandestine necessity. Without this type of equipment it would not have been possible to relay information about German troop movements and intended

Luftwaffe bombing targets in the U.K. (which ultimately led to the saving of countless lives). We were in: hook, line and sinker.

Being in good physical shape, I liked to test my endurance and wiles on weekends. I'd set goals during my leave time in Europe to see how far I could go, and still get back on time, without spending much money. (see photo) They held a "greased pig competition" where the winner got a three-day pass. * I got that little guy, but didn't stick around to eat him. I had three entire days to see how far I could go, and make it back. One time I had twenty-three days and sixty-three dollars. I took a sleeping bag (I'd sleep anyplace that was free) and hitchhiked over the Alps to Venice and got all the way to the southern tip of Sardinia, broke. These weekend jaunts turned out to be invaluable preparation for the challenges that would come later.

By the time all my training was completed, I was practically frothing at the mouth to get to the action. I could see it, smell it, and feel it. I had *earned* it, and I was ready.

But life had other ideas. By June of 1955, the war was essentially over.

To say that I was "greatly disappointed" is an understatement like none other. I had conditioned to my physical peak and was primed to fight and be brave, but I would not be going into combat. Devastated, lost, missing a purpose- all of that, and so much more. I was like a tightly coiled spring, with no place to release all that had built up in me. I couldn't simply go home like my fellow soldiers were doing. I craved adventure, and I would not be disappointed this time. I immediately went to Alaska to help my brothers launch the concrete business where I made enough money to take off.

And that is how I came to take a 32,000-mile trip from Australia to Alaska, where my brothers would be waiting for my return to help their business venture already on a measly $400 with a mischievous monkey named Chin.

In case you were wondering.

Chapter 2:

Suddenly Solo in Sydney

"Now that I'm this old, and wiser, I realize it was not that I was brave. It's probably a good thing I wasn't aware of all that was going on. Here I was going out into no man's land, thinking nothing of it. The beauty of it all was that like a drunk, or a baby, I was so naïve, so ignorant."

T.W. December 2014

I SPENT MY last night in Sydney sleeping under a Eucalyptus tree on the lawn of one of my gardening customers. I wanted to finish up a bit of hedge trimming early the next morning before starting the journey home to Alaska. My buddy Ed and I had spent the last nine months in Australia attending Sydney University under the G.I. Bill. We'd lived in a run-down apartment in Glebe, where Ed had spent much of his time in bed due to an acute bout with pneumonia, and several relapses. Ed and I had planned to hitch our way westward around the world by any means possible, provided it was cheap. Besides failing health, he had found himself in a bit of trouble with the Australian police after getting busted for importing cars for re-sale under a false bank account. Too many Cadillacs showed up at the port at one time and the usual bribed official was off that day. He was abruptly forced to leave the country.

That left me to make the journey alone.

I'd managed to save four hundred dollars by working as a streetcar conductor and gardener while attending the university. With that amount, I hoped to be able to get some 20,000 miles (turned out to be quite a bit more) within a few months. I'd already booked and paid for passage from Perth to Singapore- on a livestock ship slated to carry 3,000 head of sheep. All I had to do was get across the continent from Sydney to Perth before the ship sailed in three weeks.

Little did I know what lay ahead.

SLEEPING ON THE damp lawn that last morning was uncomfortable, and I constantly felt that a funnel web spider was looking for me. I had caught several of the deadly creatures on that very lawn prior to bedding down. I awoke early after a restless night and hurriedly finished my work so I could get on my way. I left Sydney about noon, laden with a pack containing sixty pounds of gear on my back. (see photo 4) I was aiming to make the five thousand kilometer journey on "Australia's longest straight road" to Perth in twenty-one days or less so I could catch the ship to Singapore. My pack was filled with everything from necessities like my passport and maps to a three pound Argus C3 Polaroid camera to just-in-case items like a military surplus gas mask and a business suit. I would eventually come to regret nearly everything I was carrying, but it would take me awhile to determine what could be left behind.

Rides were easy to get on the populated east coast, and the weather was warm so I had nothing to complain about as I started my journey. Mountains of baled hay dotted the flat plains west of Sydney for livestock feed reserves in the event of a drought. However, the Murray River was flooding much of the land right then (http://en.wikipedia.org/wiki/1956_Murray_River_flood) so the hay looked sodden and out of place. Nearby, hundreds of square miles of grazing land and grain fields were burning furiously with flames enveloping not only the land, but also bagged grain, stock, and implements as well. Farming across southern Australia seemed to be more of a gamble than the profits could possibly warrant.

That first night on the road, I caught a ride in the back of a small Ford truck that was headed a couple of hundred miles west toward Perth. The sky was filled with a plethora of stars and I fell asleep lying on my back against my pack looking up in wonder as we rode along. I had earned this lift by helping another trucker load sixteen tons of vinyl siding. The road was washed out in several places so we had to take a jarring detour through miles of Bunya Pine and Blue-leaved Stringybark trees, which disrupted any hopes for sleeping. At one point, we got hung up on a leaning

Gum tree, but after a bit of maneuvering and damage to the side of the Ford, we were able to roar forward.

To my dismay, the further west I got, the more abundant the biting, swarming Australian bush flies became. They left nasty swollen red marks on my arms and neck and were hard to escape. That was one thing I knew I would not have to worry about once I made it back to Alaska. No bugs, other than mosquitoes and for sure- no snakes!

While we were lunching at a dusty roadside cafe, a couple of young, ragtag boys pulled up on their beat-up Harley Davidson motorcycle. Their cycle was covered with slain rabbits, forty in all, which they had caught that morning in their forty traps. We'd seen hundreds of rabbits earlier in the day, but I never realized they were so easy to trap. The boys claimed that they often got as many as 120 bunnies in a day. They told us they skinned them and sold them for meat and were making a small fortune at it, reminding me of Art, my entrepreneurial brother and our bait shop venture.

I learned that in 1859 a release by the First Fleet triggered a population explosion in Australia where none existed prior to that. It was not long before millions of rabbits roamed the entire continent because there were no natural enemies and they multiply like, well, rabbits. They destroyed crops to such an extent that the Aussies built a rabbit-proof fence stretching the full width of their country in an effort to keep the rabbits contained to one side. But soon, there were countless rabbits on both sides of the fence, and the Aussies took to introducing the myxoma virus which causes myxomatosis, a disease known for blindness leading to starvation (they can't find food) and this trimmed the population- but only for a short time.

The Aussies are a mighty proud of their Sydney Harbor Bridge as it is the largest- but not the longest- arch span in the world referred to by locals as the Coathanger due to its design. Apart from this, there are few bridges in the rest of Australia. The recent thirty-foot flood resulting from higher rainfalls than average in North Queensland had washed away the Murray River Bridge which spanned the river between Parniga and Renmark and is still considered the biggest catastrophe in South Australia's history. Had the flood not spared the train trestle, which crossed at this point, it would have been necessary to detour one hundred fifty miles just to go from Parniga to Renmark, geographically separated by less than two miles. Vehicles were loaded onto the flat cars to cross but I took a wooden bench in the passenger car and crossed for six pence. The flood had hit Renmark hard, but now that the waters were receding, the Aussies were busily cleaning up the debris and repairing washed out roads. As a result of the flood, the Menindee Lakes were constructed to store high flows from the Darling River.

A few small boys pushing an old tire gathered about me as I plodded down the remnants of the main street lugging my large pack. "Good day, soldier" they said in friendly voices passing the tire back and forth. "You had best fill your water bag, and get yourself a camel, for a camel does not need water," they advised me once I told them I was going to cross the vast Nullarbor Plains to Perth. I thanked them for their sound advice, even though I realized that camels might be hard to obtain today in Australia. I had seen a handful of signs stating “Please don’t ask for water-as refusal often offends,” so I knew I had to prepare wisely.

A road grader operator working the flood repairs gave me a lift in his machine a couple of miles over a levee. While crossing the levee we noticed the top of a sign, which read "THIS ROAD FOR DRY WEATHER USE ONLY". We shared a chuckle at what was obviously an unnecessary notice, since the road referred to could not even be seen due to complete submersion in an ocean of water.

Arriving in Adelaide the next morning I parked my gear and self in a pub and killed a few cooling beers. Aussie beer is some of the best; so good in fact that law required them to close from 6PM until 7PM- otherwise the Aussies would forget to go home for dinner. I tried to line up a ride with transcontinental carting companies to Perth but because it was too close to the Christmas holidays- I was out of luck. The trains and planes to Perth were booked up for a month in advance, not that I could have afforded them anyway. Since the day was shot I decided to spend the night at a cheap lodge on the top of Mount Lofty some fourteen miles distant. The train took me part way up the mountain and I wasted the next five hours looking for the Mount Lofty Lodge because none of the local inhabitants knew exactly where to find it. I followed many well-intentioned leads without results. It was getting mighty cool and to satisfy a growling stomach I wolfed down the only food I possessed, a large jar of sweet, sticky plum jam. This fortified me to the extent that I continued to look for the evasive lodge until midnight, when, alas, it appeared at the end of one of many tangled foot trails with a sign on the door "CLOSED FOR THE WINTER." And my escapades for the evening were not yet over.

Catching the last train back to Adelaide, I began to look for a suitable place to bed down immediately upon disembarking. I was feeling quite weary and did not need any further delays to sleep. A distraught young woman with long dark hair came dashing out of the police station I was passing by. I did what I could to avoid being drawn in to her problem- whatever it might be.

"The police will not listen to me," she shouted as she approached.

I shrugged and kept walking. "My husband beat me again tonight, and they will not arrest him!" This time I pretended I couldn't hear. "The fools, I'll teach them to ignore me!" she shrieked. And with that, she pulled off her left shoe and attacked the police motorcycle, which was parked at the curb, bashing in both headlights and the tail light with her shoe. She broke the speedometer glass before replacing her damaged shoe on her foot. She was simply hysterical.

"I need a cab, Love, give me two bob," she commanded. By now I was a good ten yards down the road. "You cheap bastard," she shouted when I refused. "Maybe that will learn the cops to believe me the next time," she sobbed as she rounded the corner disappearing into the darkness.

I came back to stare stupidly at the damaged cycle, wondering why I had not been more forceful in trying to prevent her destructive display when a Commonwealth police officer in a formal navy blue uniform casually strolled up from the building. I stood up straight and respectfully not wanting to appear guilty of the crime. After questioning me briefly, the officer explained that the upset woman often pulled such stunts for she was "a bit insane". We shared a conspiratorial nod and I went about seeking my nighttime shelter knowing he was unlikely to give me any trouble.

I ended up sleeping comfortably under a eucalyptus yet again. I loved the peeling bark, and the sound of wind through their papery leaves but more than anything, the scent, by now quite familiar. I rested soundly and was able to rise early and be well away from Adelaide before noon. I caught a ride from a rancher who didn't want to chat which was fine by me. The sun was setting when we pulled in to Port Pirie, a small but filthy seaport just a short detour from the National Highway. Not being able to afford the luxury of a hotel I decided to spend the night in the nearest vacant lot. My confidence had been growing as the Outback became my territory, until a voice called after me.

"Where do you think you're going, Yank?" I turned around to find two blokes, one skinny and one burly, jeering at me. The area was dark and isolated.

"I'm trying to get to Perth," I said, deciding to play them as friends verses foes with my tone. I stood waiting a beat as they appraised my pack. I felt a quickening in my heart and had to work to keep my breathing controlled.

"Come on, we'll fix you up for the night, let's have a few beers."

Even though I was half expecting them to roll me before the night was over, I consented. The three of us proceeded to the nearest pub. One does not merely drink beer in Australia, one *swills*, so it was not long before we were all in a gay mood. I spent the night at the home of the skinny bloke after his wife who was in a foul mood, left the house for the night. Imagine not being happy with three smelly drunks in the house-the gall. Regardless, it was a notch above sleeping in a vacant lot.

At noon the next day I was west of Port Augusta, and on the edge of Nullarbor Plains. The Nullarbor, extremely hot, dry and almost devoid of humans, stretches for over a thousand miles, and ranches are hundreds of miles apart. The landscape is dotted with skeletal remains of all kinds of creatures. Many hopeful travelers had also perished as they crossed the Nullarbor because if one's car breaks down, it is only a matter of hours before the hot sun dehydrates the human body, depriving it of life.

It was early afternoon when I was dropped off by the car that had given me a short lift. I watched it turn down one of the unfrequented trails leading to a lonely ranch. Since it was just a few days till Christmas, the driver had invited me to spend the Christmas holiday on his ranch, some twenty miles from the main route. I reluctantly declined his generous offer, explaining that I had to catch one of the few ships that sail from Perth to Singapore within the following weeks and couldn't chance any delays.

I stripped down to a pair of shorts and the warm, dusty red sand felt good between my toes. A slouch hat protected my head from the direct rays of the sun, which was necessary. From atop a small knoll, I could view hundreds of miles around and it seemed strange not to see a house, person or a single thing that suggested man had ever set foot in that area.

Being a foreigner to Australia, I was fairly ignorant of the type of wildlife to expect in the Outback. I noticed a group of Acacia bushes that looked as if they could form a shelter for some large animal and felt my first touch of fear imagining hostile aborigines returning to their encampment that evening. Or perhaps the primitive nest belonged to some strange animal like a hopping kangaroo or nocturnal marsupial. In either event, I became ill at ease, nervous and hungry, an unhappy combination. Rabbits were numerous, darting from every scrubby bush. I had not eaten since yesterday and had failed to procure any rations out or sheer stupidity. This was one failure I seem doomed to repeat. The bones and skulls of sheep were all about me, so I began lobbing them at the evasive rabbits, hoping to stun one long enough to catch it. But they were much quicker than I, and my stomach rumbled persistently. The only hope was to catch a ride to a more urban setting.

From the top of the knoll I could see dust billowing to the east. I grabbed my cumbersome pack and ran down to the roadside, waiting as the cloud of swirling dust came nearer. I waited and waited; but it was only a dust devil.

I gulped down the remainder of my water supply. I figured it would be better this way. If I did not get a ride by nightfall, I'd be so thirsty that I could spend the cool evening looking for water rather than being driven blind in search of it in the dehydrating sun. Perhaps I could even make my way back to the kind rancher's house before sun up.

During the next several hours I hustled from the shade of the brush back to the open road several more times, certain that a car was approaching, but each time finding it to be another dust devil. My morale was sinking along with the sun when I finally saw a real car approaching! I stood by the side of the road and desperately flagged it down. The car came nearer, and roared past, leaving me choking in its wake. At first my heart sank, but as soon as the dust settled, I could see that an FJ Holden with cages full of chickens strapped to its trunk had come to a halt several hundred feet up the road. While the hens clucked and ruffled their feathers in weak attempts to shake off some dust, I hoisted my gear and wasted no time running for it, jumping in and off we sped. The driver, a young British bloke, explained that the dust and setting sun had temporarily blinded him. He handed me a bottle of the hottest beer I ever drank, but under the circumstances- it was exquisite. We stopped once in awhile so he could give the gasping hens a few sips of his beer. They'd been riding in a crate tied to the back of his car all day, and they were a bit windblown and thirsty to say the least. Besides, they quieted after each "dose". All too soon I was dropped along the highway while he turned up a side road. I rolled out the sleeping bag and smoked a pipeful of tobacco for supper.

A week into my trip, I was starting to get into a rhythm of getting up with the sun and hitting my sleeping bag not long after it went down. I liked to think of the sun as my clock and the stars as my nightlight. By dawn the next morning, luck was on my side because within two hours I had a lift. Ceduna was the next stop, a town of perhaps five hundred inhabitants. Crested on a cliff overlooking the vast aqua-colored ocean, I could immediately feel a soothing breeze. I took a dip in the waters of the Great Australian Bight (ocean bay) first thing. It was cold but invigorating, and it felt good to be clean again after days on the dusty road with no proper bath, and especially since it was the day before Christmas.

The day before Christmas, I splurged and bought a meal in a dumpy little café called McKenzie's. To prevent future hunger, I purchased Anzac bread, some Quandong peaches, carrots and a pound of cold cuts and some "Vegemite". I wasn't sure what it was but had noticed all the locals considered it a staple. By noon I had walked a couple of miles out of town to find myself once again surrounded by nothing but salt bush and sand for as far as the eye could see. I waited unsuccessfully all afternoon for a ride but there was no traffic due to the holidays. As evening came I built a fire, and dined alone beside it. What a rotten way to spend Christmas Eve. No snow, no tree, no Santa, no gifts, no family, no friends, no one to talk to, not even a ride; nothing but flies and more flies, saltbush, sand and a churning mind full of thoughts. I was trying to ignore some small pangs of loneliness that rose unexpectedly. I guess holidays can bring that out in a person. At first the feeling was in the background, quiet but gnawing. Before sleep came, I realized that I had never before experienced such loneliness. It would continue to grow until I met my traveling companion in Asia, but we'll come to that.

I awoke Christmas morning to hear Christmas carols drifting over the desert sands. Apparently some church was amplifying them over a loudspeaker. The carols struck me as being out of place in my present mood. I ate bread and carrots for breakfast, and spread a bit of Vegemite on my bread not finding it to be particularly satisfying. I later learned the brown paste was made from leftover brewer's yeast and various "vegetable and spice additives". Since I had finished my drinking water, I walked back to Ceduna to refill my canteen. It was 1,250 miles to Perth from Ceduna, a greater distance than the average person would care to give a lift to a stranger. Two blokes pulled up at a nearby gas station, driving another Holden, popular as they were assembled right in Australia. I ran over to them, introduced myself and asked if by any chance, they might be headed towards Perth. They were! But they quickly added that they had no room for a rider. And then perhaps because it was Christmas Day, they reconsidered and said that there would be room for me as soon as they rearranged their luggage. My morale soared-things were definitely looking up. Finally- a Christmas present!

"The least I can do is to buy you blokes a beer." They took me up on the offer. Only one pub was open but as you can imagine, it was booming. Would-be drinkers were forcing themselves through the windows as the queue at the door was so long. We elbowed our way in and the three of us managed to squeeze into one corner. Blokes were eight deep all around the bar. A husky red-faced German was perched atop the piano playing jazzed up Christmas carols on a classic accordion. The Aussies had figured out a way for the German to drink without interrupting his accordion playing. Every five minutes a bloke would stand atop the piano and pour some frothy beer into the Kraut's cavernous mouth. Above boisterous cheers, Pete and Ken introduced themselves. I would be spending the next several days with them en-route to Perth. As we barged out of the pub the same way we came in, I could not help but think the second half of the trip across the continent would be relatively easy. The three of us were in the best of spirits as we hopped in the car and pressed on down the dusty Eyre Highway toward Perth. (see photo 5)

We reached Penong in short order, where after waiting an hour we had a delicious Christmas dinner complete with Pavlova for dessert. I was a bit reluctant to part with the three dollars it cost because I knew that I would have to go hungry some time in the future to make up for this extravagance. I guess I was just swept up in the joyful spirit of my traveling mates.

Crossing Nullarbor proved to be hot, dusty and monotonous. There was little variation in scenery. Looking in all directions we could see nothing but level horizons; there was not even a knoll to break the irregularity. Sluggish lizards were the only form of life we encountered for hundreds of miles. We had stopped to refill the gas tank and to check the radiator when Ken noticed a rabbit. He killed it with one shot from his .22. The bunny was too scrawny to eat, so we buried it with much ceremony, feeling sorry that we had killed it when it obviously had had to work so hard to subsist on a starvation diet. Pete then brewed a Billycan of tea and we supped in the middle of the Eyre Highway. Fortunately, we had a few rations with us. We did not have to fear oncoming traffic since we had not seen a vehicle in the last two hundred miles. Given the lack of traffic, and scarcity of produce, we drove well into the night until we reached Eucla.

Eucla consisted of less than half a dozen stone buildings, which were practically buried by the huge shifting sand dunes. The nights were as chilly as the days were hot on the Nullarbor so the sight of a bonfire in the distance compelled us forward. It was here that we met a young couple with a small tow-headed baby who had attempted to drive from Perth to Adelaide to spend Christmas with their relatives. Christmas Day had passed by a few hours ago. This was as far as they had gotten due to the blowouts and insufficient funds to replace the tires leaving them stranded here three days. They had no blankets and the poor Cherub of a baby had a bad cold. We brewed some tea on their bonfire. I served them a canful as the youthful couple huddled together, the baby between them, in the front seat of their dilapidated pick-up truck. We offered them some of our clothing but they refused, saying that we would need it ourselves. I slept on the rocky ground while Pete and Ken grabbed a bit of shut-eye in the car. Encounters like these leave lasting impressions. I found myself worrying about their well-being far into the night and even to this day wonder what became of the little baby with a cold sleeping in the Nullabar desert. I made a mental inventory of any extras I had- including the half-finished container of Vegemite, and made sure to leave it by the truck sheltering the sleeping family. It was all I could do to keep from taking my jacket off and placing if over them.

We spent a cold, restless night and were more than ready to hit the road again long before the break of dawn. We purchased some gas in Madura, as well as a greasy breakfast of "mixed grill", a combination of three types of scrap meat, and washed it down with a couple of beers. During the day we stopped several times to shoot at White-bellied Sea Eagles, which could be found, perched atop power poles every few miles. We could hear the .22 shells ricochet off the feather-matted creatures, powerless to penetrate them. In each case the eagle would sluggishly flap his wings and swoop away. We judged their wingspread to be over six feet. We passed a few semi-civilized aborigines, who gave the impression of living a pitiful, lethargic existence, lacking the schooling to cope with today's machines or society. Yet they were not so primitive that they were satisfied with their struggle for survival on

Nullarbor. Their forbearers still inhabit certain areas of the Nullarbor. Since they do not come in contact with western culture they appear content with their own, perhaps the world's most backward people I had ever seen. It is the people who live on the fringe of two or more cultures who seem constantly in conflict with themselves and or their societies, unless they accept one or the other explicitly. Later I came to know such a person, and perhaps I, too, recognized I was becoming a man wavering precariously between cultures.

We reached Kalgoorlie by midnight and sacked out in a vacant lot. Kalgoorlie has long been the heart of Australia's gold mining area. It is a town with red dusty streets, shabby dwellings, and an over-abundance of beer, women, and gambling. Isolated as all the other towns in the Nullarbor, living in such a place might give the impression that the town itself was the whole world, or at least the end of it. Isolation and dust; that will be my memory of southern Australia.

The remainder of the day in Kalgoorlie was about trying to forget the heat and sand of the last few days. In order to fulfill this ambition we found it necessary to visit many of the local pubs. We won a few quid on the slot machines. A kindly old woman with hazel eyes and striking grey accents in her hair let us use her spider-filled woodshed as a bathhouse. We found an old tub, filled it with buckets of water from a nearby storage bin and before long the three of us almost looked presentable again. (Water is piped four hundred miles across the plains from Perth to Kalgoorlie.)

The drive from Kalgoorlie to Perth became more scenic as we progressed west. Nothing like driving a flat barren desert for days to make us appreciate rolling hills, flowers, trees, and animals- other than reptiles- once more.

We arrived in Perth before the pubs closed for the night. Ken and Pete booked in at a hotel and let me leave my gear with them. Having only my sleeping bag for company I toured Perth on foot looking for a suitable place to sack out. I climbed over a high fence into what appeared to be a beautiful park where I found a comfortable bed of pine needles to sleep on after crawling under some low evergreen branches. Had the bugs not been so hungry, nor the pedestrians so boisterous my sleep would have been sounder.

I awoke the next morning to find a policeman looking into the shrubbery nearby, obviously looking for derelicts like myself. I wasted no time in making a fast exit from my garden bedroom. I was on the sidewalk side of the fence in a flash! In daylight I noticed a sign in the haven I had just left which made me laugh aloud at my ignorant brazenness. It read: "GOVERNMENT HOUSE."

Chapter 3:

Killing Time in Perth

THE SHIP WOULD not leave for Singapore for ten days, which meant I had some time to explore this interesting coastal city. I had loaned two hundred dollars from my stash to a friend back in Sydney and had hoped to find it waiting for me upon my arrival in Perth. After gallivanting across the continent celebrating the holidays with beer-drinking mates, my funds were about nil. I figured the best use of this hiatus would be to work for additional income. I hitched to the outskirts of Perth, which is in the "grain belt of Australia" and tried to obtain work in a grain storage area and on farms- but no luck. If the money did not arrive before my ship sailed for Singapore I would be disembarking in Asia flat broke. It was not a pleasant thing to think about. My passport had been forwarded to me from Canberra, but without any of the visas I had requested. This meant I might become stranded in Singapore indefinitely due to lack of funds and without authority to cross national boundaries on foot.

I tried to keep my concern to myself but it was very much on my mind when I went to meet Pete and Ken at their hotel. After a few beers we went down to Roe Street, a most notorious street in Australia catering to the sale of the flesh. A real old-fashioned "red light district" reminiscent of what I imagined the Wild West was like in its hay day. One side of the street is lined with railroad tracks, while the other is lined with perhaps thirty whorehouses. A high board fence lines the sidewalk in front of each house. Men queue up by the hundreds to wait their turn for a rendezvous with the damsels who would at least take their cash, if not satisfy their customers. Several women, ranging from Oriental and exotic to dark and Aboriginal, sat wearing delicate lacey lingerie on the front porches of each establishment, protected from the eager male mob by heavy wire mesh screening. The majority of the clientele were new Australian immigrants, mainly southern European, who had difficulty in finding a date due to their inability to speak English. Many of the "caged women" were also recent immigrants. The scene of dozens of men bargaining for favors was quite similar to a cattle auction in many respects.

I suppose this is a good time to tell you about the girl. Her name was Doris Marx. On the way to Australia to attend the University of Sydney on the GI Bill, we had stopped in Hawaii and rented a car to drive around the island where she had been living. When I met her I was immediately reminded of the girl in Green Mansions- by today's standards a real hippie- but she was well-educated and a fabric designer. She had a willowy build and was wearing a colorful green Mumu. (see photo 6) She had been in Hawaii to study floral fabric pattern creation. Her personality was a bit abrasive without meaning to be so- a spitfire if you will. She joined the ship (Orosova) as it went from Hawaii to Fiji and I got to know her on that journey. You can imagine the set up: a beautiful independent girl; gliding through the tropical ocean together; with nothing but time on our hands. I almost jumped ship with her to explore the Marshall Islands where her father had once lived. But my travel mates outnumbered me, told me it was a bad idea, and if I tried, they were going to lock me up! So instead, Doris traveled to Australia with us (see photo 7), and after a month continued on with her plan to complete her studies in Denmark. But she was never far from my heart, and it was not the last I would see of her.

Even so, a man is naturally curious. I was content to just "look". As it was not yet dark when we arrived, I took a picture of a few of the girls behind the wire and made a hurried exit through the front gate. "Look out, they're after you!" Pete shouted. Glancing around I found that two of the prostitutes were in close pursuit, both wielding empty beer bottles. Given they were handicapped with high heels, I had little trouble escaping them. Many of the clientele were angry at my actions, but they did not become violent, perhaps assuming I was from the police. Regardless of what they thought, I decided not to return to Roe Street for my mates until later, when my identity would be masked by darkness.

When I came back later that night, I recognized some of the same men I had seen late in the afternoon. Either they were still waiting, or they were going to throw even more of their money away. I began at one end of Roe Street and worked my way up the entire street looking for Pete and Ken, having a chat with each of the dames at every house who were not busily fulfilling their end of a business transaction. Many of the wenches had passed their prime and were a pitiful sight to behold. I had little trouble being invited to talk with the girls due to my American accent. They were more interested in the money they thought I had than my appearance, so my two-week old beard didn't faze them. I guess they thought I was a spree-bent American merchant mariner on leave.

Out of sheer nosiness, I decided to try to see inside of one of the brothels without paying. This is a difficult thing to do when a girl will not even unlock the front door until a customer has passed four dollars and fifty-cents through the screen. Obviously they have learned from past experience that they had best get their money beforehand. I made my way to the front of a milling crowd of men at brothel number 182. One of the caged girls, a lovely Asian in a lacy bodice, beckoned to me. I approached her with a suppressed grin.

"Good day, Miss, is this a motel?" I queried, in polite manner.

"What is a motel, Love?" she responded.

"Oh, it's just like a hotel, except that one is able to park his car under a shelter at a motel," I told her.

"Oh no, Love, this here isn't no motel, this is a house for women."

"You mean it's a nurses' home?" I asked, pretending that I was completely ignorant.

"It's not exactly a nurses' home. It's more like a hotel where women live," she answered.

"Well, I like women. How much will it cost me to get a room here for the night?" I asked.

"Most of our customers don't last a whole night, honey, but if you really want to do, you could stay the whole night for eighty quid (that's about one hundred eighty American dollars)," was her reply.

"That's a *bit* more than I had expected to pay," I answered as if the amount didn't seem *too* expensive.

By this time several others were listening to our conversation. Guess they figured I was really loaded.

"Mai is my name. Look Love, why don't you come in and we can talk this over in my room where it is quiet."

To the amazement of myself and the other male onlookers, the door was unlocked and I walked in without having to pay. Mai led me down a long corridor and into a neat little bedroom. It was cheaply decorated with childish knick-knacks, and toy panda bears. It seemed so incongruous; I had been expecting erotic art. Then it dawned on me: these inanimate objects receive much affection from girls who are in the "love making business", who invariably crave affection and yet seldom attain it.

"What do you think of the room?" asked Mai.

"The bed is comfortable, that's all I care about," I replied as I bounced on the double bed, patting the flowery print bedspread.

Pretending that a buddy was waiting outside for me, my next question was, "But will my mate and I be able to sleep here undisturbed? We have driven our Cadillac across Australia and we are tired."

"Oh, but your friend can sleep in another room can't he? I want to share the room with only you, Love."

"That would be fine with me, Mai, but we can't afford two rooms at eighty quid each. Besides, there is only one bed in this room, where would you sleep?" I asked as if concerned for her welfare. "And another thing, Mai, what would your mother think, if she knew that you were sleeping in the same room with a man?" I asked? She still didn't seem to catch on to my teasing.

"Apparently you don't realize what kind of a place your in, Love. This is an infamous house, a notorious house, the same as a *brothel*," she explained with a touch of impatience.

"Well, Mai, whatever it is, I had better consult with my mate before I decide to spend the night here. I'll see if we can find a safe place to park the Caddie and then we should be back shortly, okay?"

"That's fine, Love, here's my calling card, don't forget to ask for me when you return." Mai seemed hesitant to let me go as she escorted me to the front door, not certain of what to make of me, but hopeful.

The night air was exceptionally fresh in contrast to the musty atmosphere of the brothel.

Perth was too expensive and there were few places to sleep without raising detection so I took a bus the few miles down the road to the Port of Fremantle. It was very late when I arrived and I was tired, so I made the night's sleeping nest behind some trashcans in a residential backyard. A policeman heard the rattling trashcans, shined his flashlight in my direction, and then wandered on. The mosquitoes on the other hand, had no trouble finding me.

Early the following morning I was covered in pink marks not unlike the measles, ate a poor man's breakfast in a nearby cafe, checked my backpack at the train station, and spent the day loafing on the beach. I fasted the remainder of the day, as my money was precariously low. By nightfall I had hiked down to the South Beach, constantly on the lookout for a place to spend the night. I finally bedded down behind a barricade of boulders, a few feet from the Indian Ocean. The wind became stronger and salt spray from the ocean soon dampened both my flimsy sleeping bag and my spirits. As if this wasn't enough, it began to rain. I dashed over to the only shelter I could see: a railway-loading platform on the side of a dilapidated wheat storehouse. I made a fine mattress out of a few wheat bags that I found on the platform and was thankful to be in a dry place, even though I shared it with rats.

I awoke in a panic the next morning as a loud freight train approached my "bedroom". I hastily grabbed my gear and ran across the tracks to the beach. A few moments later I saw a hobo come out from behind the same building I had just left. As he approached me I noticed he had no socks, his shirt was ripped, revealing a filthy undershirt, and his pants were just as cruddy and full of holes. He introduced himself as Jim, and bummed a few cigarettes and so we had cigarettes for breakfast. I helped him to brush some of the weeds off his jacket. He had spent an uncomfortable night on the ground. He explained how hard the cops made the life of a bum.

"They never let up on us", he complained. "Let's go down to the park and I'll treat you to breakfast. Yesterday was Sunday, so the garbage cans should have a lot in them if we get there before the others. It's good picking down there. Sometimes I've found parts of ducks and chickens!" he added excitedly.

Much to Hobo Jim's bewilderment, I passed up his generous offer. I went hungry instead! It is embarrassing to be as broke as I was in a city. Not wanting to become a beggar, I decided to take a boat to Rottnest Island, which is some twelve miles off the Australian coast. I hoped to catch enough fish to live on for the few days remaining before my ship left for Singapore.

There I found a beautiful sandy meadow adjacent to the shore, where I constructed a simple lean-to using a poncho as a roof. I purchased some bread and a bag of ripe plums at the island's only store where I also picked up a bit of octopus bait, a few hooks and a short line. As this was the last day of the year, New Year's Eve, I was unable to pass by the local pub without craving a beer, and besides, I was thirsty for something other than water. I stayed in the pub much longer than I expected to thanks to the hospitality of the locals I met there. Staggering out around sundown, I somehow managed to find my way back to my encampment where I promptly passed out. Hours later something nudged me in my sleep. I awoke to find a large gathering of weird looking animals encircling me. They were about the size of large rabbits, but had the features of rats. They had eaten most of my cherished plums, and had broken into my last pack of Craven "A" smokes. I later found out they are called Wallabies. When the island was discovered by the Dutch many years ago they named the island Rottnest, meaning rat nest because they thought these animals were some breed of large rats.

After an early morning dip, I had a full day fishing but caught not even one small fish. Had the octopus not been so rancid perhaps it would have served as a meal for me. Instead, I ate the loaf of bread. Before retiring that night I put out a couple of nightlines. The only saving grace is that the island was free of mosquitoes.

Checking the nightlines early the following morning was without reward yet again, the bait gone but no fish on the hooks. Such a lack of food makes one very sluggish and inactive. I purchased another loaf of bread and spent the day in the sun, reading a copy of the *Naked and the Dead*. A few friendly wallabies dined with me that evening, but they looked too much like giant rats to be loveable.

Life on the island proved to be cheap, but in my predicament it was monotonous and lonely, so I took the passenger launch back to Perth that evening. Once there, I ambled through a vacated house in an attempt to find a suitable place to spend my last night in Australia. The house was in shambles, every room cluttered with discarded wine and whiskey bottles, newspapers were strewn about and the charred remains of a recent fire. Apparently the toilet was out of order, for heaps of human dung were found in every room. The resulting odor was not too pleasing, so even though I had a gas mask with me, I decided to look for a more suitable shelter for the forthcoming night. A bum was stretched out under a willow tree in the yard. He was but a few feet from the sidewalk. He was fast asleep, an elderly, bewhiskered gent. By his side lay an old crutch, and a couple of empty wine bottles. No less then eight flies were sunning themselves on the old gent's penis as it dangled off to one side. I woke him up and told him he had best cover his reproductive organ lest some policeman arrest him. He thanked me, and wished me a Merry Christmas. I doubt if he was aware that Christmas had passed more than a week prior.

I made a last check at the post office to find my money had not arrived. I would be sailing for Singapore broke the following day. Ken and Pete were still at the Beaufort Hotel and insisted I spend my last night in semi-comfort, so I took them up on their offer of their hotel room floor.

After a week of bathing in salt water it was a pleasure to take a fresh water shower the next morning in the hotel. Pete and Ken treated me to my last Australian meal, a delicious breakfast of steak and eggs and saw me off at the train station where I took a train to the Port of Fremantle to finally board the Gorgon, the relatively small ship that was to take me to Singapore. The Gorgon was quite old but very clean. The ships officers were British, the crew of ninety, Chinese. As passengers the ship carried forty-five humans, one hundred head of cattle, and 2,000 sheep. It was a relief to know that I had complete security for the next eleven days while aboard ship. It meant that I would have a real bed of my own without being disturbed by onlookers, cops, insects or the elements. Though it was nothing like the dreamy passage with Doris, I would also have all the food I could eat, and for the most part, it was highly palatable.

Chapter 4:

At Sea on the Gorgon

THE WATER WAS calm for the most part, and the weather the best. When I was not too busy playing chess for beers with the mostly Eurasian passengers, I would spend my time reading on deck. Our only port of call en-route was Geralton, a seaside town some three hundred miles north of Perth, which provided important service, and logistics support for regional mining, fishing, rock lobster, wheat, and livestock. During our stop, the Gorgon took on wheat, which gave me time to browse through what was then a barren, little port. I spent a thoughtful moment at the Lost at Sea Memorial pondering the irony of my current mode of transport, and thinking of how many have not been so fortunate in their adventures at sea.

I could never quite accustom myself to the stench of the sheep and cattle below us. I noticed only one dead sheep throughout the voyage. One of the officers informed us that three hundred cattle had perished during a recent voyage to Singapore. The crew spent most of its time hoisting the dead cattle out of the hold and dumping them into the sea. It must have been a gory spectacle, trailed no doubt by flocks of sea gulls. Even though we were miles out from the Sunda Straits, sea gulls could be seen hovering around the ship, occasionally diving to the water to pick up a bit of the ships refuse as it was dumped over the fantail.

Passing through the treacherous narrow Sunda Straits in the Indonesian islands stirred my longing to explore. Despite the very deep waters, random sandbars and very strong tidal flows made the boat unsteady. Due to the catastrophic volcanic explosion of the Karaktoa in 1883, which was so severe it altered the topography of the strait, many of the smaller islands were never resettled. It had also been the site of the famous Battle of the Java Sea during WWII Sumatra when two allied cruisers were sunk. Sumatra was portside, while Java lay serenely to starboard. The dark green of the dense jungles on both islands were highly inviting. A few junks, and other small craft were plying along the coasts of both islands. Peaceful volcanic islands were numerous.

When my fellow passengers, the Eurasians, learned of my plan to hitch up through Malaya and Siam (now known as Thailand) they promptly informed me that it was impossible to do because Malaya was having an internal war against the communist insurgents after three estate managers were murdered in Perak, northern Malaya. The men were murdered by guerrillas of the Malayan Communist Party (MCP), an outgrowth of the anti-Japanese guerrilla movement, which had emerged during the Second World War. Despite never having had more than a few thousand members, the MCP was able to draw on the support of many disaffected Malayan Chinese, who were upset that British promises of an easier path to full Malayan citizenship had not been fulfilled (now known as the Malayan Emergency). The harsh post-war economic and social conditions also contributed to the rise of anti-government activity. I had no choice but to continue to Singapore and to worry about my destiny thereafter. This information was not exactly a boost in my morale, but I was learning the best-laid plans could always be trumped by changing local politics (and weather), so I adapted my mindset to become as flexible as possible.

By noon the next day we could easily see the tall white buildings of Singapore standing out against the green flat background of Singapore Island. From such a distance the city gave the impression of being immaculate, western and modern. In contrast, just before the Gorgon berthed, we passed dozens of grotesque rusting hulls of ships anchored off shore- a ghostly tribute to what had been bombed or scuttled in the harbor during World War II. It would be years before they would finally be harvested for scrap metal and cleared away.

As the Gorgon docked, the clouds burst in a drenching torrent, which promptly ended the heat, and humidity that had been with us for the last week of our crossing. A few Muslims, each leading an immaculate white sheep on a leash, were among the small throng of people that had come to the wharf to greet the Gorgon's arrival. Paradoxically, the sheep stood out as being far cleaner than their handlers. The immigration authorities came on board and stamped my visa without a lot of unnecessary ceremony.

Chapter 5:

Shore Leave in Singapore: Sewers and the Pursuit of Sleep

MY FIRST STOP was the fairly luxurious Adelphi Hotel, certainly not to obtain accommodation, but to see if my money had arrived from Australia. The official doorman was a huge Sikh decked out in a bushy beard, with a turban wound expertly about his head. He gave the impression of being proud and fierce, but his job demanded that he be courteous- which he was.

The cooling morning downpour had continued and I was relieved to go indoors. The desk clerk generously offered me an air-conditioned room for twenty dollars a night, but I had a mere twenty cents in my pocket. He informed that he had no mail for me, but advised trying the American Express office a few blocks away. Running all the way to American Express, I managed to arrive just before it locked up for the night. I was saturated with rain by this time, wishing I had thought to include an umbrella in my sixty pounds of personal freight of a backpack.

I stood at the counter dripping, waiting, watching the clerk make his way through a stack of handwritten letters with colorful stamps from around the world. I really had no option if the money hadn't made it so I was dripping more than rain. My soaked shirt clung to me and I could tell I needed a shower. Finally, after fifteen minutes, the clerk raised an envelope with familiar handwriting, asking "This it?" I was never so grateful to see a single piece of mail. My money had finally made it to me. All two hundred dollars of it, which I hoped would get me to

London, some 10,000 miles away. I had earned an additional one hundred forty dollars, which I had left with friends in Sydney to forward to London to pay my fare across the Atlantic. I dared not carry all my funds with me because I knew that I would spend it enroute to Europe, leaving me penniless if and when I ever made it to London. Another observation about the type of unplanned vagabonding I was doing came to me that evening: so much of life is about procuring food and shelter.

That two hundred dollars was the most money I had had at one time for months so within a few minutes I was celebrating by guzzling a Tiger beer in a nearby bar. Part of the American fleet was anchored in the harbor and swabbies (sailors from the Navy) were swarming around the waterfront dives. A couple sailors joined me and it was a breath of fresh air to talk to Americans for a change over the next several hours. Shabbily dressed beggars who tried to sell us everything from pornographic pictures to a living Chinese doll constantly interrupted us. At times as many as three peddlers would hawk their wares at our table simultaneously. They made so much noise arguing among them that we decided to find a quieter spot. We got up to leave but the protective proprietor came over and apologized to us, shooing the noisemakers out onto the street allowing us to finally hear each other.

During the course of the afternoon I told my companions of my predicament. They thought my proposed trip would be quite an adventure, but since my final destination was Alaska they tried to persuade me to go via Japan across the Pacific, saving 12,000 miles. I explained it would cost far more to go by ship than by land, and the little money I had would not even get me as far as Hong Kong by ship. The next bright idea they hatched was that I stow away onboard their destroyer since it was leaving for Hong Kong the following day. The proposition sounded feasible. We ordered a few more beers while we schemed out the details. The plan was for one of them to distract the deck officer while I climbed aboard via a rope ladder and then the other would escort me to the hold of the ship. I was to stow away in the propeller shaft hold, which they said was seldom entered. They would sneak food to me if the opportunity afforded; otherwise I would have to go hungry, but they said it would only be for a few days at most, since the ship was scheduled to be in Hong Kong by then.

Unfortunately, as I was about to accept their proposition one of the swabbies thought of a factor that voided our stowaway plan. He remembered that their ship was to cross the equator enroute to Hong Kong, and that the ship would be searched thoroughly in an effort to locate all hiding sailors so that they could be properly initiated in "Equator Crossing" rituals. For a stowaway to remain hidden under those circumstances would be practically impossible. In any event, it was not worth the risk because detection would mean not only punishment for being a stowaway, but as a Navy ship, a stowaway would probably be tried as a spy as well. Regretfully, we had to drop the idea.

Due to naval regulations my companions needed to return to their ship shortly after dark. I thanked them for their effort to get me to Hong Kong and saw them off at their gangway. After the buoyant conversation, I again felt how truly alone traveling solo could be. Walking alone among the crowds on Collyer Quay is perhaps when the seed I had been holding to find a traveling companion began to sprout.

Roughly eighty-percent of Singapore was Chinese at that time in what is now an international city of unparalleled proportions. The river was practically empty due to low tide. Heavily laden coolies were scurrying everywhere, busily emptying the bellies of hundreds of junks and sampans, which were wallowing in the black filth of the river bottom. Garbage was strewn everywhere. In fact, the riverbed and all the streets of the surrounding area were literally buried with garbage, and the stench was equally prevalent. A few mangy monkeys could be seen perched on second story windowsills. Pigeon droppings were so prevalent that it was difficult to discern the original color of the fronts of some of the riverfront buildings. In the street market, huge over-fed flies nearly obscured the chunks of fat they were clinging to. Yet shabbily dressed customers who could not afford the luxury of meat readily purchased this same fat. Merchants brusquely whisked away the flies before wrapping the fat in palm leaves for their bartering customers.

It was not long before I was lost, evidently in the slums, for I doubt humans could possibly live in a more extensive degree of filth. I took a trishaw, telling the driver that I wanted to go to the main part of the city. Either he could not understand English, or he pretended so. In either event, I was at his mercy. The night was black: not a single streetlight. The driver pedaled up one street, down another, into and out of several alleys and finally pulled up by an attap (bamboo hut dwelling). He led me inside where I met an older woman and her daughter. I could not understand the ensuing conversation between them but it was obvious that my rickshaw driver was a procurer. I had numerous reasons for not spending the night with the girl and ran out of the hut. I slipped down an alley, dodging in and out of the thousands of dark skinned Hindus, Malayans and Chinese who were as thick as maggots on a cadaver. The people stared at me as I passed and I soon figured out that one does not mill aimlessly around the slums of Singapore alone at night if he is white. I took another trishaw only to find myself in the same trap when the new driver led me in a zigzag course through seemingly endless unmarked side alleys eventually stopping at a shack where he fetched another witch-like hag who also propositioned me. I explained to her that all I wanted was to get back to the Gorgon (ship), and if that was not possible, to find some place to spend the night cheaply. I tried to persuade her to let me sleep on the floor in her shack, but she was obviously against it as she pushed me out and bolted the door. The Kafka-esque nightmare continued when my driver drove me to yet a third brothel, this time more lavish, apparently thinking I was passing on the quality rather than the style of the situation. This madam communicated to me that she had four charming girls, each of a different nationality. The four girls were paraded into the room dressed in costumes native to their countries of origin: Turkish, Persian, Chinese, and Hindustani. I was offered tea, which I was helpless to resist due to my own upbringing to be polite. She interpreted my acceptance as encouragement, praising the attributes of each of her girls. I declined any and all of her various propositions, and politely, but firmly explained my predicament to her: I simply needed a place to *sleep*.

By this time I was mighty tired and angry with the trishaw drivers who had been trying to pedal me off to prostitutes. I stomped out of the dump, hopped on the driver's seat of my waiting trishaw and attempted to pedal my way through the milling throngs of people. If the driver, now riding uncomfortably in the passenger seat, was unable to find the heart of the city, then I was determined to do so myself. Pedaling a trishaw in Singapore is about as hellish as it would be to drive down a busy one-way street against oncoming traffic anywhere else. After sideswiping another trishaw and bumping into three pedestrians, I was glad to relinquish my mission to the licensed driver. He promptly dodged multitudes of people in the streets, making an erratic right turn onto Serangoon Road, which, compared to the other streets I had been on that evening, seemed relatively devoid of Chinese. This was the Hindustan district and it reeked of filth and spices even more repugnant than the previous area.

I came to the conclusion that my trishaw driver had no intentions of taking me back to the Gorgon, even if he did understand that I wanted to go there, which I doubt. I motioned him to stop- but he kept forging ahead so I jumped out and threw some change at him which was all I thought he was worth. It wasn't much- and he became angry with me. That's when I ran for my life, jumping over one of the broad open sewers and around attap hovels to get out of his sight. I knew that he would not chase me; he dared not leave his trishaw unattended for fear it would be stolen. Past midnight by this time, I gave up the thought of returning to the Gorgon, which would be closed and well guarded for the night.

I was so desperate to rest that when I spotted a large, obviously well fed Malayan woman tossing a bucket of slop out her front door I approached her, and through sign language, and begged for permission to sleep on her hut floor. She was barefoot and bare-chested, with broad feet and large breasts. She wore only a lungi (sarong), which is popular in climates where heat and humidity make trousers and underwear uncomfortable. She answered me in words with a soft voice, none of which I understood, but when she stepped aside and motioned me into her hovel, I did not hesitate to do so. The roof was thatched with walls made of bamboo matting. A small oil lamp gave a tiny bit of illumination. Several sticks of incense were burning with smoke that twisted up toward the palm frond roof and filtered through its leaves. The aroma from the incense, mixed with the stench of the open sewer flowing through one end of the hut gave the place an "exotic" air. A steel runway mat formed a bridge over the sewer. This kind Malayan gave a most convincing demonstration that the sewer served as a toilet among other things. I spent the next few hours napping on a bamboo mat, frequently awakened by boisterous tenants in the adjoining attaps. Certain areas of Singapore contained as many as 40,000 inhabitants per square mile and I could hear a good many of them throughout the night.

I met my host's spouse the following morning. He had apparently been asleep upon my intrusion the previous night, and I'd fail to notice him in the dimly lit room. He was much smaller than she, but equally friendly. They brewed some tea, which tasted exceptionally good after my unprofitable night on the damp earth floor.

I was consumed with my old friend "Hunger" when I left their company. I'd last eaten at noon the previous day. I walked along the planked sidewalk, dodging slop buckets that were dumped from second story windows with apparent disregard for unsuspecting pedestrians below. I came upon a small cafe that seemed a bit cleaner than the others I had passed, so I took a seat at one of the small, dirty tables. Pointing to the dough the chef was kneading, I indicated that I would like to eat some. It turned out to be chapatti, an Indian creation resembling a pancake and looking fairly edible- until the chef poured a sauce of goat meat and hot spices over it. There were no utensils, so I did as the other customers and ate with my hands. As a small boy I had often thought that the use of forks, knives, and spoons presented too many problems, but now that I had no choice but to eat the greasy chapatti with my fingers I realized just how glad I was that our culture uses eating utensils. The sauce was so hot that I gagged. I motioned to the cook to bring me a glass of water. He did, but the glass was so filmy I ordered a bottle of Pepsi Cola instead, and drank it straight from the bottle much to the astonishment of the cook who had fetched a second filthy glass. Throughout the meal I had all I could do to keep the flies from eating faster than me. The flies were exceptionally bold, perhaps realizing they had strength in such numbers.

I will never forget what happened next. As I passed a small Chinese printing shop, a youthful Asian man rushed out of the building. He pushed his way through the crowds and halted a few doors down, leaning weakly against the portal. Upon reaching him, I noticed that his right wrist was nearly severed. He held his right hand in place with the aid of his left hand. Blood flowed freely through his fingers and splashed on the pavement. He uttered no sound, but from the contorted expression on his face it was an obvious he was in extreme agony and terrified. A motley crowd gathered about within minutes. Several of the more aggressive onlookers were arguing among themselves as to how to treat the bleeding youth. One produced a roll of toilet paper. The others wrapped the youth's arm like a mummy with the tissue paper, but the blood soaked completely through before they finished. As I was of no help, I left the sobering scene. I could not help wondering how the accident happened, and whether or not the youth would lose his hand. At the rate he was bleeding, he would die from loss of blood before long if proper help were not found. The vivid red blood draining the life out of this young man made me think of war, of the combat I'd missed, and how it must have felt on the battlefield, especially when death could be so imminent, and for this moment, I was grateful fate had delivered me different challenges.

To clear my mind, I spent time loitering around an open-air Chinese bizarre. Old women and small children squatted before their humble handmade wares and homegrown produce. Sometimes their inventory consisted of only a few items or vegetables, which they spent an entire day trying to sell. The return on such small stock would be but a few cents, yet that is how they spent their lives. How they managed to exist was a mystery to me. This was not the first time I thought about the fact that we are all united in a universal need for food and shelter. Ninety-nine percent of the world's population spends the majority of life fulfilling this fundamental need.

As I crossed over the Rochor Canal, which dissects the central region of Singapore, I stopped to watch a power shovel dropping its clam bucket into the black, soupy water. The bucket would come up heaped to the brim with refuse, revealing the unfathomable fact that the canal bottom was several feet deep with garbage and trash. While I stood looking out over the railing, a bloated dead dog floated beneath the bridge with its feet sticking out rigidly toward the sky. The putrid odor of the canal was overwhelming in the heat and made me long for the fresh, glacial air of Alaska.

As mentioned, the open sewers of Singapore are used as public toilets and it was not uncommon to pass persons in the squatting position adding their share to a hungry sewer. Occasionally a sewer would get plugged, and overflow. The resulting mess was as bad as might be expected. The Singapore Canal had overflowed its banks that day, flooding an area of several blocks in the Chinese District to a depth of over a foot. People were sitting in an open cafe near the river, their feet propped on the rungs of their stools to keep them out of the liquid filth. That they managed to smell their food- let alone taste it- over the smell of the floating debris is highly doubtful and merely illustrates that one can adjust to most anything if necessary.

Just one block from the filth and squalor of this area was Raffles Place, a modern, westernized shopping area where one could find most anything imagined or desired from Europe or America. Just beyond the luxurious shopping center sits the Britannia Club, a large modern service club for members of the British military forces. I spent part of the afternoon talking to Malayan soldiers on leave from fighting in the jungle. Communist guerrillas, mainly Chinese had been ambushing government installations, both civilian and military. Many lives had been lost on both sides in the past eight years. The leader of the guerrillas was the notorious Chin Peng, who seemed to be everywhere at once, yet had never been caught. Vast numbers of Britain's forces were scattered in small units throughout Malaya. In addition to the famous British "Red Berets" were Fijians, Gurkas, and trackers from Borneo. The majority of the soldiers advised not to attempt hitching lifts up through Malaya: to do so would be more than risky. They told of existing curfews, and explained that anyone out after dark would be shot on sight. One soldier advised me to check with the Kings Dragoon Guards, an armored outfit that protects northbound convoys. During this time they were involved in counter-insurgency operations in both mounted operations (armored car) and on foot in the dense jungles. It was several miles to the K.D.G., too far to go before the duty hours ended, so I sat down to a snack of clean, fly-free food. It was a relief to be in hygienic surroundings once again; the interior of the Britannia Club was immaculate.

I took a trishaw to the notorious but blissfully air-conditioned Straits Cabaret, one of Singapore's favorite hangouts for seamen of all nations. The price of beer was outrageous; however the beauty of the amorous females more than compensated as evidenced by the number of seamen buying drinks for the erotic creatures. The music was western and the vocalists sang in English, although the majority of seamen were unable to understand it. A small boy was the star attraction. He sang and rolled around on the floor with the microphone to animate his songs. Unfortunately I had to conserve my money or go hungry in the near future, so I left the Cabaret and headed for the Gorgon after one beer. I hoped to sneak into my bunkroom where I could get a much needed good night's sleep. The Gorgon was a wonderful sight to behold, brightly lit and standing out in its whiteness like an elaborate resort (in contrast to the previous night's place of rest). I managed to get past the security police without interference and continued on undetected as I climbed up the gangplank. I wasted no time in getting down to my cabin where I bolted the door behind me for my last night on the Gorgon.

Despite a good night sleep I awoke with a fever the following morning that sapped what little strength I had remaining. Apparently the flies, sewers and dirty glasses had finally won a battle against my immune system. Laden with a sixty-pound backpack, I barely managed to descend the gangplank. The Gorgon would be sailing back to Australia later that day, so I had to find a new place to spend the night. Rod, a Eurasian student I had met on the ship en-route to Singapore had invited me to live with him and his parents while I was in Singapore. I had never before visited persons who had extended me such invitations, for I did not want to become a mere parasite. Often I had heard of others speak of the numerous "contacts" they had lined up in foreign countries that they intended to visit. The so-called "contact" was quite often no closer than a distant relative, or friend of some casual acquaintance. I preferred to make my own contacts, rather than to be dependent on others to do so. I did not want to be a "sponger" or a "string- puller." Rod was the only person I knew in Singapore and I set aside my pride in the interest of frugality and called on him.

On the way to finding Rod's home, I had to pass through the Tanjong Pagar railway station filled with hundreds of armed Malayan soldiers boarding a north-bound train to join in the war against the guerrillas up country. The energy was palpable and this scene stayed in my mind as I pondered a quiet urge building inside me- could the K.D.G. use my skills?

I found Rod's house on a hill overlooking the Port of Singapore harbor. It was the first spacious house I had seen in the city, surrounded with a well-kept lawn and beautifully tended gardens. Much to my relief, Rod and his parents received me with open arms. His mother, a beautiful, gracious lady of Asian ancestry and his father, tall and slender- almost Italian-looking but in reality a mixture of Asian and Scottish- made a handsome couple.

After a welcome rinse of buckets of fresh water from a clay container three feet deep, I was served a delicious lunch of rice and curry. It was exceptionally appealing to me coming from a clean kitchen. Back home where sanitation is taken for granted, such things never entered my mind. My fever had passed and I was feeling on the mend. Rod, Derrick and I spent the afternoon bicycling to various points of interest. It had rained every afternoon in Singapore so far and that afternoon was no exception. We got drenched in the downpour but it did not matter: it was warm and we were dressed in shorts. As weak as I felt it was still a pleasure to get out of the city of Singapore into relatively open spaces. We spent much of the afternoon in the famed Tiger Balm Garden (Haw Par Villa), an elaborate and detailed accumulation of ancient Chinese legends depicted through statues. The majority of them were of a sadistic nature. It was undoubtedly one of the largest gardens of its kind in the world. Most of the scenes were portrayed by mammoth figures, much larger than life-size. Torture scenes were common: a captive being sawed in two symmetrical halves by two cruel soldiers wielding a crosscut saw; men pulling the bowels out of their captive while the conscious captive looked on; an old woman sucking nourishment from her daughters full breasts while the daughters baby lay bloated from starvation by her side. As repulsive as these scenes were, they portrayed events that had happened in the past. An afternoon looking at such atrocities made me realize that all of us so called civilized humans are often more beastly than the most vicious beasts. Even today we quickly and consistently suppress memories of equally heinous tortures. We want to believe that only the Nazis and Japanese committed such crimes during World War II, but as difficult as it is to believe, some of the "clean-cut boys" of American mothers were capable of such atrocities. Fortunately we are able to say that it was not an American policy to torture, but committed in rage by individual soldiers. Such isolated instances were seldom revealed to America for fear of shocking the public.

In 1956, racism toward Eurasians manifested in much the same way the American south treated Negros: swimming pools and club memberships were separate. Given my hosts were of mixed origins, when it came time to take a swim we were directed to the Asiatic pool. This was my first experience feeling the direct impact of racism and I took but one dive into the murky yellow water of the “Indian pool”.

I left the Rod’s house the next morning before breakfast and bicycled from one dispensary to another, trying to locate a place where I could get a cholera injection. After several hours of pedaling I found one. Next stop was the Burmese consulate to apply for a visa. I filled out the necessary form and was told to return the following day to pick them up.

On the way back to Raffles Place, I passed the American Club. It was the most modern building I had ever seen complete with an entry drive lined with well-trimmed Palms. The spacious lawn and elegant gardens were well cared for by a few poorly dressed coolies. I wheeled around and pedaled up the steep drive. I was dressed in khakis, which were far from being respectable looking, a bit soiled and never ironed. I consumed a couple of hamburgers and beer in solitude. A few socially- minded American women were chatting over cocktails at a table on the veranda. The whole atmosphere struck me as being so incongruous; a block away people were living in abject poverty.

Pedaling on to the Raffles Place, I ran into a couple of New Zealanders. They were even more shoddily dressed than I. They were broke, so I treated them to a couple of beers in the nearest bar. It was there they told me they needed an extra hand and a few hundred dollars to get their small freighter down to Australia. They had purchased a ship in London and had gotten it this far, but now it lay idle in the Singapore harbor for they had run out of fuel. Had I not just come from Australia I would have been eager to toss in my two hundred dollars and sail with them. Their plans included trying to locate and salvage an old sunken frigate that supposedly lies off the Australian coast, laden with gold. Shortly after they took off, I met Jim Smith, an athletic American from Boston. Jim invited me to join him in a drink on the rooftop restaurant of the Asia building. He claimed to be an ex-marine lieutenant, on his way back to the States after participating with the American rifle team in the Olympic games in Melbourne. He was returning to Harvard to continue law school, but rather than fly back the same way he had come he had decided to see the world by flying home through Asia and Europe. His father was footing the bill. When I asked him what he thought of Singapore, he replied that he felt it was less poverty stricken and more sanitary than many cities in the states. I could hardly agree with him! It was apparent that he had seen little of Singapore but Raffles Place. He ranted about his pure British ancestry as he sipped his tea. A more pucker, snobbish American I had never met; he would even have disgusted a native Brit, I'm sure. Jim's ambition upon graduation from law school was to work with the Australian Customs Department using his training to help the Australians circumvent high American tariffs. I have great admiration for the British, yet Jim was pro-British to the extent of being anti-American. His attitude was repulsive, yet when he asked me to accompany him to Change Alley I did so, eager to watch him get taken by one of the sharp hucksters. Small open shops lined both sides of the alley and awnings above them formed a roof across the narrow alley jammed with throngs of aggressive vendors and persistent bargain seekers.

A Hindu merchant immediately whisked Jim into his clothing shop. Jim begged me to help him choose a suit and to advise him as to whether or not it was a decent bargain. I reluctantly joined the naive snob. The salesman was high pressuring both of us into buying a suit. He offered us both a beer, but since Jim preferred tea, I obliged by drinking both of them. Jim walked out with a Dacron suit for a reasonable price, but given how eager the salesman was to make a deal, I could have gotten the same suit for $10 or less. It was a pleasure to depart Jim, and a stark reminder of how I did not want to behave as a guest in a foreign country.

Chapter 6:

Venturing into Burma: Fear and Friendship

I PICKED UP my Burmese Visa early the next morning. Passing through the Hindu district I had a chance to witness one of their annual religious festivals purportedly aimed at raising spiritual awareness, a piercing/hooking ritual. Several Hindus had been selected to have the honor of undergoing what appeared to be outright torture. Amid smoking pots of incense the chosen men were worked into a trance. Then they were pierced by more than fifty needles, which supported varying types of paraphernalia. Others were pierced in the chest by ten hooks, which supported heavy silver balls, which pulled at their flesh. (see photo 8) As if this were not enough, the men then shouldered a huge log. A small arrow pierced through both cheeks, and a similar arrow pierced through their tongues, which prevented them from drawing their tongues into their mouths. The Hindus then proceeded down the street from the temple, as if sleepwalking. The crowds joined in an eerie chant. The amazing thing was that the pierced men did not bleed. Watching the bravery, the chilling endurance, and the purpose with which these believers moved together triggered that niggling urge to pursue previous thoughts of using my hard-won skills in some purposeful way.

I returned to Rod's house, gathered my gear and took off for Neesoon, where the British had a large military base. I trudged up to the guard gate hoisting my burdensome pack and was stopped by a Malayan guard. When I told him I was from Alaska, he asked if I was the advance party for an Alaskan military contingent, affirming that I did look like a soldier dressed in khaki pants, shirt, and carrying my pack. He let me through and before long I located the King Dragoon Guards who were busily pulling maintenance on armored vehicles. I reported to the battalion orderly room. A young lieutenant listened attentively while I told him of my desire to go up north with a convoy. He escorted me into a rear office where I was introduced to a Major. He pointed to various points on a large wall map of Malaya with his swagger stick, explaining as he did the overall guerilla operation.

He was more enthused when I told him that I had prior military training and that I would be willing, in fact eager, to link up with a British jungle unit. He apologized for not having any of his group in action at the time, but did suggest that I try their headquarters in Johor Bahru. The Major was headed that way in his jeep, so he gave me a lift. While crossing the causeway to the mainland of Malaya the Major's driver balked at taking me any further, for fear that his jeep might be stopped for inspection by military police. My unauthorized ride could possibly cause him trouble. However the Major intervened on my behalf and I was able to ride into Johor Bahru, all the way to the customs check.

My confidence building, I flagged down the first army truck that approached. Clambering on board with my gear, I sat beside a small, but husky dark skinned driver. He was a native Malayan and spoke no English. It was obvious that he picked me up thinking that I was a British officer. As he drove through the main gate of the large military installation on the outskirts of Johor Bahru I returned the guards salute. He dropped me off in front of the headquarters. But I was too late, arriving after duty hours. Rather than spend the night in camp I decided to try to get as far north as possible before darkness and the curfew set in. It was a half-mile walk back to the main gate. While still several hundred feet from the gate, two English guards darted out of the sentry house toward me.

I had no choice but to be apprehended by them. They were both hardened non-commissioned officers. They escorted me to the sentry house for interrogation. There they demanded that I explain who, what, and why I was here. I showed them my passport, but they did not accept it suspecting it could have been counterfeit. They demanded further identification, so I dumped all of my papers in a heap on the table. After they looked at such things as my Army discharge, a deed to land in Alaska, my boat ticket from Australia and other irrelevant papers, they told me to have a seat. I explained to them that I was trying to get to Alaska the cheapest way possible, and that Siam was my immediate destination. The more boisterous of the two guards left to make a few phone calls to confirm what I had told him. Half an hour later he returned, carrying a tray of tea and biscuits.

While relaxing with a cup of tea, my would-be custodians explained that I had been cleared. They explained that they had mistaken me to be one of five American marines who had deserted a ship recently. They added that the five marines were undoubtedly being seduced back in Singapore, rather than risking detection by roaming the streets. One of the sergeants then gave me a lift back to Johor Bahru.

While trudging through the town, children darted out of sight upon seeing me. It made me feel a bit awkward and embarrassed to scare them so. At first I thought it might be my beard that frightened them. I soon learned that many of the communist guerillas wore clothing similar to mine. No wonder the innocent children were afraid of me! I had not walked very far when a military ambulance stopped beside me. The driver was a young English chap. He gave me a lift to a nearby hospital. En-route he warned me to spend the night in the village compound where there would be armed protection against the terrorists. He told me that the curfew would be going into effect in a couple of hours: anyone on the road between 7 p.m. and 5 a.m. was just asking to get shot; in Malaya, it was customary for terrorists and the British alike to shoot first- and ask questions later. They had learned that it was the safest way through past experiences. I felt not unlike a hunted animal, in "open season" being in as much danger of being killed by the friendly British forces and the Malayan police as by terrorists themselves. I felt a bit uneasy as I left the safety of the ambulance and proceeded at a slow pace up the road.

Luckily I got a lift with a smiling Malayan. He was headed for Kluang some seventy miles north. He explained that we would have to spend the night in a protected compound if we were not able to reach Kluang before the curfew went into effect. Every couple of miles we were halted by roadblocks. Well-armed soldiers searched every vehicle, especially cargo trucks for supplies that might be destined for the terrorists. Even food was on the list of illegal cargos, for they were trying to starve the terrorists out of the jungles.

We passed by several small native villages, where every building was constructed of palm leaves and bamboo. Strands of entangled barbed wire encircled each of these compounds.

Sentries patrolled cautiously along the inner perimeters. Tension filled the air.

Between roadblocks, the driver floored the accelerator in an attempt to reach Kluang before curfew. We whizzed by miles of graceful olive and palm groves, well-cleared rubber plantations, and fields of Sarawak peppers known to thrive in the hottest tropics with one hundred inches of rainfall every year. Dusk and the curfew were not far off as we sped past the last roadblock on the outskirts of Kluang we were able to see the high gate swing shut for the night. Frantically the driver blew his horn. Luck was with us; the police opened the gate and let us through without incidence. A few minutes later we were in the heart of Kluang. Darkness came quickly, but even so, I could see that much of the town was extremely modern. In contrast to the modern buildings were the open sewers, unpaved muddy streets and tumbledown shacks. The night streets were jammed with people, perhaps finding it particularly desirable to roam the streets while a curfew was in effect outside the city limits. Before dropping me off, the driver advised me to seek safety for the night in a certain hotel, and warned me not to loiter about the streets alone, for Kluang was one of the strongholds of the terrorists. According to him, the throngs of people filling the streets and alleyways would be saturated with agitators and informers. I thanked him for his concern for my welfare, and the lift he had given me. "Many people have vanished recently in Kluang, remember what I have told you. I wish you luck for you will need it," were the parting words of that kindly Malayan gentleman.

The number of Asian faces staring at me had me feeling somewhat like a freak. Undoubtedly they were curious to learn what had brought a bearded, militaristic-looking white man to their town. In any event they did not appear too friendly so I tossed my pack on my shoulders and worked my way down the street forcing myself through the masses of mankind. A hotel for the night or for that matter any other night was out of the question; it was a luxury that I could not afford. At the rate I was going I would be lucky to have enough for food, let alone visas and the numerous other essentials of my journey. Perhaps I had been consuming too much beer, but at least it did not give me a morbidly profuse discharge from my intestines (diarrhea) like most of the other contaminated foods. Besides, beer was good for the health, as well as relaxing. At any rate I convinced myself that I should keep drinking beer while I still possessed the strength to lift a bottle to my lips. Each day I seemed to feel a bit weaker, a gradual loss of strength that did not feel like a real sickness. I jostled through the crowds for more than an hour, constantly on the lookout for something clean and cheap to eat. My stomach began to growl, but my eyes and nose found nothing appealing. When I reached the end of town without finding a suitable place to eat, I crossed over to the other side of the street and worked my way back into town. A few hundred yards down the street I found a decent looking restaurant. The only trouble was that it seemed too decent for me to afford. But for the first time that day my senses enjoyed the sight of clean and western food and my senses finally aligned with the desires of my old friend, Hunger. The power of the two was overwhelming! I found myself saying, "To hell with the cost, I'm going to eat anyway!" In a moment I found myself seated at a table. The restaurant had real class! Tablecloths on every table. Clean tablecloths. The waiter was a short, well-built Chinese youth. I really splurged by ordering a couple of beers and a steak. Even the rolls tasted extraordinarily delicious. My only lament was that the servings had not been more generous. I could easily have eaten a second helping of everything, even a third for that matter. A glance at the check indicated that only the one serving had cost me more than I could afford to spend in three days of travel. However, the thought that I would have to go hungry sometime in the future to pay for this gluttonous extravagance did not seem too distressing to me as I paid my bill and headed once again for the streets. Some things are priceless.

Chapter 7:

King's Own Scottish Borderers: A Brief Stint

FOREMOST IN MIND on my search for tonight's place to sleep were the bugs, mosquitoes and soggy saturated earth. My summer sleeping bag was about as worthless as teats on a boar hog, but I had reconciled myself to accept it in Australia for financial reasons. I found the pathetic sack in a second hand shop in Sydney for two quid ($4.50). It was no more than heavy cheesecloth stuffed with a bit of cotton, and it soaked up moisture like a sponge. If I had any common sense I would have sacrificed a few beers for mosquito netting long ago. It was useless for me to complain of my stupidity at this point. However, I could overlook these minor deficiencies; the only thing I considered a prerequisite to a good nights sleep this particular night was that I not be bothered by curious- and possibly dangerous- onlookers, thieves or terrorists. Finding such refuge outdoors in Kluang's crowded streets would not be possible. I lugged my heavy pack around for an hour finding no place to hide for the night. Then I spied two white men sitting at a small booth inside a cafe, engaged in beer swilling.

They eyed me suspiciously as I walked up to their table. My first impression was that they had a chip on their shoulders, eager for someone to nudge so they could "let all hell fly loose." They said not a word while I eloquently but briefly introduced myself, responding only with a boisterous belch. The heavier of the two stood up, hollered for a third beer and introduced himself as Will and his seemingly uncouth mate, Craig. They spoke with a husky

Scottish brogue, fitting for members of the K.O.S.B. (Kings Own Scottish Borderers). They were both sergeants assigned to a company battalion in the area of Ayer Hitam, a rest town known for its ceramics some thirteen miles distant. They had been in Malaya a little over a year, but had served together in Korea as evidenced by a few distinguishing scars.

It was a relief to be speaking English again, despite their difficult accents. I asked them if they knew of any outfit that was in need of a replacement, explaining to them that I had been a former paratrooper and ready for a little adventure. They both appeared enthused at the idea of having a "Yank" in their outfit, claiming that it might be good for morale purposes. Will left the table to phone his company commander on my behalf. A few minutes later he returned to the table smiling broadly. He had not told the commanding officer that I wanted to go out on patrol with the K.O.S.B., but the C.O. did give Will permission to let me spend the night at the camp solving my one chronic problem for the night. My companions were raring to forget the military for the rest of the evening because they seldom had the opportunity to leave their jungle camp and wanted to make the most of their passes.

The three of us jogged down the street in search of a livelier place, pushing our way through a battered doorway and up three flights of rickety stairs. To my surprise, we ended up on the roof of a building. It seemed an odd place to find an open-air cabaret, but I was far from disappointed. A gentle breeze brought clean, fresh air, a genuine relief from the stench permeating the streets below. Before the waiter could fill our order, three Chinese maidens descended upon us. They may not have been bona fide virgins but, as being gentlemen, we offered each a place at our table. We passed the next few hours dancing between drinks. By midnight Will, Craig, and I came to the conclusion that our female suitors were a greater financial burden than they were worth even though in spite of our stinginess, they communicated they would like to stay with us.

Will, plastered by now, was all for it. Craig was sober enough to realize they would be late for duty if they allowed themselves to be seduced. The next time Will left the table to chunder in the latrine, we figured out a method to get him away from the temptation and into Craig's car. When Will came staggering out of the latrine like an inverted pendulum a few moments later, we realized that we would have little difficulty escorting him safely to camp. We expected him to sink in a heap to the floor with his next pained step. By the time Craig and I reached him, he was hanging desperately to a chair for support. We put one of his arms around our each of our shoulders and dragged him out of the cabaret and down several flights of stairs, his feet creating a hell of a racket as they thumped on the steps behind us. Will's body was so limp when we reached the street, it was all I could do to keep him braced against the wall to prevent him from falling face first into the muddy street, while Craig hurried off to get his car which he backed up on the sidewalk. We dragged Will into the back seat and our tires squealed as the car roared off the sidewalk onto the street.

Craig finagled his way past the Gurka sentry who was guarding the road gate on the outskirts of Kluang. By rights, the road was closed to everyone except military vehicles during the curfew hours, but the British were broadminded enough to break their own regulations to allow their troops an occasional bit of relaxation. Craig warned me to keep my head below the level of the dashboard until we reached camp, explaining that we were sitting ducks for an ambush. He raced along the narrow winding road for all the car was worth, taking curves at dangerous speeds. I understood his recklessness was much safer than driving at a slower speed which would enable terrorists to get a much more accurate shot at us, if they wanted to do so.

We drove up to the K.O.S.B. compound about 3:00 a.m. where Craig parked alongside a couple armored cars. We aided Will into a squad tent were he fell asleep in his clothes, and covered him with mosquito netting. Craig led me to a cot in the far corner of the tent; it even had the luxury of a mosquito net! Before we dropped off to sleep he warned me of the grave malaria problem and was shocked to learn that I had been taking no pills to counteract it. I was not even aware that malaria was prevalent in the Ayer Hitam district. Such ignorance on my part could cause me some real strife if I did not begin to wise up before it was too late. He then gave me a couple of paludrine tablets (proguanil hydrochloride, an anti-malarial medicine), which I swallowed before falling asleep.

I awoke early the next morning to find the blazing hot rays of the sun staring me in the face. I sat up on my cot to escape the sun and the deadening heat. I had a fever, a bit of a hangover and the sun had completely sapped any remaining ambition. Craig was afraid that I might have gotten malaria so gave me a bottle of the tablets and told me to take at least one a day.

Craig then introduced Sergeant Trott who slept in the cot across from me. Trott was a tall, heavy-set Irishman, who although only twenty-four, had been fighting most of his life. He had been a renegade with the Irish independent rebels as a youth, and more recently, had been fighting in Korea with the U.S. Marines.

The three of us showed up in the Sergeants' mess along with the other non-commissioned officers. It was so hot we wore only shoes, socks, and shorts. A gaunt looking, dark-skinned Hindu sat next to me at the breakfast table. He looked similar to an emaciated Negro, except that his jet-black hair was straight. He was the outfit's interpreter. In addition to English, he spoke Malayan, Chinese, Hindustani, and Rhodesian. The chow was plentiful, and apart from being too greasy, enjoyable. Sergeant Major Murdock dropped his obese corpus down long enough for a cup of tea. He then suggested we raid the beer cooler as a means of lessening the effects of the tropical heat. We eagerly followed his suggestion.

Accompanied by a couple of grunts, Murdock managed to lift himself out of his chair, blow his whistle to call a company formation, and waddle out the door. Within seconds more than a hundred well tanned, husky soldiers were standing at attention outside the mess hall. I observed them drill and was sincere when I remarked to Craig that K.O.S.B. was much sharper than most American soldiers in marching drills. Impressive for mere ploughboys from Scotland. After the drill most of the troops were assigned to details: building an officers mess, cleaning up latrines, and other mundane chores. Being Saturday, most of the non-coms had the day to themselves, with nothing but time on their hands because they could not leave the two acre compound. Machine gun emplacements were located at each corner of the camp along with a perimeter of tangled barbed wire and sentries to keep it well protected.

Adjacent to the rear of the compound was a small Malayan village. I had the pleasure of shaking hands with Mando and Kina, both small but extremely wiry ex-headhunters from Borneo. (see photo 9) They wore their jet-black hair in bangs over their golden brown foreheads, and sported pierced ears and necks covered in dark purple tattoos. Mando and Kina were attached to the K.O.S.B. as trackers, having a tough sixth sense enabling them to ferret out communist terrorists while on jungle patrol. They were invaluable to the K.O.S.B. in this environment because a well-executed ambush could annihilate a large armed patrol using the simple element of surprise. With Mando and Kina as point men, the ambushing terrorists would often be discovered before they could do any harm. They could not speak a word of English, an advantage as far as the discussion of work details were concerned. Terrorists had shot down Kina's brother the previous week so he was more than eager to get a chance to retaliate.

Because of their value to the outfit, they were exempt from the harassment the rest of the troops faced. Much to the embarrassment of the company commander, Kina and Mando were the only two men in the outfit that left the compound when they pleased. The Commanding Officer was also unable to punish them for fear they might turn on him with their knives at some opportune moment. While not on patrol the two Borneans could usually be found in the native village adjoining the compound. According to the Hindu interpreter, Mando and Kina were playboys as well as trackers. They were often seen smuggling military rations into the natives' houses, presumably in exchange for the favors of the owners' daughters.

Craig showed me a colored photograph of one of Mando's headhunting trophies. The gory picture revealed the hands, head and neck of a communist terrorist that Mando had stalked and killed on a recent patrol. The severed neck resembled a bloody stump more than anything else. For some unexplained reason the "Old Women's Anti-Vivisection Society" or its equivalent (American Anti-Vivisection Society an organization created with the goal of eliminating a number of different procedures done by medical and cosmetic groups in relation to animal cruelty in the United States), disapproved of such handy knife work, hence put so much pressure on the military that the trackers had to discontinue the beheadings.

As soon as we finished lunch, I located the company barber. He was the only other Hindu in the outfit. I had not had a haircut or trimmed my beard during the past five weeks, and I wanted to look my best when I spoke to the company commander about joining the K.O.S. B. for a while. The barber carried his shop in a small leather valise. He seemed to be in a state of ecstasy as he dragged his long straight razor through my bushy beard about my throat. With a modest pair of scissors and a small comb I could see in the wooden-framed hand-held mirror that he did a very professional job.

Corporal Jodie stopped by as the barber was finishing to invite me over to the corporals' mess for a little party in my honor, since I had been a corporal at one time. I told Jodie that I wanted to speak with the C.O. (commanding officer) before I joined his party, but he advised that one should be well fortified before approaching the "Big Bloody Bastard". Jodie was the Chief among the Corporals, having been promoted- and demoted- a good many times in his long army career. What he lacked in rank, he made up in experience. I spent the whole afternoon with my own rank. Before I could finish one bottle of beer, they would have another opened for me. The more I protested to drinking too much, the more the corporals insisted that I was deliberately lagging behind. The drunker the corporals got, the more they became argumentative. Arguments escalated to brawls. Then peace again, followed by more drinking. By five o'clock all of us had stopped drinking. Two of the corporals had passed out and laid in a listless stupor, others staggered out to chunder, and no doubt swore off of beer as they did so, for they did not return. Jodie and I were the only ones left and stopped because there was no more beer.

I had to act sober as I practically staggered across the compound to the commanding officer's private house for my interview, a challenging proposition. The house was high off the ground on stilts to benefit from any breezes, and was a bit drier as well. Luckily, there was a railing affixed to the steps leading up to the front door of the "castle" housing the "Big Bloody Bastard" because it took all the strength I had to pull my body up those steps. My semi-paralyzed legs were not much help. As I reached the top step, I tried to pull my faculties together so that I could make a good impression. I made an impression all right, almost battering the door down when I pounded it with my fist.

"Come in," said a baffled voice from within. I shoved the door open and entered to find two officers rising from the dinner table to greet me. The size of the commanding officer, Captain Scot, astounded me! He was a veritable giant, well over six and a half feet tall, and nearly as wide. He easily must have exceeded 300 pounds. He was clothed in shoes and shorts only. Beads of sweat were dripping so profusely from the uncovered mass of his hulk that he gave the appearance of being slimy. His head was abnormally large even for his frame, perhaps as large as a large well-fed hog. His beady, deep set eyes, and his blubbery jowls would have been the envy of any prize swine beyond a doubt. The sides and back of his head were close cut giving one the impression that his thick mop of auburn hair atop his head must be a toupee. To further enhance his appearance, it was parted in the middle. As we shook hands his powerful chubby hand completely enveloped mine. Compared to him, I felt like a dwarf.

"So you're the Yank I've been hearing about. I've been expecting you to call." This is Lieutenant Bristol. He's fairly new around here, too. Take a seat," Scot mumbled as he plopped his massive hulk back in a chair. Newspapers and clothes cluttered the floor.

Without uttering another word Captain Scot resumed carving a leg of lamb that lay across his tray. He was prying a chunk of meat off the leg when his knife slipped, knocking the majority of food off his tray. Diced carrots were sprawled the full length of the table. He seemed highly embarrassed at his own clumsiness and at a loss for an explanation. A moment of silence as he peered at Bristol and me was followed with: "The BLOODY WHORE!" I could hardly restrain my urge to roar with laughter. A portion of his bulging stomach protruded a couple of inches onto the table. Gauging from the amount of food before him, it was no wonder he was so fat. He would have been the envy of any flat-chested female, and in fact his superiors referred to him as "Tits". "Blubber Guts" would have been just as appropriate. The only other striking thing about his appearance was that he sported an extraordinary mustache stitching from one ear to the other.

"You do drink, don't you?" he asked in a tone that implied that to be a non-drinker was a sin.

"Why yes, of course I drink. Are there people who don't?" I answered jokingly.

"What will it be, beer or Drambuie?" he asked.

"Either will be fine, Sir."

"In that case, you will have both," he asserted in a commanding voice.

"Help! Help!" he shouted, pounding his massive fist on the table. Seconds later a meek, youthful recruit stumbled into the room through the rear door.

"What is it, Sir"? He asked in a faltering voice, his body trembling.

Captain Scot ordered his batsman to keep us supplied with beer and drambuie until he was notified otherwise. The batsman pulled down a bottle of drambuie from a large wall cabinet behind the Captain. I noticed that the shelves were well stocked with liquor. The batsman poured us each a mug of beer. Before leaving the room he asked, "Will there be anything more, Sir?"

"No, but be quicker the next time, Boy!" he snapped. As Captain Scot reached for his drambuie, he knocked over his mug of beer. I quickly realized the Captain had been doing much drinking prior to my visit making it an opportune time to ask permission to join his unit. He pondered my request for a moment, and then told me to be prepared to go out on a ten-day patrol the day after tomorrow.

Captain Scot found it necessary to explain what an important and powerful man he really was. He conceded that Lieutenant Bristol was on officer- but merely a *junior* officer. Right, or wrong, whatever Scot ordered was carried out without question. To prove how powerful he was, he banged on the table and hollered, "Help! Help!" The batsman hurried into the room, exceptionally nervous, and asked the Captain, "What is it Sir?" He was exceptionally nervous.

"Just an experiment, boy, just an experiment," Scot answered.

Throughout the afternoon Lieutenant Bristol did not say much, but when he did speak, he enunciated clearly. He was recently graduated from the Royal Military Academy Sandhurst in Surrey, England's foremost military academy. During the course of conversation, he frequently interjected quotations from a number of military manuals, as though an expert in military strategy. “A good battle plan that you act on today can be better than a perfect one tomorrow.” “Everyone wants peace- and they will fight the most terrible war to get it.” It was plain to see that Bristol was greatly disturbed and embarrassed by Captain Scot's actions that afternoon, but nonetheless tried to lower himself to the Captain's intellectual level so that he would be appeasing to him. Lieutenant Bristol was striving for a promotion. At the rate he was bucking he would undoubtedly attain rank, most skillful in the military art of "ass-kissing."

The grog session continued late into the night. He swore that he was the complete master of the Company. As if to prove the supremacy of his authority, he ordered several of the recruits to police up the entire camp. It would have been less ridiculous had it not been after dark. The main topic of discussion was the forthcoming patrol. Our little group finally broke up and it was a relief to get into bed.

Morning came all too soon. Those of us who were to go out on patrol the following day spent the day drawing rations and getting briefed. I was issued jungle boots, fatigues, and other essentials. Captain Beans and his simple henchman paid a social visit that afternoon. Beans was a slob and a loudmouthed big shot. He was Chief of Police in the nearby village of Yong Peng, where he obviously ruled with dictatorial authority. When he learned that I was an American and about to go out on patrol with the K.O.S.B. he accused me of being a spy. Beans made no effort to conceal his unwarranted dislike for me. Glaring at me he shouted,

"If I catch you in Yong Peng, I'll blow your head off, or lock it up for good!" I offered to show Bean my credentials in an effort to clear myself of being a spy. But he was not interested in my *credentials*. Luckily the K.O.S.B. officers intervened on my behalf or I might be rotting away in Yong Peng today.

As evening drew near Craig suggested that we go into Ayer Hitam to take in a Chinese burlesque show. We showered under improvised water tanks and headed for town. It was cold comfort to know that the only thing that protected us from terrorists' bullets was the thin-sheeted steel body of our civilian station wagon. The road gate on the outskirts of Ayer Hitam was locked and unguarded. I volunteered to search for the guard. In a flash I scaled the high barbed wire fence and dashed toward the lights of the town. Before getting very far I was stopped by a Gurka wielding a long, dangerous curved knife. Through sign language I indicated that we were British soldiers and wanted to get through the gate. We gave the Gurka hell for leaving his post and drove on to the burlesque show. It was performed in Chinese so we caught none of the spoken jokes. Strippers were clothed in exquisite oriental gowns as they began their act. The odd thing about the show was that they would toss a bit of her finery on the floor every few seconds, and before long would be alone on stage, completely nude. To this day, I have not been able to learn why they took off those beautiful costumes.

After breakfast, Lieutenant Bristol picked nine men from the ranks for a reconnaissance patrol. I was one of the chosen few. I drew a carbine and a few clips of ammo from supply, clambered aboard a steel plated troop carrier and roared northward. The sound of grinding gears was the only noise that could be heard above the roar of the engine. Looking around at the grim, uncomfortably seated soldiers reminded me of the times I had been equally as nervous as a paratrooper. The only one of us in any possible danger was the lookout-man who stood with his head and shoulders poked up through the observation hole in the roof.

Even though he was armed with a sten-gun (British 9mm submachine gun known for simple design and low production cost making it an effective insurgency weapon for resistance groups), he stood little chance if we should be suddenly ambushed. A new man took over the lookout position every five minutes. The rest of us were safer than the National Guardsmen for the time being: our steel-plated rolling vehicle was safe from small arms fire.

Several miles down the road our "Trojan Horse" screeched to a halt. With the exception of the driver, we all jumped out into a ditch, under cover of the tall jungle swamp grass. Once the last man leaped from the troop carrier, it pulled away and continued north serving as a decoy of sorts. We assembled at the command of Lieutenant Bristol. He looked rather debonair in his camouflaged parachute silk scarf, and sporting a weird long sword that looked more like a museum piece than a deadly weapon. I guess he was trying to make a reputation for himself- or maybe he was bucking for a "Section 8" (deemed mentally unfit for service, and at that time, homosexual).

At any rate, we headed into the dense jungle in single file, spaced about five yards apart. Our weapons had no shoulder straps which meant that we had to carry them in our hands. Feeling skittish, none of us were in a mood to sling them over our shoulders anyway. Our little patrol possessed a lot of potential firepower with two stens, two brens (light machine guns) and a few new Belgian FN rifles (bolt action sniper rifles), plus pistols and other miscellaneous firearms. However, all the firepower in the world would not help us if we were suddenly caught in a well-planned ambush. We penetrated deeper and deeper into the darkness of the jungle, the vegetation so thick that the plants seemed to be struggling against one another for their very existence. Our eyes became sore, and our bodies exhausted as we taxed all our senses to the utmost in an effort to survive.

Later in the day we came upon a mammoth rubber plantation. Several Malayan natives and their children were busily tapping the trees gathering the milky white latex. They were dressed in rags and children under six were working along with their mothers. It took us more than an hour to check the natives' identification cards. They were tight-lipped and unsmiling as we approached, reluctant to show us their cards, some out of fear and others out of hatred. Many of the rubber workers were either informers or terrorists themselves, but it was a difficult task to pin anything on them unless they were caught with a weapon in their possession. Of those searched we found no incriminating evidence. One of the terrorists killed in a recent raid was a fourteen year-old girl; therefore these tight-lipped women were by no means being questioned for the mere fun of it. None threatened us with a gun, but didn't give us any information either, which undoubtedly was possible. When we finished with our search, they carried on with tapping of the rubber trees.

We passed through the plantation and entered back into the jungle, continually plotting our route on a map. If we failed to find an ambush, the entire company would use this same route the following day. It was impossible to tread quietly through the thick tropical vines and undergrowth. We had been ordered to shoot to kill upon sight of anyone outside the plantation, but no targets had appeared. We trudged back, reaching the roadside at a pre-arranged hour to meet the armored troop carrier for our return to base camp.

No sooner had I disembarked from the troop carrier than I was told to report to Captain Scot. I did so immediately and it was as I had expected, disheartening news. Apparently Captain Beans of the Yong Peng police had informed the Colonel in charge of the K.O.S.B. at their regimental headquarters that I was currently a member of the K.O.S.B. The Colonel had then called Captain Scot and informed him that I could not go out on any patrols with the K.O.S.B. for fear that complications might arise. In the event that I was wounded or killed there would be a lengthy investigation as to why I had been allowed to join them in the first place. It would also have been embarrassing to the U.S. Department of State. Captain Scot apologized for having to go back on his word, but I fully realized that he had already done more for me than he was actually authorized to do. Therefore when he suggested that I remain with them in the garrison, I decided to be on my way. Perhaps I could join the famed British Commandoes, the Red Berets, further north.

Within minutes my backpack was stuffed with my paltry possessions and I passed through the front gate, starting up the road. I was surprised to hear the shouts of the K.O.S.B. troops behind me. Glancing around I realized that they had come out to the barbed wire barricade to say good-bye. Their thoughtful gesture certainly brightened my spirits. I returned and shook hands with them over and through the fence. Many of them said they wished they could accompany me, but they added that they did not envy my chances for a long life, heading north into a "no-man's land", with darkness falling in a couple of hours. I felt a bit sad as I turned my back on them and began walking up the lonely road. They were great guys and I could at least hope Anglo-American relations might be a bit stronger as result of my sojourn.

Chapter 8:

Malacca: Nuns, Red Berets and a Lack of Maps

MALACCA, THE THIRD smallest state in Malaya and located in the southern region of the Malay Peninsula (now a World Heritage Site), was my next destination, some ninety miles north. As I plodded along I could not help but worry that I may have to walk the entire distance. I doubted that anyone would give me a lift due to the political situation, not to mention my coarse appearance. Yet, within an hour a car did whiz by and come to a skidding halt several hundred yards up the road. I wasted no time running to the car, despite not knowing whether the occupants were about to assassinate me- or give me a lift.

It was a great surprise to find two Catholic nuns in the back seat. Resting across their laps lay a large statue of the Holy Mother, which they lovingly protected. The driver, obviously in a hurry to reach Malacca before the curfew, was a pleasant English speaking Italian, and a building contractor. He had just finished building a convent in Malacca where the two nuns in the rear seat were going to teach. The nuns were also Italian but with limited knowledge of the English language. The contractor drove like a maniac, many times careening the car from one side of the road to the other to avoid hitting water buffalo. A young white goat literally lost its head when it was whacked by the front bumper as he didn't bother to slow down for smaller animals.

We waited in the village of Bandar Maharani to board a small barge, which later ferried us across the murky Muar River to Malacca. The slight delay gave me a chance to wash a few pieces of my rancid clothing, in the equally rancid water. Since I didn't carry washing powder, it was debatable as to the value of the effort.

We raced into Malacca as darkness closed in on the ancient city. It had originally been settled by Portuguese and many of the ruins and relics were still intact. The Italian contractor dropped the two nuns at their new convent and then took me on to a large western hotel overlooking the Straits of Malacca. He apparently assumed I would spend the night there because it was the place for white people to stay. It would not have been proper for a westerner to spend the night at one of the less expensive native hotels. So I said I would spend the night at the elegant hotel rather than shock him with the truth. I checked my pack with the clerk and then joined him for a fine Chinese meal at his favorite restaurant. He thought I had a lot of courage, and insisted on picking up the bill for the meal. It would have been most embarrassing if he hadn't been so generous: I had less than sixty cents in Malayan money in my pocket.

I decided the safest place to sleep would be on the lawn under the Indian gooseberry trees of Bandar Hilir Park. I crossed through the park to the hotel to pick up my checked pack, but found the hotel doors to be locked. Since it was still quite warm, I returned to the park and crawled into a pile of wet leaves next to one of the ancient Portuguese cannons that used to guard the port of Malacca. I awoke several times the first few hours to find that it was getting much cooler. Mosquitoes were feasting on me, but as there was no one to issue me a T.S. card (tough shit), I had to grin and bear my misery. By two a.m. it started to rain and I could take it no longer. I walked back into town passing a Portuguese graveyard. The dead were in stone vaults above the ground and I momentarily considered crawling into one of the vaults to get free of the rain and mosquitoes. Surely there would have been room for me: the bodies would have rotted away hundreds of years ago, but the tops of the stone caskets were secured with cement.

I continued into the heart of town searching for a more suitable bed. Only a few teashops were open. Most of the street's inhabitants at that hour were mangy dogs and healthy rats. A group of drunken Chinese hoodlums seemed to be trailing me so I dodged in and out of a few alleys to shake them. On the corner of one of the alleys I found a large piece of burlap in a garbage heap. A bit slimy and stinky, it could serve as a blanket and was better than nothing.

Dragging the burlap behind me, I set out to find a place to lie down, and roll up. Luck was with me this time. On the next block I found a bed standing on the end next to a small spice shop. The bed was of simple construction, more like a cot, except that in place of canvas it had a mattress of twine. Merchants would use such beds to sleep in front of their shops to protect them. I dragged the bed out near a streetlight and as soon as I became accustomed to the smell of the burlap, fell sound asleep where I slept until awakened by three Hindus who were trying to push me out of bed; perhaps it belonged to them. I pretended to be asleep until they finally left. As they walked off, I heard them mumble as if highly displeased. Maybe they had wanted to rob me, and upon seeing how poor I looked, had given up. I slept until I was awakened by the noise of early morning shoppers, embarrassed to find myself surrounded by curious natives in broad daylight likely seeing for the first time a white man sleeping on the sidewalks of Malacca.

Once I retrieved my pack, I had to walk several miles outside of Malacca in stifling heat before a car stopped to give me a lift. There were a couple of other passengers in the car. Each got out in different towns, paying the driver upon exit. I wondered why, and then it dawned on me: I was riding in a *taxi.* I did not have enough in Malayan currency to get me ten city blocks. The driver spoke no English. When he let me off in the village of Tampin, some twenty miles distant, I offered him the few cents I had, but he graciously refused. So many times in my travels I would observe those with the least to offer were the most generous.

Early in the afternoon I got a ride on the back of a truck headed for Kuala Lumpur, the capital of Malaya. I spent the remainder of the afternoon perched atop the truck cab along with the assistant driver. Most of the trucks in South East Asia have an assistant driver on the roofs of the truck cabs to direct any vehicle that wishes to pass. The country near Kuala Lumpur was hilly, rugged, and full of hairpin turns. The usefulness of the assistant driver was immediately apparent as he prevented many head-on collisions by signaling tailing vehicles to not pass when oncoming vehicles were in sight. I was sun and wind-burned by the time we arrived in early evening on the outskirts of Kuala Lumpur. A British officer gave me a short lift, and directed me to the 22nd S.A.S., a contingent of the Red Berets.

It was after duty hours when I approached the guard gate. One of the M.P. guards came out to ask the purpose of my visit. Upon learning that I wanted to join the Red Berets he told me that I would have to wait until the following day when I could report to the 2nd in Command (2IC). He ushered me into the guardhouse where he and one of his cohorts, an orderly, thoroughly examined my passport, visa, and other credentials. They were much more security conscious than the K.O.S. B. had been. The orderly was a young, muscular, loudmouthed trustee. It seemed that he was also a ladies' man, so much in fact that his women had recently taken more of his time than the military, something that the military frowns upon. He was tossed into the stockade for a month to see if his bad habits might be corrected. The guards shared their supper with me, while the untrained orderly served us from a large pot with a ladle till our trays overflowed.

After chow I washed my khakis on the floor of the improvised shower-room, and bathed to look my best when reporting to the 2IC. From the troops I had seen, the Red Berets were some of the sharpest dressed soldiers on earth. Anything I could do to improve my filthy, wrinkled khakis would lessen my shabby appearance. I beat them on the concrete floor until the darker stains faded and hung them on the eaves of the stockade. A guard warned me that the clothes would have to be out of sight before reveille the following morning.

The Red Berets were as rough and ready a bunch of blokes as I had ever seen. When they were not jumping deep into the jungles ferreting out terrorists, they were down in Kuala Lumpur tearing the bars, broads, and Alien British troops apart. It was a bit like old home week to be with the troops that were highly respected, if not feared, by their comrades in other outfits. One of the boys changed some of my American money so that I could do my share of the buying.

A new guard relief was on duty when I returned to the guardhouse for the night. They were friendly, but a bit more skeptical, so they locked me in the stockade with the orderly and a deserter for the night. It was a far cry from the previous night's bedroom, but I could not have been safer from the terrorists. I slept well.

My fellow inmates were awakened earlier than the rest of the troops as a harassing element, so I rolled out of bed at the same time, taking my khakis down from the eaves. My khakis were not dry, but I put them on anyway figuring they would be by the time I got around to seeing the 2IC.

I watched the Red Berets at reveille that morning. A more formidable parade of soldiers I had never seen. Certainly the

American military had nothing to equal them. They drilled with the precision of a fine watch, their discipline far greater than ours.

I reported to the Regimental Sergeant Major in his office, which overlooked the drill field. The Sergeant Major was tall, lean, and mustached. He commanded more respect than any officer in the regiment, even though he was only a non-commissioned officer. He barked at enlisted men and officers alike as they came into his office. He had tea brought in which we drank while I explained to him that I would like to join his outfit. He was flattered when I told him that the Red Berets were known the world over. He excused himself to make an appointment for me with the 2IC.

I walked into the 2IC's office with as much of a military bearing as I could muster. My khakis were in sad shape compared to the clean pressed uniforms of the Red Berets. The 2IC was a Major so he remained seated as I entered. I told him that: I had been in American 10th Special Forces Airborne; its mission was similar to that of the Red Berets; and I was anxious to join his outfit on their next jungle mission. He found it difficult to understand why an American would want to risk his life with a British outfit. I explained that both the U.S.A. and Great Britain were waging a fight against communism, and that as long as both nations were fighting a common enemy I may as well join up with the British. After all, they were currently engaged in warfare against the communists whereas the U.S.A. was not. But the Major and I realized that officially I could not join a British outfit unless I forfeited my citizenship. The Major seemed eager to sign me up for a few months, but it would have to be done unofficially, without any paperwork, for his protection as well as mine. The only drawback was that when the Red Berets jumped into the jungles, I could not possibly board a troop transport; the names of the troops are carefully checked on the flight manifest. Our plan would be foiled even before I was airborne.

I thanked the Major for his efforts and left with officers headed to Kuala Lumpur in a land rover. After changing some of my U.S. money into Malayan currency I went directly to the American consulate where I hoped to obtain a map of Siam, which I hoped to reach within a week, with luck. It was a real shock when Vice Consular Cummings addressed me as Mr. Wallace when I entered the Consulate. I had never reported to any other American Consulate since my arrival in Singapore, therefore the only way they could possibly have known my name is through my associations with the British military. All sorts of ideas ran through my mind, for I knew that I had violated passport regulations by being with the British. The American Consulate could invalidate my passport on the spot, or arrest me, impose a fine, or effect all three if they wished. I dared not ask how he knew my name.

Cummings asked me to take a ride with him in his staff car, while he made a few calls. I was extremely concerned this had to do with my breach of conduct and he was just gathering information to prosecute me. Neither one of us said a word, until he broke the silence by inviting me into a respectable looking restaurant for a refreshing beer. While downing our beers he allayed my apprehension by telling me that he had been informed of my little episode with the Red Berets by one of the officers. I noticed that he was wearing a tie clasp made from paratroopers jump wing, which meant that he too had been a paratrooper. I felt an immediate sense of ease. He said that he admired my courage, but he quickly added that if I were to openly fight any communists I had better not let the State Department know about it for it could cause a lot of embarrassment for all concerned. Had he not been married, he added, he would have liked to be doing as the same.

We returned to the consulate where he introduced me to his staff and showed me available maps of South East Asia, outdated and not much help. I wanted to know whether or not there were any roads traversing Southern Siam to Bangkok. No one seemed to know. Modern maps were unobtainable due to security reasons. The Vice-Consul advised me to be cautious of the people I associates with: terrorists were to be found almost anyplace. Since the Royal Air Force was engaged in concentrated bombing of the terrorist jungle strongholds, many of the guerillas found it safer to seek refuge in the crowds of Kuala Lumpur. Five guerillas had been killed in a gun battle on the golf course this very morning, while two more had been shot down as they tried to escape from a city bus they were riding. The police found hand grenades in their trouser pockets.

That evening, as I finished my dinner in a local café and got up to leave, an attractive English woman called me over to her table. Margaret seemed lonely and melancholy and offered to buy me a beer. She spoke of her marriage to a Jewish-German intellectual who taught at the local university and how her husband would spend his evenings in his study, engrossed in books, rather than spending any of his free time with her. She was frustrated, as she didn't enjoy all the social gatherings where foreign-stationed wives spent their time. She implied that we could have a mutually comforting evening together. My loneliness was the constant companion that was not going away. It gnawed at me, especially at night, and over empty café tables. I ached for companionship and perhaps this is part of why I was so driven to join a military company. I sympathized with her, but then I had my very survival to think about, let alone my happiness. As tempting she might have been, further entanglement with a married woman was not in my range of consideration, and certainly could not end well. I excused myself after my second beer to look for a more suitable option for the night and found a Christian mission, which was new, very clean, and came with a comfortable bed- all for thirty cents.

Chapter 9:

Finding Chin

THE NEXT MORNING as I was trying to find my way out of Kuala Lumpur through the Central Market, I passed a pet store. Two large gibbons were tied up on the sidewalk in front under an awning, seeking shade from the sun that was starting to press the cool morning air away. As long as I could remember, I had always loved animals and always wanted a monkey, but these looked too big and fierce. They were probably expensive, too. But it would cost me nothing to retrace my steps to take a closer look to see if they had any other monks. The noisy little shop was piled high with cages of parrots, cockatoos, parakeets, lories and macaws, some hanging from the low ceiling causing customers to bump their heads into the poor pets in waiting. There was also a fair selection of long-tailed Macaque monkeys which I knew have a long history alongside humans; they have been alternately seen as agricultural pests, sacred animals in some temples and have been used in many medical labs of late. They are "opportunistic omnivores" and have been documented using tools to obtain food.

One monkey appealed to me more than all the others combined. He was the size of a small cat, with a scruffy grayish brown pelt, a blue belly and moist, downcast amber eyes. Once I spied him, I stopped looking at the others. He seemed so young, small, vulnerable and unhappy in his bamboo tiny cage. When I spoke to him, he looked up, and extended a delicate paw tentatively toward me through the reedy bars. I put my finger within reach to touch his "hand" and was struck by how cool and papery it felt. I sensed an immediate connection.

The shopkeeper wanted five dollars for him. I was not about to part with that amount, unless the monkey was well mannered enough to make a good traveling companion. I asked the shopkeeper if I could take the monkey on a little trial jaunt. Leaving my pack as collateral, I opened his cage and tugged on the end of his leash. He promptly jumped out of the cage, gnatted his teeth at me, and then bit my hand! I dropped the leash and the monkey ran wild about the shop, climbing over the other monkey cages until he reached the ceiling. He then hopped across the parrot perches much to the dislike of the parrots who tried to peck at him. The monkey's leash finally got entangled in the stands holding the birdcages enabling me to catch him. I dragged him out of the shop to the crowded street and headed towards the bazaar. The monkey did not like being on a leash, constantly balking to grab at a piece of refuse on the street. Walking down a crowded alley he grabbed hold of a woman's pink blouse that had been hung out to dry, pulling one it off the line and down into the filth of the alley. I scolded him sternly and we continued without incident until the rascal knocked over a bowl of soup from a pushcart cafe. The Chinese vendor was furious, the onlookers laughed, I was embarrassed, and the monkey was completely oblivious.

Once his antics settled down (perhaps he had just been in that cage too long), he agilely climbed up on my shoulder, and remained peacefully while I strode around the market, occasionally grabbing at the sundry wares that were hanging from the awnings we passed under. Every once in awhile he would take his miniature hand and comb through my side burns or beard, mostly curious I think. I decided that I would keep him, and name him Chin Peng after the notorious Chinese leader of the communist terrorists in Malaya, for the monkey was certainly a trouble maker, and could be fierce at times. I returned to the monkey shop and argued with the shopkeeper that the monkey was not worth the five dollars he was asking because he was undoubtedly young and untrained. We came to a compromise where I paid three-fifty for Chin Peng and he tossed in a large leash to lead him. If only Chin could have known what his future held I am sure he would have committed suicide on the spot, if monkeys do that.

CHIN AND I ambled out of Kuala Lumpur with a lightened spring in our steps. He was free from his cage, and I was no longer alone. People smiled at the two of us as though sensing a desirable friendship brewing. I was suddenly no longer invisible, and had an instant point of conversation. We passed by a Chinese funeral procession. The deceased was stretched out on a two-wheeled cart drawn by many coolies, all haggard looking. A motley band filled the air with inharmonious tones. It was a colorful, incongruous sight, almost laughable. Adding a white man with a monkey on his shoulder to the crowd seemed fitting. Chin was completely mesmerized by the spectacle.

For our first ride together, we hitched on the back of a truck for several miles north, enjoying the refreshing breeze after the stagnant city market air. It wasn't long enough until we were dropped off at a lonely fork in the road, a desolate area surrounded by nothing but deep, dark jungle emanating frightening sounds. After the wind of the open aired ride, we needed water and tumbled down a steep embankment to a stream where we were able to splash around and cool off. Chin was not entirely sure what to do with the water and entertained me with his exploratory poking and flinches, confirming my hunch that he had been raised entirely in captivity.

As we clambered up the bank to the road, a British patrol approached on foot- startling us. They checked my papers thoroughly as their two bloodhounds sniffed at Chin, who quickly scampered up my leg to my arm and landed on my shoulder, his new perch for safety. The patrol leader boasted that he had just killed a terrorist (communist insurgent) with his trusty Belgian FN rifle, but two others had escaped. They said that I had best get out of the area for my own protection. They then formed a roadblock, stopped the first vehicle approaching from the south, and ordered the driver to give me a lift.

I happily tossed my gear into the rear of the green Morris IB van and we headed northward towards Ipoh, the capital city of Perak State and one of the largest cities in Malaya, famous for its booming tin industry. The driver was a pleasant English government official, who had recently relinquished his command to his Malayan understudy: Malaya was to get its independence in a few months (August, 1957). The driver had served in Malaya for twenty years, but he believed that Malaya was ready for its independence despite the national state of emergency facing the country. He added that he felt his understudy was a most capable and reliable man for the job.

We reached Ipoh by late afternoon where yet again assumptions were made and the driver dropped us off in front of the town's most respectable hotel. As an American, I would demand the best. The hotel looked far too respectable for me to eat in, let alone afford to spend the night. I had not eaten since the previous evening so I decided to go "whole hog" and eat a decent meal at a nearby café as soon as he pulled away. Two British soldiers sat at the next table. I let them hang onto Chin's chain as I busied myself with the food before me but he managed to spring up on their table and knock over a glass of beer before any of us could stop him. I realized that I had a lot to learn about keeping Chin out of mischief.

I wanted to get to Kuala Kangsar before darkness set in, so after eating hastily I headed up the main street. Pausing at an intersection with Chin contentedly resting on my shoulder, I tried to figure out which road led north when a car pulled up beside me. I asked the driver if he could direct me to the northbound road. Without answering my question, he introduced himself as Goh Sin Tub, a reporter for the Singapore Tiger Standard newspaper. (see photo 10) He was Chinese, but his English was better than mine. Goh asked me to spend the night in Ipoh as a guest of his employers. I found it difficult to refuse his offer, and that is how Chin and I ended up in front of Goh's office a few minutes later where a photographer took our picture for the front page of the newspaper (on the cover of my book). After checking my passport, Goh asked numerous questions about my trip. Although he seemed fascinated by what I told him, he found much of it difficult to believe. In fact, he phoned Kuala Lumpur in my presence to make sure that I was not a *spy*. He spoke in Chinese over the phone so I was not aware of his evil intentions at the time and only came to understand this later.

Once reassured, Goh encouraged me to leave Chin in his office and took me to meet a friend of his, a young, heavy-set Chinese named Yibby who had obviously been standing at the bar too long. Goh explained that Yibby was the wealthy son of a tin mine owner, and also had a mine of his own. Yibby was a backslapping boisterous character, and he was "feeling no pain." He bought us a few drinks of whiskey, which I had to force down at his command. Yibby then insisted that we accompany him to a cocktail party, which he claimed was in progress at Choong Sam's palatial estate. I was far from being appropriately dressed, but Yibby said my appearance would not matter since it was so late, everyone would be drunk by the time we got there. As we drove to the outskirts of Ipoh, Yibby told me a bit about Choong Sam. Choong Sam began his life as one of several children of coolie class Chinese parents at the turn of the century. Choong spent his childhood working in the tin mines, rather than attending school.

He worked harder, and lived more frugally than his fellow workers, until he was able to purchase a small piece of land of his own. Luckily for Choong, the small plot he purchased was rich with tin deposits. He sold it at a huge profit and kept reinvesting his money until today he was the richest man in the state of Perak, owning ten tin mines around the world.

Goh pointed out Choong's estate glowing in the distance when we were still two miles out. Spotlights brilliantly illuminated the main house, and a massive crown of lights on top gave the place an imposing palatial appearance. As we drove up the long driveway to the hilltop estate several expensive looking foreign cars passed by on their way out. Yibby swung the car around the circular drive and parked. Yibby and Goh approached Choong Sam as he waved to the last of his guests, and then I was introduced.

Goh told Choong the story he was writing about my journey and apparently it struck a chord with Choong. He not only shook my hand but also hugged and kissed me on both cheeks as well and welcomed us into his awe-inspiring castle. More than half of the main floor was devoted to a cocktail lounge. One wall was floor to ceiling fully stocked shelves filled with liquor from all parts of the world. Choong spoke not one word of English, so we had to speak to each other through Goh or Yibby. Choong told us that the guests who had just left were fellow tin mine owners, and said they were a "rather stuffy lot". Now that they were gone he wanted to get down to some serious drinking. Choong was an excellent host. He ordered the bartender to put our preferred choices of whiskey on the bar so that each could mix his drinks to his liking. Choong's selections of whiskey would have been the envy of the majority of the world's bars. Choong believed in giving a good measure, so he had done away with small shot glasses in lieu large, tumbler-style glasses. For a primer Choong poured us each a potent glassful of Hennessey's Five Star Cognac. No sooner had he filled the last of our glasses than he toasted with "Yum Seng" which means "bottoms up". I hesitated a moment, but Goh told me it was a Chinese custom, and that to refuse to "Yum Seng" was an insult. The top of my skull tingled as I gulped down the potent liquid. With our glasses refilled, Choong led us upstairs to the balcony where we looked out over one of his large tin mines. Goh emphasized that Choong Sam had done much for the welfare of his employees. Nearby were several modern workers' huts, far superior to the majority of workers' huts I had seen in Malaya.

Choong then suggested we visit a private club in Ipoh for a midnight snack. We piled into Choong's shinning chauffer-driven Mercedes and roared into town. The chauffer was a Hindu, and he was an expert at wheeling the big car as we sped into the heart of the city. Eventually we came to an abrupt halt in front of a large deserted-appearing three-story structure. Two elegant, young Chinese women escorted us to the second floor where Choong met us at the front door. There we entered an immense ballroom where we seated ourselves around the only table in the otherwise empty hall. Within a few minutes our table was covered with all sorts of delicacies, and several bottles of Hennessey's cognac. Choong tutored me in the proper use of chopsticks, and with a little practice I was able to pick up a peanut. I had no idea what most of the savories consisted of, but it really didn't matter since the cognac had deadened my taste buds.

After a couple of hours of gorging with food and drink, we were hardly able to move-such a contrast to my days of bread and water in the Australian Outback. Goh told me that we had better leave before we all got so plastered that we could not even crawl home. Goh looked at his watch and feigned surprise, announced that it was 2 a.m. and that I was to have called the American Embassy at twelve on urgent business. He had hoped this would serve as an excuse for us to leave. But Choong Sam was nobody's fool, and he reprimanded Goh for trying to pull a fast exit. Goh was unwilling to leave influential Choong without a good excuse, so we stayed put. A vivacious Chinese girl dressed in a graceful sari joined us for a while. Before long the girl was running her fingers through Yippy's hair, caressing his lips and blowing into his ears. Yippy became uneasy for some reason, and allowed the oriental maiden to whisk him away to the privacy of a small room.

Half a bottle later when Yippy rejoined us, he had a look of contentment on his face. We toasted to anything that entered our minds: to the downfall of the terrorists; to the beauty of Chinese women; to Malaya's upcoming independence; to finding Chin-and other worthy causes. Throughout the drinking Choong embraced me, shaking my hand after every toast as if to confirm its sincerity. By five a.m. neither Choong nor I were able to stand up to go to the latrine. Goh and Yippy were in better shape, so they supported us as we staggered out of the building into the street where I wretched my guts out. Choong yanked a handkerchief from his pocket and pushed it against my sagging head. I filled the hanky with more chunder. Choong was so unstable that he dobbed my whole face with the contaminated hanky. I wretched again. Choong grabbed the hanky which his chauffer held out for him and repeated the well-intentioned effort. I felt much better physically having spewed my fill, but I had sobered up enough to feel highly embarrassed. Choong's last intelligible statement was that he wanted me to be his guest the following night at a press party he was throwing. Before I had time to respond, Choong had passed out on the back seat of the Mercedes.

The chauffer dropped me off in front of the news office just as the sun showed itself for the new day. The night watchman who let me in was a dark, mean-looking Hindu. I fell asleep on the springs of an army cot in the back room as soon as the bed stopped swaying. Chin chattered softly, so happy to see me he was clawing at my jacket. It was but an annoyance at that moment and seared its way into my growing headache. I swore off of drink for life.

I awoke at noon drenched in sweat, and laden with a colossal hangover. Goh was busy writing his article in the front office. He was not feeling the best either. I took a shower and then Chin and I went out to fetch a few bananas. I was still in a daze after I washed my clothes while taking a second shower. Goh reminded me that we had been invited to Choong's party that evening. Miraculously by eight p.m. both Goh and I felt well enough to take off for Choong's estate. This time Chin insisted on joining us and with a nod from Goh, was allowed to ride on my shoulder for much of the upcoming evening.

I noted that all the guests were dressed in tropical suits- twenty male reporters in all. I felt highly conspicuous as I was dressed in khaki trousers and a flannel sport shirt. But my appearance made no difference to Choong. After a few preliminary drinks we sat down at a long table laden with oriental delicacies. I had the honor of sitting next to Choong at the head of the table. It was indeed a dubious honor, for Choong filled my water glass with straight cognac and said "Yum Seng." I refused to unless he joined me with an equal portion. Without hesitating he filled his own glass, stood up and toasted. He called my bluff so I had no choice but to gulp down the lethal potion as the other guests looked on approvingly. Hindu waiters placed the first course before each of us. A large bowl of white, blubbery sharks' fins! It was followed by fried strips of pigskin, shrimp omelets, salad, relishes, and finally placed before me was a small featherless bird, a young pigeon known as "squab". It lay in two symmetrical halves, cut perfectly through the head and even its tiny beak. One of its eyes seemed to be looking up at me so I flopped the piece over before tackling the nasty chore of devouring such a delicate creature. I watched the others and sucked the flesh from its spindly bones, and ate its minute mushy brain. Choong and most guests even plucked the meat from the toy-like heads, but I had not consumed enough cognac to follow suit. And I was *determined* to stay more sober than I had the previous night.

After a few more doses of collectible Scotch, Choong suggested that we all head for the Celestial Cabaret. I rode with Choong and one of his wives in his Rolls Royce, the only Rolls Royce in the State of Perak outside of the Sultans. Because Choong ignored the advice of his brother and the other guests, I was delegated to the impossible task of keeping Choong fairly sober. He had been drinking the whole day as it was, and had been warned by doctors that he would soon kill himself at the rate he was going.

Our party of twenty-one revelers entered the cabaret was met by the headwaiter who promptly found tables to accommodate us, despite the crowds. To do so he had to evict several patrons from their chairs, but they did not seem to mind, as he was not only important but also well- liked by the local populace. Waiters brought on several bottles of champagne and cognac. In efforts to prevent Choong from getting plastered, as well as myself, I encouraged him to do some dancing. He followed my suggestion, but carried his glass of cognac when he left the table to find a suitable partner. We spent a good deal of the evening dancing but each time the orchestra stopped, Choong would invite me to the nearest inconspicuous table he could find to sit and drink with our partners. As the evening wore on Choong began to feel the effects of the cognac, all at once. His brother came to the rescue suggesting the elite Chinese Kinta Club would have fresher air. And indeed, the party moved to enjoy a complete modern orchestra and exotic Chinese delicacies.

Thus was Chin's introduction to life on the road with Thillman.

Chapter 10:

Butterworth and a Mad Dash to Penang

SLEEP CAME EASILY that night, but a scrawny Hindu awakened me before dawn. He was headed one hundred miles north to Butterworth, principal town in the state of Penang and site of an integrated transport hub linking rail, bus, and ferry, with plans to deliver newspapers to towns enroute. Within a few minutes I gathered my gear and Chin- and we were off. We reached Butterworth by noon where Chin and I boarded a ferry for George Town on the island of Penang. I hoped to visit the Siamese consulate to apply for a visa. Chin perched himself on a railing during our short ferry ride so that he could get a better view of the sampans taking cargo from a Russian freighter.

Upon arrival, we went to the American consulate to get directions to the Siamese consulate, but because it was Saturday, was closed. I had completely lost track of days. In Asia the shops do not close on Sunday. The religions of the orient do not hold any particular day of the week to be more conducive to righteous actions, visiting their temples any time of the day or week when moved to do so.

We passed the afternoon at the Mariner's Club with a group of English seamen. The seamen had a great time giving beer to Chin from their glasses. Chin was a bit tipsy as he and I left to find a place to sleep. I had hoped to spend the night in the seaman's club. However, management, upon learning that I was not a seaman was highly indignant that I had so much as purchased a meal there.

Just around the corner from the Mariners Club an old Hindu gentleman approached me. He knew that I was in search of something, and was curious. Speaking Pidgin English he asked if he could be of assistance. He was poorly dressed in rags, and barefooted and called himself Salman. When I told him that I was in search of a cheap place to spend the night he led me down a back alley. We climbed up a set of rickety stairs and entered what appeared to be a flophouse. The manager showed me the only vacant room, which had a simple, single cot and small window with gauze covering the portal, but asked too much- so we left. Salman informed me that I would not be able to find a cheaper place to spend the night on the island. He explained that he was a guard for the building where we had met, and suggested that I could sleep on the sidewalk with him if I desired. I took out my sleeping bag and stowed the rest of my gear in the building and left Chin with him while I went down to the wharf to try to change some money.

Scores of trishaw drivers tried to whisk me away to various brothels, or to buy my money at a poor rate of exchange. The heat was getting to me and it's always worse when you are hungry. I was getting frustrated at having to fend so many shysters off. One weary fact of travel in countries with citizens less fortunate than our own- which is most countries around the world- is that there will always be someone trying to abstract whatever you have, with any method they can muster. It requires vast stores of patience to tolerate this without becoming angry.

Just when I was about to give up, a Eurasian lad pulled his trishaw up next to me. He spoke English well, introduced himself as "Dunc" and asked me what I was doing. When I told him that I wanted to purchase some Siamese money, he told me not to do it with any of the trishaw drivers who had formed a circle around us. He told me to be cautious when dealing with them, and added that I had better get away from the dimly lit wharf before they robbed me. Then he offered to show me some of the sights for nothing if I agreed to do half the pedaling. I was highly suspicious of him, too, but it would be a lot easier for me to cope with one than the mob so I took off in his trishaw.

We pedaled far out of George Town along the shore road of the island. Dunc was barefooted; dressed only in a pair of blue shorts, and a torn dirty t-shirt. He explained that he was a misfit as he was of mixed of blood, thereby feeling out of place with Europeans or Asians. He had a defeatist attitude, believing that life was hardly worth the struggle. When I told Dunc that I had left my monkey, cameras, and clothing with some Hindu, he said that it was a stupid thing for me to do, for the Hindu had probably pawned everything. Dunc pedaled as fast as possible back into town. We noticed a large gathering of pedestrians in front of the building that contained my gear. I expected to find the old man auctioning off my possessions, and learned my second lesson in assumptions on the trail. After I pushed my way through the crowd only to find Salman in the middle, playing contently with Chin, I felt prejudiced and foolish. Dunc remarked that I had certainly been lucky to find such an honest keeper, but I was beginning to learn that I could in fact trust my intuition. As he pedaled off, he shouted over his shoulder that he would return in the morning. And I had no doubt he would.

Once the crowd dispersed, I rolled out my bed, and fell asleep on the hard sidewalk. Salman stretched out on a narrow bench nearby, and Chin curled up beside me. I awoke several times during the night when pedestrians stumbled over me. Just before dawn, Salman told me I would have to move away from the front of the building he guarded. If his friends were to find a white man asleep there, they would ridicule him endlessly. Without arguing I moved across the street and finished my sleep on the concrete floor of a vacated little guardhouse.

When Dunc showed up about 7 a.m., we piled my gear into the trishaw and pedaled off to his home. He lived with his mother and father who had never married. We had a cup of tea, unloaded my gear on his steps, and then Dunc and I took off with Chin on my shoulder. Pedestrians and other trishaw drivers looked in awe when they saw me, a Caucasian pedaling a trishaw with a Eurasian seated comfortable in the passenger seat- not to mention carrying a monkey on his shoulder. We saw much of Penang, truly a tropical paradise for the well to do. We spent most of the day ambling through the mysterious Ayer Itam Pagoda, also known as Kek Lok Si Temple, the tallest pagoda in Malaya. The odor of burning incense permeated the air. Endless lines of flags flanked approach to the temple. Chin was tempted to run off with the scores of wild monkeys populating the property, but clung steadfastly to my jacket, now beginning to show tracks of small tears from his sometimes frantic ascent to safety.

In the afternoon we took the air-conditioned Penang Hill Railway cable car to the top of Penang Hill. Chin's fare was half again the amount of a human fare. I could not see the reason for such an outrageous fee! I guess Chin couldn't either, for he took the liberty of dropping a stool on the cable car floor. I was so angry about the fee that I left it right where he dropped it.

From the peak we could see all of the lush greenery of Penang, and far into Malaya proper. When we stopped for lunch, Dunc ordered rice and curry for both of us. I was surprised that it cost so little, far less than I had been paying. Dunc explained that many people would take advantage of me, for I could not expect to be able to read their menus.

Chin and I were on the road early the next morning. The sky was thick with dark purple clouds, and the heat and humidity were stifling. Rain would have been a relief, but soon the clouds passed over to allow the tropical sun to beat upon us. Chinese peasants were busily threshing rice by beating the stalks over boards, in the adjacent paddies. A grotesque vehicle approached, but failed to stop. I realized that it was a homemade armored car, probably belonging to a nearby plantation. It was a dull, grey 41' Ford. The windows were covered with steel plating with small slits in each for the driver to see through. From the number of dents in the plating, it was obvious that the car had survived enemy attack.

Eventually an overloaded truck gave us a lift into South Pattani, right next to the Siam border (now Thailand). As I plodded through the town, I came to a group of government buildings. A Hindu, dressed in white, accompanied by a soldier, shouted at me as they came running out of the central building. They asked to see my papers. When the Hindu saw my American passport he was speechless, for he later explained that he had mistaken me for a Tibetan medicine man! The Tibetans occasionally wander from far off Tibet selling herbs along the way. Like me, they carry all their possessions on their backs. The Hindu looked through my passport and delivered shocking news: my Malayan visa would expire within the next *twelve hours*. I had neglected to pay much heed to the number of days that had passed since my arrival in Singapore.

He advised me to get to Alor Setar (forty miles away) as soon as possible where, if lucky, I could catch the afternoon train for the Siamese border. The border was yet another sixty miles north of Alor Setar. If I failed to make it then I would be spending time in the security of some rudimentary jail until unknown parties could clear up the mess. The Hindu gave me a couple of rolls of fish wrapped in banana leaves because I "would have no time to stop" if I "want to beat the deadline".

Chin and I immediately began jogging out of town. Several vehicles passed us by without even slowing to look our way. With just three hours to get the forty miles to Alor Setar I had no choice but to put on my Aussie slouch hat and stand in the middle of the road pretending that I was a military check point. The first truck approaching from the south fell for my plot rather- than run me down. They were headed for Alor Setar so my troubles were over, unless the truck broke down, as they so often did. While the truck did not break down, it moved so slowly that we did not reach Alor Setar until after the train's scheduled departure. I wasted no time, running through the town to the northbound road where I prayed we'd be able to get a lift to the border in time. A stocky Malayan youth sauntered up. Upon learning that I was desperate for a lift to the border, he told it was useless for me to try to bum a lift because there was very little, if any, northbound traffic so late in the day. He then told me that the train was late, and if I hurried I might still make it.

The train chugged into the station as I ran up to the ticket window. But the ticket seller could not understand me. Bursting into the station master's office, I explained that I *had* to board this train. He refused to sell me a third class ticket, until I explained that it was the best I could afford. He then said that Chin could not ride on the train unless I could produce his health certificate. I had none, and fibbed, telling him I would let Chin go loose, for I had to get past the border today, with or without a monkey. By this time the train was fully loaded and starting to pull out. The station master ran out and signaled to the conductor to wait. He then wrote out a ticket. I paid him the thirty cents, dashed out of his office, stuffed Chin under my shirt and jumped onto the steps of one of the ancient passenger cars before the train chugged out of the station.

The passenger cars were so crowded that the over flow of locals had to content themselves by huddling together dangerously on the platforms and steps between the cars. I was standing precariously myself on the bottom step, hanging on to the railing lest I be thrown off as the train jerked, and swayed. Chin poked his head out of my shirt. I was unable to restrain his movement for my hands were firmly affixed to the railing. I was not about to let go for Chin's sake. He wormed out of my shirt and climbed nonchalantly up the railing, dragging his leash behind where he growled at the locals, barring his teeth. Then he attempted to jump on a few of them in search of a higher, safer position. They were so afraid of Chin they forced their way into the adjoining cars, stumbling over one another, but leaving extra room for us.

I watched the jungle roll by as a feeling of great relief washed over me, grateful yet again that luck, timing and goodwill had been on our side.

Chapter 11:

Siam: Jungle Night Terrors

JUSMAG (JOINT U.S. Military Advisory Group) is a political, economic, and military device whereby the American government spends millions of dollars supplying Siam with military equipment, advisors, and instructors in the hopes that Siam will be obligated to join us in our effort to check communist expansion. The idea was praiseworthy, but few of the American instructors and advisors speak Siamese, or are able to comprehend Thailand's manner of life. The Thais seem to resent being instructed in the use of our firearms, and complicated heavy equipment. To make matters worse, the Americans connected with JUSMAG each have a government vehicle and free gas at their disposal, they live in great comfort with ample servants while the average Thai must content himself with a coolie's existence. An American Sergeant earns as much as a Thai general. Many of the Yanks resent being stationed in Siam and therefore flaunt their money and weight around as if they owned the country. Time means little to the Thai, who are seldom in a hurry, but the American is highly frustrated, having been brought up in a perpetual rat race. He has yet to learn that blowing his car horn incessantly on the streets of Bangkok, besides being ineffective, is not apt to make us any more desirable to the Thais.

The road leading north was out of commission, and I possessed no elephant, so we took a slow moving train to Chumphon, an agriculturally based community in southern Thailand set between the Gulf of Thailand and the mountain peaks of the Phuket Range. No sooner had the train pulled out of Haad Yao than one of the many Thai soldiers aboard dashed out in the front of the crowded carriage. I followed him out of curiosity. A pool of thick red blood larger than a pie tin lay at the end of the corridor beside an elderly Thai, whose was bathed in blood. Pieces of broken glass were scattered about. We dragged the unconscious body to a nearby seat, where a fellow passenger wrapped the victim's head in a towel. An attractive girl using limited English that was difficult to understand explained that probably some communist insurgent had thrown a large rock through the window. That was one reason so many soldiers rode the trains. Their protective capacity seemed questionable.

Later that night, the train slowed to a snail's pace as it lumbered over a mountain. I strolled out on the platform between the carriages to get some much needed fresh air. A person could have walked faster than the train was moving. It was so dark that I thought we were passing through some sort of manmade tunnel, but as my eyes became adjusted, I realized that we were passing through a natural tunnel of dense jungle. The mammoth ferns and palm fronds brushed along both sides of the carriage. Droplets of water splashed on the platform; moisture was everywhere.

Suddenly shouts of jungle natives filled the blackness. Not wanting to get my head split open by a rock, I darted into the carriage and slammed the door. The soldiers were alerted while the other passengers ducked low in their seats to avoid shattering glass. The shouts came closer and closer, terrifying the passengers. Much to our collective relief, no further violence followed.

The train reached Chumphon at two a.m. I stumbled out of the train dragging Chin and immediately found us to be surrounded by a crowd of trishaw drivers. I indicated that their service was a luxury I couldn't afford. Then the rain came down in torrents, scattering the trishaw drivers to seek shelter. One of them motioned for me to accompany him. He took me into the heart of the village where we found a protection under a leaky shop awning. Chin and I spent the night huddled together in my sleeping bag on the earthen sidewalk. A crowd of trishaw drivers and coolies were surrounding us when we awoke, as well as a few mangy dogs that had curled up beside us, asleep.

A few minutes later I was eating a bowl of plain rice in a nearby cafe. I had a bit of trouble with the chopsticks, but by placing the bowl to my mouth and scooping the rice, I managed to fill my stomach. The mangy dogs were barking hungrily at Chin who was having his breakfast on the earthen floor. I washed down the rice with a cup of weak green tea, and headed for the cafe's only toilet. It was quite a challenging set up, for there was no toilet bowl or seat, with only a four inch hole in the floor which the needy aim for, but seldom hit. Hence the floor was covered with human dung, and as the natives use their hands in lieu of toilet paper, the walls were smeared with shit because the usual finger-bath vase was missing. Welcome to rural southeast Asia.

I asked a shopkeeper which road led to Bangkok. He pointed straight ahead but didn't seem completely confident so I asked another. He indicated that it was the road to the right. In the end, I had to ask nine people which road led to Bangkok before I got three reasonably matching answers. I hoped they were right as Chin and I marched down the muddy road, presumably bound for Bangkok which lay two hundred sixty miles to the north.

Not that it wasn't an interesting walk. Elephants were lazily performing their tasks of dragging huge logs out of the dense jungles. The sun appeared and within a couple of hours, the muddy road was changed from mud and puddles back to dusty and dry. Natives cast suspicious glances at us as we strolled by their bamboo huts. No vehicles appeared for a couple of hours so we took a rest under a coconut tree on the side of the road. Sometime later an old truck rattled to a halt beside us. We scrambled into the back which was already crowded with barefooted coolies and carried us but a few miles before it was engaged in repairing a washout.

We continued on foot for a few more miles to a nearby stream where I washed off streaks of the mud and caked red dust. Chin was beginning to smell so I tossed him into the stream. I was able to lop the top off a large green coconut with my machete and shared the unripe milk with Chin. Before we had finished, an American Jeep stopped for us. It was a part of JUSMAG and crowded with six Thais, three of who were young women. We bounced along at top speed for several miles until the driver turned by swerving into a ditch and pressed forward through a soggy plowed field onto a trail. Assuming the new route to be a bona fide detour I did not try to get out of the Jeep. Half an hour later we pulled into a small clearing where a gathering of colorfully dressed natives came out to greet us from a solitary bamboo hut. Once the Jeep came to a halt, I grabbed up my gear and started off back toward the direction we had come from, realizing I was not on a detour after all.

However, even before I had crossed the clearing the natives were motioning and shouting for me to join them. It was evident that a feast was in order. A blood-stained lambskin lay on the kitchen floor, and the rest of the lifeless animal hung from a hook in the ceiling. With nothing but a bowl of rice and coconut milk in my stomach, I decided to hang around and partake of the feast. I had to tie Chin to a banana tree after a romp on the roof resulted in Chin pulling a section of the roof apart within a few minutes. A large dog saw to it that Chin would not be leaving his post.

I joined the men in the group who were engaged in smoking a large bamboo pipe. We squatted around a mat on the earth and passed the pipe around and around, guzzling rice whiskey from several bottles between puffs. To counteract the effects of the whiskey, we ate bitter red fruits, quite like a plum in size and shape. I had to eat bananas to counteract the taste of the biting red fruit, and the bananas made me thirsty. It was a vicious circle, so I left the men folk before over-indulging to help a dreamy young Thai princess pulverize herbs and spices. It took the two of us more than an hour just to mash and grind the spices in a stone bowl, using a stone pestle. An elder gentleman cut the lamb into small chunks and threw them into a large pot. When we had finished grinding the herbs I tossed them into the same pot, and my exotic aid put the conglomeration over a small charcoal fire to cook.

The head man poured out two glasses of lamb's blood, which had been dripping into a wooden basin. He kept one for himself and handed me the other. It was thick and still warm. The others looked on, wondering if I would drink it. One of the girls rubbed her hand over her stomach and gagged as if ready to wretch. I offered my share to any and all of the onlookers, but they politely refused. I had to drink it or insult my guests. I diluted it with rice whiskey, but that only seemed to make it coagulate quicker. My host raised his glass and devoured the contents and I followed suit. My stomach churned as if it were undergoing a convulsion. My only recourse was to forget about it, so I again took my place on the bamboo mat and drank heavily. I forgot about the blood, but when I could no longer sit straight I staggered into the jungle to lie down lest I should make an ass of myself.

I stumbled over fallen trees along a narrow path overgrown with ferns. Within the first few hundred yards I found a bamboo platform, about two feet off the ground and one-third the size of a normal bed. I sat down on the hard, corrugated bench-style bed and tried in vain to pull my senses together. I feared I would be unable to sleep because of my discomfort. But sleep I did, and soundly, too. The gentle nudging of a girl's tender hands and her excited shouting awakened me. She was obviously reprimanding me for wandering off alone, for she made slithering movements with her arm and pointed into the dense undergrowth, indicating that snakes are prevalent. I felt obliged to her, for it was already dusk. Had she not found me I would have probably awakened in the dark, unable to find my way to the clearing. She steadied me as she led the way back to the clearing. No one was anywhere in sight. Then I followed her into the hut and she pointed to the others who were passed out on the reed mats. We joined them!

Sometime later after dark, people began to stir and laugh, and light a few candles. The girls reheated the leftovers from the afternoon's feast, which I had missed, and we spent the next couple of hours eating rice smothered in spicy lamb curry, along with green tea, and bananas. The Thai soldiers left in their Jeep as soon as they had eaten their fill. The bamboo pipe was passed around at the end of the meal and we all retired for the night on the raised floor inside the hut, safe from tigers and snakes.

I was sober the next morning and felt pretty good after dousing myself with refreshing water from a huge clay vase. When my hosts awoke, they served me a bowl of rice and a cup of tea for breakfast. As I plodded across the clearing to continue my journey, my hosts ran after me with a handful of green peanuts for me to take along. I thanked them for their kindness, and though they did not understand where I was going, they pointed to the elephant trail that would lead me back to the northbound road. It was too hot to carry Chin on my shoulder so I made him walk. We carried on for several hours before needing to stop in the shade for a break.

Chin was drinking water that had collected in the deep impression left by an elephant's hoof, when all of a sudden a thunderous crash put an end to the peaceful stillness. I looked cautiously in all directions, not knowing what to expect. Even Chin sensed danger, shrieking and scampering up my body like a tree. Assuming the noise could only have been made by a large beast I did not know whether to shinny up a vine entangled tree--or to run. As soon as the omnipotent thrashing came closer, I ran for all I was worth, not stopping until I reached the main road fifteen minutes later. Chin was as exhausted as I. I was dripping with sweat and he was panting to catch his breath in the heat. He resembled a wet dishrag more than a mischievous monkey.

That's when we saw our predator: a massive bull water buffalo. He lowered his head and pawed the dust with his fore hoof, reminding me of a bullfight I had seen in Madrid. We gave him plenty of clearance as he passed. To do so, we had to leave the road and slog through a rice paddy. The bull did not follow. The first vehicle heading north, a '56 Ford truck, gave us a lift. We were jostled around in its rear as it bounced over minor washouts before coming to a sudden, abrupt stop. Dust swirled about us and I stood up to peer over the cab to see what was causing the delay. A large Keeled Rat snake stretching from one side of the road to the other was sluggishly beginning to move toward the ditch. Its silver-grey silken form shimmered in the sunlight. As soon as the snake had cleared enough of the roadbed to allow the truck to pass, we proceeded forward another few miles further where the truck parked in a gravel pit.

Several waiting coolies stopped leaning on their shovels and began to fill the truck bed with earth. A heavy set man, better clothed than the others, motioned for me to follow him. He led the way to a bamboo hut nearby, where he asked me in poor Pidgin English to produce my credentials. He took a seat in the sole chair, and he stared at me across his crudely constructed desk as if he were a demigod. Perhaps he felt so important because he was able to understand a few of the words I spoke. To the large motley gathering of natives who observed us, he gave the impression that he not only understood perfect English, but capable of handling such an unusual happening as my appearance presented. I laid my passport on the table, which he flipped through. I then spread a map of the world across his desk, pointed to the countries I had come through, indicated and the general route that I expected to take.

He turned the map sideways, then looked at it bottom side up, trying to make sense of the document. He was completely bewildered, did not even know what the map indicated, although he did understand it was a map, which is more than his fellow countrymen could comprehend. Through pantomime, I tried to explain that I was trying to get to the other side of the earth. To save face he nodded occasionally but his eyes would widen, skeptical if not disbelieving entirely.

He offered me a seat on a continuous bamboo bench that lined all four walls. Slipping the passport and map into my pocket, I shook his hand and smiled, hoping to assure him that I was harmless. I took a seat on the bench and stared at the small crevasses in the earthen floor while the spokesman uttered meaningless phrases at me. All I could say in reply was "Bangkok", "Sawadee", and "Kob kun kaa " meaning Bangkok, hello and goodbye, and thank you. Finally, he shrugged and gestured that I could leave.

Gathering up my gear I strolled out of the hut and ambled down the road a short distance where I came upon some elephant dung. It would require the combined efforts of numerous humans to equal that elephant's monumental deposit. It was dry and light, so I tossed large chunks into a stream and watched it drift away with the current. There was not much else to do. Chin and I spent the remainder of the day waiting by the side of the road for a single car or truck, but nothing on wheels came our way.

As the sun began to set, the "gatekeeper native" came to fetch me back to his hut and became a host of sorts. He placed a bowl of rice and two black pieces of meat before me. The rice was tasteless though filling, but the meat resembled well-worn shoe leather more than flesh. Its appearance I could overlook, but its rancid odor was more than I could endure. I tossed the greasy meat to a mangy dog that had been eyeing me hungrily. He sniffed the meat- and backed away. His tail was a bloody stump covered with flies. I discretely buried the meat in a corner of the hut, to avoid offending my host by leaving uneaten food.

When he returned, I asked him how the hound had lost its tail. He understood my question (after several attempts using charades), and judging from the gestures he made in return, a tiger had gotten hold of the dog. Between the snake I had seen earlier, and this information of the possibility of a hungry tiger, I made a mental note to not be wandering off into the jungle alone, even if I was fortified with whiskey.

As darkness fell, candles were lit. My host explained to me through simple stick drawings on the powdery earthen floor that a bus would come tomorrow early in the morning, headed for Bangkok. According to him there was seldom any traffic on the road that would ever go more than few a miles a day; if I wanted to get to Bangkok I had better catch the bus. I had to conserve my limited funds, but on the other hand it would cost me more to linger for weeks in one spot. Bangkok was yet two hundred fifty miles away. My host had reversed his attitude toward me. Instead of regarding me with suspicion, he now showered me with friendliness. At an early evening hour, he motioned for me to follow him to an adjoining, more elaborate hut. He closed two gates as we ascended the stairs to the first floor. The cages were to keep animals out, and the house was on stilts. Chin and I had a miniature room to ourselves. The plank floor was not as comfortable to sleep on as the matted bamboo of the previous night, but we were safe, dry and protected so I thanked him with a full heart.

Sometime during the night I awoke in utter agony. My stomach was in knots and bulged as if it would blow apart with the slightest movement. I had an acute case of the "runs." I looked out through a crack in the wall wondering if I should chance going out into the night of snakes and tigers to relieve myself, or if I should make my toilet on the floor of my host's hut, such a lousy thing to do to someone who had been so kind to me. It was bound to be a messy ordeal, so I felt I would be a martyr and risk my life rather than commit such a faux pas.

I tiptoed out of the house and down the steps being careful not to make a lot of noise when I opened the protective gates. The darkness was an impenetrable solid pitch black: I could not even see my hands before my face. The air was moist, and not a sound could be heard from the surrounding jungle. I breathed so hard, and my heart pounded so loudly that I was certain it would attract some lurking beast, unless I should have the misfortune to tread on a poisonous snake beforehand. I tiptoed all the way to the road. With a trembling roar, my intestines cleared themselves in a single blast. It seemed loud enough to wake the natives in the surrounding huts let alone any carnivorous animals. I raced blindly back toward the hut, and feeling my way along the supporting stilts I managed to find the stairs. I slammed the gate behind me and bolted up the stairs, the whole hut shook. Lying down on the floor once again I sighed with relief, but at the same time I realized that I had been trembling with fear.

My host shook me violently to wake me early the next morning. I could hear the bus rumbling nearer as I became conscious of my surroundings. I had no time to spare so I ran out to the road with my gear in my arms, dressed only in shorts and a light shirt. A cloud of dust could be seen in the early dawn long before the bus was in sight. As the rickety bus skidded to a halt, I bade my host "sawadee" and clambered up a ladder on the rear of the bus to the cargo carriage on the roof. Before I even had a chance to secure my gear, the bus rolled forward. A heavy mist hovered about eight feet above the ground, just low enough for us to be caught in its cold moisture.

I fastened Chin to the spare tire. The roof was piled high with coconuts, several baskets of lively ocean crabs, tomatoes, bundles of sugar cane stalks, coconut husks, tropical melons and a heap of shabby individual baggage. Chin feasted on stalks galore of bananas. I joined him. I was deeply chilled at first, but after two hours the sun came out to drive the mist away. From then on it was sheer luxury to be able to ride on the roof in the hot sun, getting wind-burned while eating tropical fruit. The first stop was in the beautiful little town of Bang Saphan Yai located on the shores of the Gulf of Thailand. The bus laid over long enough to permit the passengers to get their morning rice.

One of the passengers spoke understandable English, a friendly, comely but not overly attractive young woman in her mid-twenties. "Kanya" told me that I would have to ride inside the bus until we got out of town for the police frowned upon those who rode on the roofs of buses. I purchased a few chunks of juicy pineapple from an adolescent street vendor and then climbed over several of the other passengers to a seat that my new friend had saved for me. The bus had a Ford chassis and motor that were products of the pre-war era and was fully ornamented on the exterior with Siamese symbols and dragons. The bus body was made of wood, long before my time judging from the way it rattled. The handful of unbroken windows were made of ordinary glass. The interior of the bus was so crowded with jungle natives that it reeked with the smell of body order and Pons (betel nut). My seat was greasy with sweat that had accumulated through the years.

The bus rumbled out of the village. On the outskirts we stopped to wait for a procession of laborers to dump their baskets of crushed rock, carried on their heads to the roadbed, which was under repair. Most of the workers were women, grandmothers and granddaughters working side by side, the wrinkled and haggard in contrast to their bright-eyed, smooth skinned descendants. Chin startled one of the passengers by dangling at the end of his leash outside the window. I excused myself, explaining that I had better get back on the roof before Chin hanged himself. It was a relief to get out of the bus into the fresh air. Kanya and the assistant driver accompanied me.

The bus rolled on. As yet no one had approached me for my fare. I hoped that by riding on the roof I would not have to pay so much. As the bus continued north, it picked up more passengers; so many that the overflow had to ride on the roof with us. It was difficult to smoke my pipe in the air resistance created by the speeding bus, which invariably blew the tobacco out of the pipe bowl. Behind me the pile of husked coconuts lashed to the bus roof flared up, leaving a trail of smoke behind the bus. I was momentarily puzzled as to why there was smoke coming from the bundle when it dawned on me that the ashes from my pipe might have caused it. The driver's assistant, perched above the cab, was alert and banged on the roof for the driver to stop. Several of the local passengers helped me pull the pile apart and pour the water from my canteen on the nucleus of the fire. The driver and owner of the coconuts climbed up on the roof to inspect the charred heap. They both laughed, for the meat and milk next to it were not damaged.

The bus broke down several times during the day. Each time the driver, assistant driver and a couple of natives would look under the hood, probe around and then, as if by magic, the bus would run without trouble as long as an hour before quitting again. By late afternoon we had reached a paved road near Hua Hin. Those of us on the roof were summoned to get in the bus. The bus clipped along at a much faster pace on the surfaced road. I enjoyed seeing glimpses of the Gulf of Thailand flashing through coconut trees for the next few hours.

Suddenly the bus careened violently, accompanied by the sound of skidding tires. Immediately ahead in the middle of the road a bus lain broadside, its roof completely torn off, and the seats bent back. Cargo and passengers were strewn about the paved highway. Three of the bleeding victims were helped onto our bus. The only fatal victim, a woman, was stretched out under a palm tree. Our driver maneuvered around the sprawling mess and raced on to Petchburi where the injured were taken to a medical clinic. It was handled in a matter of fact manner that left an indelible impression.

Unlike the American Greyhound system, there were no organized rest stops. Whenever two or three passengers needed to make a nature call, the bus would stop to allow they needy to work and elbow their way out of the bus. Usually the other passengers would take the opportunity to stretch, or enjoy a "beedie" (cheap slim cigarette popular in Asia).

During one such stop, Kanya gathered a few stalks of sugar cane from an adjoining field. She presented them to me to eat. Next she took a battered aluminum pan and scooped it full of stagnant murky water from the ditch. It looked more like tea than water. She offered it to me, but when I refused, she seemed hurt. So like a fool I drank part of it and then gladly returned it to her to finish. She smiled broadly. Back in our seats she rested her hand on my arm. "I lub you, Mr. Thill. Do you lub me?" she asked. I felt a bit embarrassed and I was at a loss for tactful answers. Fortunately the bus broke down before I had time to answer her. To escape our awkward conversation I joined the driver and other others as they poked their fingers around under the hood, trying to locate the trouble.

It was virtually a free-for-all with so many hands tinkering with the motor simultaneously. The driver expected wonders from me since I was a westerner and would therefore be supposedly familiar with motors. The driver pointed to the amp meter on the dashboard and indicated that it was not charging properly. The fan belt was too loose to turn the generator, so I tightened it. The passengers gave the bus a push and it started immediately. The amp meter indicated the generator was working. As reward for my handiwork, the driver offered me a cigar and insisted that I sit beside him in the driver's seat along with the assistant driver. They had apparently taken me to be a master mechanic, and from my position in the front seat I kept checking the various gauges. Luckily my duties as chief engineer were not needed again, for I know next to nothing about motors. It was much more pleasant in the front seat with fresh air blowing in through the window, as opposed to sitting in the rear of the bus where the air sifted through all the other passengers first.

Chapter 12:

Bangkok: A Private Tour

WE REACHED BANGKOK at 10 p.m. which was over five hours behind schedule. It did not matter though: a few hours meant nothing in Asia. I got off the bus just after it crossed the Menam River (now known as Chao Praya River). I offered the driver some money but he refused to take it. I gathered up my gear and plodded across the littered street, slimy garbage oozing between my toes. From there, I took a taxi to Bankapi Villa, a service club for American soldiers stationed in the area. The taxi driver tried to get twenty bahts out of me rather than the ten he had originally agreed to charge. Rather than argue the whole night I paid him fifteen. Bangkapi Villas was truly a westerners' paradise in an oriental city. It was more like an estate than a servicemen's club. The lawn was spacious and well perfectly groomed, with a large lily pond in one corner. Easy chairs were carefully placed about the grounds under awnings overlooking magnificent gardens.

Sergeant Glover, whom I had met a few days earlier in Haad Ya, had insisted I stay with him upon my arrival in Bangkok. He had flown to Haad Ya via military transport to spend a few days repairing equipment which is how he came to be ahead of me in arriving in Bangkok. He happened to be at Bangkapi Villa, so I had to look no further. For one dollar, I feasted on western food in the Villa. It was an extravagance, but by limiting myself to one decent meal a day I could last longer physically than if I depended on Asian food three meals per day for less money.

Sergeant Glover's wife was due to arrive in Bangkok from the States within a couple of weeks, but in the meantime he lived alone in a private house which he had rented in advance to make certain that he would have a place for his wife. We were both beat from our various travels so we took off for his home in his jeep, a new civilian model, donated with free gas by the Thai government. But before the Thai government was able to give our soldiers (under JUSMAG) such an expensive gift, the American taxpayers had to first grant Siam millions of dollars in economic aid. Siam in turn could spend a considerable portion of that aid making our boys happy.

As the jeep pulled up before Sergeant Glover's house, he apologized for not having a more elaborate lawn. I marveled at the first building I saw: a two story wooden house, complete with a garage on the first floor. Glover explained this was only the servants' quarters. Glover's house stood 100 feet to the left with a gleaming white plaster exterior. Beyond it was *another* smaller house- for his maid. I could hardly believe that a Major in the American Army could afford such a luxury, let alone a Sergeant. They certainly never had it so plush in the States. The government also supplied him with free DDT bombs, which he did not use sparingly in this tropical, infested region of the world. We killed a beer in his living room while being cooled by a large fan that hung from the ceiling. It was real luxury to sleep on an American bed- complete with mattress!

When I awoke at nine in the morning, it was already so hot and humid I had to take a cold shower before I could muster the energy to descend the stairs. Sgt. Glover and I had lunch at the Villa where I met several of his friends. I queried many American civilians connected with the S.E.A. Supply (South East Asia Supply) in hopes they might know how I could best get to Burma. There was no overland traffic between Bangkok and Rangoon because there were no roads, or even elephant trails, listed in the recently published military map of Siam. To make matters worse the border between Siam and Burma was officially closed due to considerable fighting among the various tribes of natives in the jungles. No one seemed to know what they were fighting about and surmised it could be lack of anything else to occupy their time.

Glover spent the remainder of the afternoon showing me the sights of Bangkok from his jeep. Those with cars had chauffeurs, but the majority of the people were barefoot in the street. Driving was hazardous because the streets were teeming with rickshaws and pedestrians. To run a pedestrian down with a car in Asia can often prove fatal to the driver of the car, for pedestrian onlookers frequently become vigilantes so enraged that they kill the driver before the police arrive. If the driver is spared street justice, he will be heavily sued. Therefore the majority of cars in Bangkok are chauffer driven, thereby shifting much of the responsibility from the owner to the driver.

Bangkok is a city full of canals, weather-beaten houseboats, beautiful women, smelly fish markets, and scurrying Chinese. In contrast to the filth and open sewage systems are beautiful government estates, foreign consulates, and majestic wats (Buddhist monastery-temples). In 1956, only one street in Bangkok was western and modern consisting of travel agencies, hotels, and international business firms.

I spent the following day, Sunday, walking the city mapping out the various places I wanted to go during business hours the following day. Teenage boys were swimming in a pond across from the American Embassy. The water was black and filled with trash. Bloated dead dogs, almost iconic in Thailand, floated on the surface nearby. The swimmers were oblivious. That night on the way back to Glovers' mansion I passed a streetcar surrounded by people. A body lay sprawled on the tracks. I passed it up, not wanting to become involved, realizing for better or worse, I was becoming inured to third party suffering, processing quickly and moving on with my own life and concerns.

The next morning I visited the American Embassy. It was a beautiful modern building with simple lines, surrounded by the ubiquitous immaculate Asian gardens, and a very closely cropped lawn, almost golf course perfection. I had let my khaki trousers hang low in hopes that they would conceal a broken shoelace, which I had replaced with a shiny piece of wire. I checked with the 3rd Secretary to learn if he had any up to date information on crossing overland from Siam to Burma. He was a slim, pleasant chap who scrutinized my passport. When he found that I had no stamp authorizing me to be in Siam, he told me to visit the Siamese Immigration Bureau without delay. He advised me that the only way to get to Burma would be to fly. I could not take the monkey unless I got him vaccinated. I thanked him for his advice and bummed a ride with a staff car in the direction of the Thai Immigration. The youthful chauffer let me off in front of the Russian Embassy by mistake. The building was nothing more than an old mansion. I entered in hopes of getting a visa for Russia, figuring if I were alive by the time I got to Persia, it might be shorter to go to Europe through Russia. But the girl who received me said that it would be several weeks before I could get a visa. In addition to the time element, she informed me that there were few roads if any that connect Russia with Persia.

My next stop was the Siamese Immigration Building. A soldier stopped me at the foot of the stairs leading up to the offices. After a look at my passport he escorted me to one of the officials. The official took me to another official who spoke English. I was interrogated, essentially given the works. They could not understand how I managed to get by their immigration checkpoint in Southern Siam, travel some five hundred miles and roam for a whole week in their country without ever having been caught by the police or the numerous soldiers who are supposed to check the credentials of foreigners. They were not only flabbergasted, but also embarrassed. If I could pass undetected through their security barriers, then communist infiltrators could as well. They found it inconceivable that I had never been able to find the border checking station, and that no one had checked me since. Apparently they believed me, (after all it was the truth), and requested I write out a lengthy description of where and how I had crossed into Siam and why I felt that I was not apprehended at the border. I explained to them that I had merely walked two hundred yards up the railway tracks from Malaya into Siam with a Thai man, then hopped in his car and took off to Haad Yi.

The paperwork and questioning took three hours in total, finally resulting in having my passport stamped with an attached explanation as to why I had no border entry stamp, just in case some alert official might detain me when I tried to leave the country.

I found a veterinarian late in the afternoon on Plern Chit road who agreed to vaccinate Chin, the only drawback being that he charged me more for the vaccination than I had originally paid for the monkey. At this point, he was family. I was unable to evaluate his companionship on an economic level so I agreed to pay. (see photo 11&12)

I decided to try the Burmese embassy to see if they knew of any land route from Bangkok to Rangoon. They said it was not only impossible physically to go by land, but unlawful for the border was closed due to all the civil unrest aka tribal warfare. The administrator was highly disturbed that their attaché in Singapore had issued me a visa without travel restrictions stamped. At this point I was beginning to feel stranded. My only choice was to spend thirty dollars on an airplane ticket from U.B.A. (Union of Burma Airways). The flight was to leave the next afternoon. Completely discouraged and not ready to endure the financial hit,

I trudged to the ticket office. At the same time, an Australian airplane captain and his wife entered the ticket office. When they learned that I was bound for Rangoon, they advised me to keep out of the place, for as they put it, "You think Bangkok is bad, just wait till you get to Rangoon! Why you can't even get twenty-five miles outside of the city because the communists are about ready to storm Rangoon. Police will turn you back. You couldn't possibly get into northern Burma by land. You had better fly straight to Calcutta and forget Burma, altogether."

This news was disheartening to say the least. I had but ninety dollars remaining, plus my ticket to Rangoon. To fly direct to Calcutta would fifty-five dollars in my pocket. I could not reasonably afford to fly direct to Calcutta. I would have to go to Rangoon and worry about the consequences later. The Australian couple wished me luck.

I returned to Sgt. Glover's house and washed and packed my gear. Glover's amiable house girl sewed a patch on my trousers. I piled my junk and Chin into Glover's jeep and we took off for the Villa club where I had a light breakfast. Had I been able to foresee the future I would have gorged myself with clean western food, for it was to be my last decent meal for a *long* time to come.

Upon arrival at the airport, the clerk insisted that I get a cage for Chin. This was another financial hit (approximately ten dollars) for the cheapest one I could find. I stuffed Chin into the woven bamboo basket, but even before I boarded the bus for the twenty-mile ride to the airport, he had chewed his way out of it. I ran back around the corner to purchase a small, inexpensive flight bag. I needed to make sure that it would hold Chin at least for the duration of the flight. I tried to grab the little ape, but he had never liked to be handled. He fought with all his might, squealed, wet on the floor, and bit me several times before I finally got him zipped safely in the bag, much to the amusement of a throng of onlookers. I had no time to haggle over the price of the bag if I wanted to catch the bus, so I paid the Chinese shopkeeper his first price and dashed out of his shop.

As soon as we arrived at the airport I got permission from the pilot to carry Chin aboard, and then we cleared customs and immigration authorities. While waiting to board the plane I watched thousands of Thai airmen parade up and down the airstrip in their American style uniforms. From a distance they looked exactly like American troops except that they marched with a sort of a goose step. Even their weapons were made in the U.S.A.

No sooner had our plane gotten airborne than Chin made an exit from his stifling flight bag. The charming Burmese flight attendant said that Chin could stay out of the bag providing he did not disturb the other passengers. To play it safe I kept his leash nice and short. The plane passed over nothing but jungle covered mountains for the next few hours. Occasionally, a native's hut could be seen in a clearing far below. The only other sign of life was the occasional tendril of smoke as it twisted its way into the heavens from hidden fires far below. The plane crossed over the seaport of Mawlamyine located on the Salween River. The river was crowded with sampans and junks laden with rice harvested from the surrounding endless miles of paddies. The plane passed over the Gulf of Martaban, which is part of the Bay of Bengal, and then it descended minutes later into the ultra modern Rangoon air terminal. The modern airport was highly incongruous with the crude way of life surrounding it: attap huts and water buffalo treading on rice to thresh it. Chin and I cleared customs without any trouble. When the immigration authorities asked the purpose of my visit, I said that I was merely a tourist to avoid any further delay.

Chapter 13:

Rangoon: Pagodas and Penicillin

RANGOON'S MOST STRIKING landmark is a fabulous three hundred twenty-five foot Shwedagon Pagoda, also known as the Great Dragon Pagoda, which stands on a hill overlooking the city dominating the skyline. It resembles a gigantic Prussian helmet, and is awe inspiring as the setting sun reflects from its diamond and ruby crown, and golden plated bricks once called a "beautiful winking wonder that blazed in the sun, of a shape that was neither Muslim dome nor Hindu temple-spire" by Rudyard Kipling. The pagoda is roughly thirteen hundred feet in circumference at the base. It has weathered earthquakes and wars only to be rebuild with improvements. It is said that once every generation the Buddhists of Burma completely recover the Shwedagon Pagoda with pure gold. It contains personal relics of Buddha himself.

The air terminal hostess of U.B.A. addressed me in English. She was a sweet, friendly and curious to learn what brought a person of my appearance to Rangoon. She advised that I stay at the local Y.M.C.A. as it would be cheaper than any other reputable hotel. She seemed eager to show me the sights of Rangoon, but her father did not trust his innocent daughter with foreigners such as myself. While this eloquently groomed hostess was giving me directions to the Y.M.C.A. by contrast, Chin was busily picking through the contents of a spittoon that he had just tipped over.

Rangoon was in sad lack of maintenance since it was built. Everything was broken, dirty, or worn out. By the time I located the "Y" the sun had set, and the damaged streets and sidewalks of the city were teeming with night crawlers: trishaws, hawkers, pimps, and thieves. It was common to stumble over some starving derelicts who lay limp on the crowded sidewalks. The streets and walks had not been properly repaired since World War II. The "Y" finally appeared, not far from the center of town. It was a shabby looking three-story structure, but looked no worse than the majority of buildings in Rangoon.

I entered the "Y" and queried a couple of Chinese lads about obtaining accommodation. They informed me that the chief administrator was off duty, but that an English chap might be able to assist me. I waited in the clean, but dismal empty lobby until a tall, lanky Caucasian ambled toward me. He introduced himself as a free-lance journalist named Reggie. He explained his emaciated, pallid appearance as being the result of a recent bout with jaundice and hepatitis.

Reggie introduced me to a stocky young Finnish reporter who was writing articles for a political paper back in Europe. Sorka, as he called himself was hunched over a typewriter in his cluttered cubicle. He was trying to write a letter of thanks to the Chinese Communist government in Peiping- in English. Sorka's main drawback was that he could barely speak English, let alone write it. His reason for choosing English rather than Finnish was that he doubted if the Chinese would be able to translate it. Sorka looked every bit the part of a struggling journalist, as he peered at me through his heavy dark-rimmed spectacles. His thin sparse mustache twitched as he twisted his mouth to speak. He asked me proof read his letter of thanks while I puffed away on one of his cheap Burmese cigars. The text of the letter explained how pleased Sorka was at having been granted permission to enter China. He had tried for weeks to enter the country while his finances drained away in the heat of Rangoon. His letter of thanks was far from being understandable. If he had any talent as a reporter it was well hidden! I retyped his letter and spelled the words correctly enough to be understood. He was clothed in a wrinkled, spotted, double-breasted suit. It looked as if he had received it through C.A.R.E. and had not bothered to have it pressed or cleaned since. He ran his left hand through his thick mop of curly hair as he shook my hand and thanked me for my efforts. He was short and stocky, only twenty-five, yet he carried himself with the air of being mighty busy and important. He was laughable, yet I could not help but like him for he was full of "piss and vinegar".

Sorka advised me to be leery of a fellow countryman of his who was also staying at the "Y". According to Sorka, Rollo, the other Finn, had jumped ship in Rangoon to spend some time with a girl he had met while on shore leave. The girl must have been captivating; by the time Rollo got back to the wharf his ship had already reached Singapore. Rollo had blown through his money and was apprehended by the authorities for stealing food. As he had no travel papers he could not leave the country. He had consulted his own embassy but they said the he would have to fend for himself; they were glad to get him out of their own country. For the time being, he was a man without a country- and desperate.

Sorka rounded up a key for me and showed me to a room. He at least had the guts to get me a room, even if he did lack the authority. As fate would have it, the only vacant bed was in the same room as the countryless Rollo. He was sitting on the edge of his bed with his head in his hands as I entered the large, dingy room. Rollo was slim, blond and sallow of complexion. A mosquito netting covered his bed, but there was no mattress. He slept on his extra pair of pants. He explained to me that he was a nonpaying guest of the "Y" therefore not entitled to a mattress. I felt a bit reluctant to leave Chin and all my possession in the room with him, but I felt they were probably safe since the "Y" was his only refuge in Burma. No other agency seemed to care whether he continued to exist or not. My bed had no mattress or mosquito netting, but it did not disturb me for I was not going to worry about sleep for a few hours to come. The room's only window looked out into the courtyard three stories below. A single twenty-five watt bulb was the one source of illumination. The walls were dark wood halfway up the wall in a sort of pony wall and from that point to the ceiling, consisted of heavy wire mesh only, allowing one to peer into the adjoining bedroom by standing on the bed stead.

I joined Reggie for supper when he mentioned that he knew where we could get a cheap edible meal. We went down the street and climbed to the second floor of dingy Chinese flophouse where we were greeted by an shriveled, elderly Chinese couple who served us a greasy meal of rice and duck eggs- followed by green tea.

After the meal Reggie and I browsed through a busy Chinese bazaar. A funeral parlor was getting out the paraphernalia needed for a procession the following day. Next door, a casket shop was bustling with craftsmen working late into the night making simple caskets. We purchased some Burmese corn from a ragged woman squatting beside her flaming charcoal pot on the curb. Had she not blown her nose into her hand just after we made the purchase, we might have enjoyed it more freely.

Reggie explained the political situation of Burma as we sipped a pot of tea in the Chinese slums. Teacups were not washed in Burma; it is the custom for a customer to rinse out his cup with a bit of tea and to throw the tea rinse onto the earthen restaurant floor. According to Reggie, Burma is plagued by communist rebels who have been unable to bargain with the government to their satisfaction. Therefore they are currently engaged in sabotaging roads, bridges, railway stations, and tracks. They recently derailed a train, which resulted in the death of thirty passengers. Six days ago they raided the railway station in Pegu, and blew up the large suspension bridge crossing the Sittang River. The communists were operating on the theory that if they created enough havoc then perhaps the Burmese Republic would give them a few concessions. In addition the communists were actively engaged in capturing outlying villages, either capturing or killing the officials who opposed them. To augment the terror of the communist activities, local bands of dacoits (armed robbers who were deserters of the Chinese Nationalist Army) were doing a brisk business of plundering villages and ambushing trucks and busses for loot.

According to Rangoon press, one out of every five civilians had been armed in an attempt to ward off the threatening communist attack on Rangoon proper. Reggie advised that we "keep to the strait and narrow" as we walked through the nearly deserted streets of Rangoon after leaving the teashop. Each night in the past week, communists had kidnapped worthwhile victims off the streets. The next day's newspaper would devote about one sentence to each victim, as it was so commonplace. The arming of twenty percent of the civilian population did not seem like a wise move, for chances are that a good many of the recipients were communists themselves. We walked on to the Hlaing River and as we passed in front of the Grand Hotel, Rangoon's finest, we noticed scores of Burmese troops guarding the waterfront, and the embassies, which lined the opposite side of the street. Regi advised me to get out of Rangoon as soon as possible, but added that I definitely should not attempt to venture north in doing so. The only way was to go by air or sea to Calcutta. This was news I didn't cherish hearing again.

Back at the "Y" as I was entering my room, the guest in the next room poked his head out the door. Since he was white, I asked if he was English. He replied that he was Morris Spevak, an

American Jew. He was not more than five feet tall and could not have weighed over eighty pounds. He was clothed in a stained undershirt, and baggy black trousers so long they dragged on the floor. He held a bunch of bananas in his hand and he was wearing a battered, shapeless hat, which he removed to show how he had stuffed it with an extra pair of long johns. He was from Brooklyn, and his accent supported this claim. He explained he had put up with the modern American pace for the past fifty-three years and could take it no longer. He was now in search of an island paradise where he could live in peace and simplicity for the rest of his days. I felt sorry for the mousey little man, truly a lost soul. He wondered if I had been attacked by any of the people of Rangoon. When I explained that I hadn't and asked him what he meant, he said in a mournful tone that people were continually sneaking up behind him and hitting him on the head with clubs, pottery, or their fists. He looked at his padded hat admiringly and said that it helped to soften the blows, which he received every time he ventured into the streets.

Spevak claimed to be an author of several books, but when I asked him to name a couple of them he merely explained that he could not recall their titles for his memory was slipping. He slept alone in his three bed room. Even though the "Y" was full up he would not allow the management to put a stranger in one of the empty beds. He said that his parents would send him a dollar if he ran out of money. As I said good night to the confused creature, I could not help but wonder what mental institution he had escaped from. Or how he had gotten a passport, if he had one at all.

Rollo was snoring loudly as I entered the room and stretched out on the springs of my bed. The buzzing of famished mosquitoes soon filled the air. I pulled my sleeping bag over me, but it was too hot to crawl into. Try as I may the unrelenting mosquitoes gorged themselves with my blood all night long. It would less traumatic had they not concentrated on my lips and eyelids. I spent the first hour swatting at them, and even though I squashed hundreds of them, there were thousands waiting their turn. My lips became swollen, and I was in such misery that I left the security of the room for the street, anything to get away from the mosquitoes that were driving me insane. Maybe, I thought, that is what happened to Spevak!

By this time it was well past midnight and the streets were deserted except for the homeless beggars who slept on them. There was a slight breeze, but the mosquitoes were still prevalent. I squatted next to a Hindu who was draped in a shawl as he slept in a squatting position. I pulled my light jacket over my head, but the mosquitoes found an opening through which they carried on their assault. It was not quite as bad as the "Y" until the Hindu next to me started wailing his prayers. He chanted on and on, half singing, half crying. I swore at him to shut up. He stopped for an instant- and then continued. I felt like breaking every bone in his scrawny body but opted for removing myself from his company.

I could hear eerie music coming from down the street. I stumbled along through the trash until I found the source: five men sitting on a well-worn reed mat in the cross-legged style of Hindus. Two of them were beating primitive drums while another produced weird sounds from a bamboo flute. Candles illuminated a canvas lean-to behind them. I took off my boots and took a place on the mat. One offered me a small cigar, and between the smoke from the two of us we kept the mosquitoes at bay. Inside the lean-to was a dead man stretched out on a cloth-covered slab. Three of the Hindus had hair that stretched to their waists. It was thick, black, matted and unclean. They belong to a small sect that believes it is wrong to wash, cut, or comb their hair. Through the years it becomes heavy and thick like a cow's tail that has been lying in the manure for many months. The only advantage I could see was that it formed a natural pillow for them when they slept on the streets. I joined in the chanting, but merely humming since I could not follow the words- if there were any. A beady-eyed bold rat was nibbling garbage in an open sewer not three feet away. Rats are so numerous in Rangoon that they frequently attack sleeping babies. I wondered if the corpse was in any danger. We smoked cigars until dawn.

When I returned to the "Y" to pick up Chin, the mosquitoes had virtually disappeared in the morning daylight. I was in a foul mood for I had not slept a wink. I bought a couple of bananas, one for Chin and one for me. Then I wandered over to a well and washed as best I could much to the amusement of several Burmese women who were bathing themselves by sloshing buckets of water over their bodies. They gracefully replaced their wet lungis by letting them fall to the ground as dry lungis fell into place unrolling down from their shoulders. The Rangoon women were far from being the beauties of Siam. In Rangoon the majority of the Burmese had flat, pudgy faces. The women wore purple lungis from the waist down, and transparent white blouses on top. Most carried umbrellas to shade themselves from the merciless sun. To further protect their faces from getting too suntanned, they smeared a white flour-like powder on them, making them look like corpses made up for a funeral.

As soon as the Indian Embassy opened, I applied for a visa. The clerk told me that I would not be allowed to enter India except by sea or air, and he demanded that I produce the tickets before he would grant me a visa. I told him that I planed to fly to Calcutta from Mandalay, which was four hundred miles north of Rangoon. Luckily he did not realize that no flights originated from Mandalay to Calcutta, or to any other city outside of Burma. All foreign flights in Burma originate from Rangoon only. The clerk explained to me that the reason I had to fly to India- or go by ship- was that the border was dangerous, as had been detailed to me several times before. He told me to return the following day to pick up my visa.

I figured there must be some way to get out of Burma other than taking a commercial flight, which I could not reasonably afford so I proceeded over to the American Embassy. I tied Chin outside and climbed up two flights of stairs to the Air Attaché's office. A large, friendly colonel, dressed in loose fitting civvies, invited me to have a seat in his office. I told him of my predicament and asked if there was any chance of getting on an American courier plane bound for Calcutta. He said they had nothing flying west because all their mail went via the east. It looked as if I was going to be forced to try to cross overland through Burma and attempt to cross the border illegally so I asked the Air Attaché if he knew where I could get my hands on a map of Burma. He advised that my only hope was to get one from the government. Maps were not freely circulated in Burma for fear that the communists would be able to use them to facilitate the planning of their attacks.

The Government Printing Department was housed in a huge brick building in the same general area. I was politely refused a map on the grounds that they had recently destroyed their maps and were now in the process of making an updated map. Next I tried the Office of the Director of Survey for a map. A young clerk ushered me in to the director himself who queried me as to why I wanted a map of Burma. After I convinced him that I did not want it for political purposes, he agreed to let me have one. He stamped it with his official seal, which would indicate to any doubtful officials I might encounter that I was authorized to have the map in my possession.

I spent the evening scrutinizing the crude, vague map over a pot of tea in a Chinese teashop trying to determine the best route to get to Calcutta. I would have to go as far north as Mandalay no matter which way I tried to get to Calcutta. I did not try to plan my route any further in advance than couple of days since available information was often not reliable for distances of over fifty miles, let alone hundreds of miles. I had learned that it is better not to worry about hardships and obstacles that lay ahead until actually confronted with them.

When I left the teashop to head back to the "Y", I passed by an open air puppet show. I could not resist the desire to take a seat among the hundreds of Chinese who were sprawled around on woven straw mats watching the show play out on a colorful, hastily constructed platform. An intricately decorated Chinese temple was adjacent to this "stage" and a five-piece band played penetrating Chinese music. I could not follow the story the puppets portrayed, but I gathered it must have been a comedy judging from all the laughter. Nearby a second group of comedians was performing a slapstick routine on a float. I guess they figured my appearance alone would make the audience laugh, because the two female actresses beckoned me to join them in their act.

Soon the audience shifted all eyes to a Chinese dragon, which jogged and wiggled like a snake on the street against a backdrop of exploding fireworks. The dragon was more than fifty feet in length, made of strong paper and carried by scores of shouting Chinese. It looked as if the celebration would go on throughout the night so I wandered back towards the "Y, placing a few coins next to a sleeping, legless derelict who lay in a grotesque heap on the ruptured sidewalk. I hoped I would never be too poor to help someone like that.

We finally slept soundly in the "Y" till late in the morning after my complaints had yielded both a bed with a mattress and mosquito netting. I was awakened at a reasonable hour by a knock at the door by the administrator bringing a bowl of rice to Rollo. He seemed to have it made, free room- and board! I took Chin's leash off for the first time since I had purchased him figuring he could not get out of the room and I was anxious to see just how agile he was with no holds barred. He promptly climbed over the mosquito netting frame and jumped onto the wire screening that separated the upper portions of the adjoining rooms. Chin climbed up the wire mesh with ease and crawled through a small opening into the adjoining room inhabited by Spevak.

To my dismay, I was unable to catch him when I tried. Fearing Chin might destroy something of value, I banged on Spevak's door to arouse him, but he had already left for the day. I had to get down to the Indian Embassy to pick up my visa before they closed for the day: embassies have a habit of closing early in the afternoon. I hated to leave Chin loose, but I could not spend any more time trying to catch him or I would not get there in time. I put all of my belongings in the backpack and strapped the cover tight so that Chin could not destroy any of my valuables. I told Rollo to do likewise, but he replied that he had no possession other than the clothes on his back and the extra pair of trousers that he used for a mattress.

I ran down to the Indian Embassy, picked up my visa without delay, and raced to the to check on Chin's activities. I looked through the keyhole to see Chin chewing on a roll of Polaroid film. I turned the doorknob only to find it was locked. I rushed down to fetch the key from the office and raced back to the room. When I flung the door open, Chin dropped his playthings. I surveyed the damage. My maps were torn apart, film strewn about, my toothpaste tube was chewed in half, and a pile of cigarette tobacco was heaped on the window sill. Chin had completely destroyed all four packs of Kools, which I had been able to purchase from the American Villa Club in Bangkok and was rationing out judiciously as it had been a splurge.

Reggie popped in to see me just as I was chasing Chin around the room with a broom. Chin jumped up on the window ledge and then climbed to the outside of the windowpanes, his only footing the half-inch molding framing the window. I could not reach out to get him without risking Chin would lose his footing and drop to the concrete courtyard sixty feet below. From the expression on Chin's face, it was obvious that he was frightened as well. His body was trembling as his muscles grew weaker. Scores of Asians lined the two balconies across the courtyard to watch the drama unfold; it seemed inevitable that Chin's body would be splashing on the courtyard within mere seconds. Reggie ripped the mosquito netting from my bed and raced down the stairs into the courtyard. Three onlookers helped him make a net out of the mosquito netting and they stood directly under the window to catch Chin. I backed out of the room, so as not to frighten little companion. Somehow, the attempted escape surprised even Chin, because he worked his way along the molding tentatively and climbed back into the room. He was so weak from the ordeal that I scooped him up off the floor without any trouble. I had learned not to unleash him again.

By now it was afternoon, too late to leave Rangoon. I decided to scout around in search of reliable information on what to expect up-country. According to *The Nation*, the major English newspaper in the country, conditions were not the best up north. I scanned the headlines and learned that several villages had been overrun with insurgents. The communists had derailed a train. The Burmese army had barely rescued another train from an ambush. In Rangoon, a wealthy businessman's son had been kidnapped. A bus had run over a child, which angered the onlooking crowd to the extent that they burned the bus and stoned the unfortunate driver to death before the police intervened. Thirteen hundred homes had been razed by fire on the outskirts of the city. They were only bamboo structures, yet they were all the owners possessed.

Apart from this, things in Rangoon were relatively quiet enough for me to explore. I dropped into a Hindu cafe for lunch consisting of rice and curry so hot that I had to wash it down with four glasses of polluted water from a greasy glass. Even with the water, I could not finish the meal; it was that spicy. The Hindus also eat with their fingers, a particularly messy ordeal for me as I tried picking up curry slop in my fingers and getting it to my mouth, sauce dribbling down my chin only to lodge into my beard. Further down the street, I checked with several of the Hindus who were seated before typewriters on the sidewalks in the heart of Rangoon. Many of these Hindus speak English and act as notary publics, clerks and sages to the ignorant masses who are in need of legal advice, written contracts, and general information.

None of them could give me any information on upper Burma, but the last one did know of a doctor where I could get treatment for my chronic dysentery which had all but sapped the life out of me since the midnight explosion in the dark of jungles of Siam. The Hindu motioned to a youthful Anglo-Burmese lad, and told him to direct me to a particular doctor. The youth led me on a zigzag course through the city, and finally pushed open a lopsided door where we climbed three flights of stairs. My guide pointed to a closed door. “Is good doctor here,” he said, holding out his hand for baksheesh.

“I do not have much money, how much do you want?”

“One kyat.”

“One kyat! I can’t afford to give you a kyat, I have thousands of miles to go yet, and I don’t have enough money as it is! Half a kyat is more than I can spare- but here,” I said firmly, as I dropped a coin into his outstretched palm. He snapped his fingers around the offering and vanished without saying a word. The doctor, hearing the commotion, had come to the door. He spoke English exceptionally well. When I told him that I had constantly been sick, and run down for the past month and continually plagued with diarrhea, he said he could "fix me up". If he was a doctor, he was the most disorganized one I had ever encountered. His desk was littered with books, papers, vials, and a pan full of needles. I told him that I had been roughing it a bit and explained how I was trying to get to the States. "I am going to give you an injection of penicillin that should rid you of your illness," he said as he jabbed a rusty needle into my buttocks. "You may have malaria, dysentery, or perhaps Beriberi (thiamine deficiency brought on by poor nutrition). You must take better care of yourself."

"How much do I owe you for the injection, Doctor?"

"You owe me nothing. You have many hardships to face. I admire your courage. Our country and its people are very poor, and you are as one of us. We must help each other in time of need." I thanked him sincerely, and as I descended the steps to the street I realized the importance of the kind doctor's advice. While I did crave adventure, I was not willing to die for it.

I checked the map against my passport and its visas the following day so that I would be heading in the right direction, if nothing else. My Indian visa required that I enter India within a month of its date of issue. Surely I would cross the border much before then! The map indicated that one road went to Mandalay. It looked like the only sensible choice; there were no roads leading west to the border, not even so much as a trail between Rangoon and Mandalay.

Chin and I had to force our way through the crowded bazaars at sunrise in the morning to get out of the city. Chin alarmed many women as he snatched at their turban-covered heads from his advantageous perch on my shoulder. I stopped before a woman dressed in the usual htamein and jacket who was selling rice. I pointed to a bowl, she shoved her cheroot cigar in her mouth, and handed me the rice. In the old days, people ate pounded rice, called maung-htaung, which retained most of the nutritious bran covering. Nowadays rice is milled, and refined during processing which causes it to lose its healthful bran covering. The white grain rice only serves to fill the stomach. It is no wonder that the death rate in Burma is the highest in the world, and also probably no mystery as to why I might have beriberi, if I did. Sixty-percent of those who manage to live are physical wrecks, dependent on medicines and herbs for their continuance. At this rate I had a distasteful choice: to get beriberi, or indulge in other types of food and prolong my dysentery. Even Chin had diarrhea, and he had been brought up in Asia, so I did not feel like there was much I could do about it.

The rice bowl emptied, I asked the seller if she knew which road led to Mandalay. After a brief moment, her blank stare broke into a smile and she ushered an English speaking shop keeper toward me who explained how I could get onto the road to Mandalay. I followed his jumbled directions, ending up on the road to the airport where I removed my hot boots and bathed my feet in a pond of muddy water. Looking back toward town for one last impression, I could see the blinking wonder herself, Shwedagon Pagoda, as it towered into the sky, glittering in the rising sun like a gigantic jewel.

Chapter 14:

On the Road to Mandalay: Navigating Around Ghosts of Past Wars

IT WASN'T LONG before an old battered cargo truck came chugging down the road. There was no room in the cab so Chin and I piled us atop the shifty load it was hauling. The road was full of deep potholes. I had to hang on for all I was worth as the truck bounced along the rough, narrow road for the next two hours. Each time a truck approached from the opposite direction, either our truck or the oncoming vehicle would have to pull off onto the shoulder to allow the other to pass. The terrain was level and dry, the earth scorched, and the fields criss-crossed with gaping cracks. When we pulled over to pass bullock carts, a cloud of dust would envelope the pedestrians and carts in our wake. Fields of stubble left from harvested rice formed a golden rust-colored sea from which ancient pagodas in various stages of disintegration protruded. In the distance to the east and west, mountains bordered the deep blue skyline.

Finally the cargo truck pulled off the road and stopped, shutting down the engine just outside Pegu (port city in southern Burma). I hopped down and asked the driver why he had stopped. He pointed down the embankment to the railway station, and said in understandable English, "Pegu, much trouble in country. Better you take train, more safe." So Chin and I slid down the embankment and plodded down a dust-covered footpath to the train station. It looked as if a tornado had struck. Charred timber and rubble were scattered about the grounds. The roof and upper section of the walls were missing from the center section of the station. As I stood gaping at the scene of destruction, a handsome Burmese soldier ambled up, his arm in a sling.

"What you want?" he asked in a friendly voice.

"I want to get to Mandalay. I was told to take train. He say is better if I take the train. He say not safe to go by road." I answered in semi-baby talk so as not to confuse him.

"Train is not safe. Communist bad men bomb station two days ago, shoot two friends- dead. They do not hurt me so much." He pointed to his bandaged arm and smiled. "Come, we have tea, my wife, she fix."

He led the way to his small hut, which stood on stilts eight feet off the ground like all the nearby huts. He introduced me to his wife and his baby son. We sat on his steps sipping green tea from handle-less Chinese cups while he excitedly explained how the communists had blown up the station house. His wife quietly passed around lumps of solidified brown sugar candy, her young son resting on her hip.

I thanked my hosts for the tea, and their advice. Chin and I climbed up the steep embankment to the road. Everyone in Pegu turned to stare at me as I passed by. I came to a three hundred-foot long suspension bridge, which was badly twisted to one side. Several of the planks in its flooring were missing. A heap of earth, several truckloads in all, was blocking the approach to the bridge. I looked around but could not see any other way to cross the broad Bago River, other than to work my way across the bridge like an acrobat. I clung to the suspension cables as I stepped over missing floorboards. The yellowish water drifted lazily far below. Shouts of natives caught my attention. I looked up to see scores of people waving their arms high above their heads and shouting at the top of their voices from the far bank. I could not understand what was triggering the commotion. Then it dawned on me: this must be the bridge that the communists had bombed a few days previously, and that it was likely not officially open to any kind of traffic, vehicle or pedestrian. Retracing my steps to solid earth, Chin and I scrambled down the embankment to the river's edge, where we waited for a dugout canoe to reach us.

The dugout had very little stability, rocking even after I was seated on the bottom of it. The dark bare-chested pole man pushed us toward the opposite bank. Looking up at the underside of the mangled bridge, I could see that I would have encountered great difficulty had I tried to cross it on foot: large sections were blown to bits. I later learned that the communists had sabotaged the bridge the same night they had attacked the rail station. I climbed out of the dugout onto the north bank where a crowd of natives surrounded me and started jabbering. Guess they were trying to tell me that the bridge was not safe. The pole man from the dugout canoe pushed his way into the center of the crowd and held out his hand. I dropped a five pyak coin into it and he backed away, smiling.

The north bank was lined with rundown bamboo huts. The odor of fish mixed with sewage permeated the air. I passed through the narrow alleyways where baskets of mashed minnows were being sold. I was hungry, but nothing looked appealing so I walked on until I got to the northern outskirts of Pegu. I waited on the shoulder of the road for two hours, but nothing faster than an oxcart passed. A gentle breeze scattered flaming butea blossoms over the ground. The gilded heights of Burma's second largest pagoda, the Shwemawdaw towered far above the trees and huts at its base. Children began to gather around until there were so many that they blocked the entire road. I moved further off the road into a rice paddy so that no one would get run over should a truck happen to appear. A uniformed man pedaled up on his bike. He brusquely dispersed the crowd and then addressed me in English.

"Your papers, please! I am Police Officer Yone. What brings you to Pegu?" I handed over my passport and explained my situation as he thumbed through it. Luckily I had gotten my Burmese visa in Singapore and there were no restrictions on it; likewise with my Indian visa.

"There are communist insurgents here, not to mention the dangerous Dacoits. You have not registered with the police here, why?"

"I'm sorry, but I did not realize that it was necessary."

"It is for your own protection- as well as ours. Come, you will not get out of Pegu today, all of the trucks leave early in the morning. After you register with the authorities, you can return to my house for the night, we will take care of you."

I followed Officer Yone to the local authorities and registered with them. Since he was still on duty, I left my gear at the station house and took off through the paddy fields towards the pagoda. I passed through a poorly kept cemetery with only three oxen to caretake the grounds by grazing the greenery to keep it in check. The vaults containing the dead were above ground. All the vaults had been broken into, and human skulls and bones were strewn about. I had never seen anything like this, and it was haunting.

Buddhist monks in loose fitting saffron robes dotted a brilliant green landscape as I neared the pagoda. The three hundred twenty foot Shwemawdaw Pagoda, also known as the Golden God Temple, was like a mountain; it looked so near, and yet was so distant due to its enormous size. The entrance was guarded by massive Chinthe lyogryphs (lions) of brick and stone. Surrounding the main pagoda were smaller shrines, containing figures of Buddhas inlaid with jewels. Faithful Buddhists touched their foreheads to the ground to make obeisance, and presented their offerings of food or flowers in humble well-worn bowls. Only the tinkling of the golden Hti's binaural bells broke the stillness. Each round of bells ringing signified a prayer. I slowed my pace to savor the gentle, peaceful scene. These moments found in world travel, and spent in rapture of newly discovered magic, are treasured for life.

As dusk came I headed back toward the police station. I hopped onto the back of a slow, bumpy bullock cart. It moved slower than I could have walked, but it consumed far less effort. Yone was off duty, and waiting for me. He pushed his bicycle along as we walked to the police officers' compound where he lives with his wife and two young girls. The house was a small two-room affair, without electricity or running water. Yone changed into a lungi and suggested I take a bath. I took a lighted candle into a tiny cubicle at the back of the house, smiling to myself. Indeed, 'twas a grand idea. However, in the center of the floor was a toilet hole, and the surrounding floor, splattered with human waste. I did not like the idea of standing on the floor in my bare feet to bathe, but there was no alternative. The usual clay vase filled with cold water was standing in the corner. I doused my body with the icy water, and while standing on the back steps to warm and dry myself, a group of native women walking by stopped to giggle.

Yone's wife had gathered her son under her arm and taken off for a nearby cafe here she had a tea and cake concession stand. With a loan of a lungi and a pair of sandals, the two of us went over to the café to get our supper. Yone ordered a bowl of rice and gap-htaung (dried fish) for each of us. He molded the rice into balls with his fingers and dropped them into his mouth. I found it impossible to mold the rice into balls that would stick together. I had to force it into my mouth making a mess of the task.

"You eat like a baby!" teased Yone.

To change the subject I asked him about the damaged grave vaults I had seen earlier in the day. He explained that the graves of the rich are plundered for their jewelry. "The poor are buried in a temporary vault which is broken apart and the remains strewn about to make way for the future dead. Many Burmese are too poor to afford a permanent burial plot."

Chin and I spent the night huddled together with Yone and family on a mat, on the floor. After a cup of green tea in the morning, Yone led me back into Pegu to the new bridge that had been hastily constructed to replace the damaged one. He rounded up couple of police inspectors and assigned them to the task of stopping all northbound trucks. The inspectors were told to check the cargo holds for smuggled goods, and to locate a truck that would take me far north. Yone and I took a seat in a cruddy little tobacco shop next to the intersection. There was barely room for us along with a small pig and a flock of disheveled chickens that were busily searching the floor for edible droppings. We smoked cheroot cigars and chewed bettle nut for the remainder of the morning.

Meanwhile, the traffic jammed up for blocks while the inspectors checked every single truck as instructed. Throngs of local natives stood around to watch all the activity. Most of the trucks were only going a short distance, but early in the afternoon Yone's men halted a truck that was bound for Meiktila, over two hundred miles north situated in Central Burma on Lake Meiktila and home of an air force base due to it's strategic location. I tossed my gear on top of the cab and climbed into an outside seat beside the driver, making a total of five of us in the cab. None of them spoke English. I passed around a handful of cigars. Even when we all smoked at once the smoke did not bother us since the cab had no doors and wind blew the smoke out as fast as we generated it. The only drawback was that the cigars were cheaply made. They were more like huge cigarettes, and hot chunks of tobacco kept blowing onto our clothing. The bitumen road got worse the farther we went along; potholes were so deep I thought we would lose a wheel. We passed two trucks that already had torn axles. I doubt if the road had been maintained at all since the last war.

The road to Mandalay has been so well publicized over the years that it was even the subject of a romantic song. While indeed an interesting route, I can attest that it is hardly romantic. Of the hundreds of streams and culverts we crossed, the majority of them were partially blown away by the insurgents' home made bombs. Larger bridges were guarded by machine guns. Gates blocked all approaches, and no vehicle could cross until its identity had been determined. The assistant driver had to get out in many instances and guide the trucks across what was once a bridge, and now mere random rubble. The machine gun placements and the huts of the soldiers who manned them were protected by two feet of earth reinforced by bamboo stakes on either side.

Countless times, the truck had to be maneuvered around disabled Japanese and British tanks that had been abandoned right where they failed. The Burmese had nothing powerful enough to move heavy steel hulks off the roadbed. Nor does the Burmese government have enough money to cut the tanks up with acetylene torches. Evidence of the last war is prevalent everywhere. Without exception the twisted wreckage of bridges in postwar conditions are found in the streams and rivers below today's sabotaged bridges. On three occasions during the afternoon we had to ford the riverbed because the communist insurgents had succeeded in blowing the bridge above us to bits. Coolies were sledging away on a fourth bridge, trying to break the reinforced concrete into moveable chunks. The twisted I-beams curved grotesquely towards the heavens, an unintentional monument to senseless destruction likely to remain for a very long time.

Since the insurgents operated after dark for the most part, there was little danger that a bridge would blow up as we crossed it. Late in the afternoon our truck stopped in a peaceful little village where everyone piled out and headed into a thatched restaurant. The truck driver motioned for me to join him. I sat down at the fly covered table and started forcing rice into my mouth as soon as the chef put it on the table. There were chunks of blubbery chicken fat and small pieces of chicken meat in a common bowl. Trying to keep the hungry flies off the food was a full-time occupation. They swarmed all over us and clung to our greasy hands like parasites and it was a feat to keep them out of our mouths. My cohorts were spitting the fragments of chicken bones onto the floor. In Asia, it is difficult to discern what you are eating when you eat meat because most of the animals were chopped into little particles by a cleaver, bones and all.

The truck rattled on all afternoon, past bullock carts laden with rice, and the families of the driver. They were protected from the hot sun and rain by a curved roof of bamboo matting. At dusk the truck pulled into a large village and parked in front of a cafe.

Across the street was nothing but smoldering ashes covering an area of three city blocks. Peasants were picking through the debris in search of their belongings. The fire had flared up a few days back, consuming over three hundred bamboo and attap houses in less than four hours. The devastation was appalling. The entire village reeked with the smell of charred flesh. A thick grey blanket of smoke hovered over the ruin. I stumbled through the deep ashes, shocked by the magnitude of the devastation. Regardless of the wealth of the individual families, the common denominator of fire had reduced every structure to rubble. Where once peasant huts had stood, nothing but a few cracked clay vases remained. A lone chimney and a distorted iron bed were all that remained of the most elaborate structure. I crossed over onto the adjacent street and started to head back to the truck for the night when a soldier stepped out and ordered me to follow him.

I followed him down the road a short distance, through a gate into a fenced compound and up a flight of stairs on the outside of the building. My escort shouted something in Burmese and a man from within the whitewashed stone building opened the door. We had to wait until it settled in place to form a drawbridge between the building and where we were standing at the top of the stairs. We entered a very large room with a hand-hewn beamed ceiling. A burly man seated at the only desk in the room motioned for me to take a seat. I placed my papers on his desk and he sent my escort out of the room.

A few minutes later he returned with a small-boned man dressed in western clothes who introduced himself as being "in charge of investigating insurgents". He looked very young to be holding such a position, yet he spoke English very well. He checked over my papers and asked me to explain my presence. When I finished, he told me that I would have to spend the night in their compound. It was okay by me, for it would save me the trouble of finding a place to spend the night. He explained what an impossible task he was performing. According to him the insurgents would often blow up bridges right under the noses of the soldiers who were supposedly guarding them. The insurgents had little trouble getting blasting material since so much of it had been left behind after the last war. The insurgents were seldom caught in the act, leading him to think the army itself was plagued with saboteurs for the communist activities. He warned me not to be alarmed during the night if I heard explosions; that it would only be another bridge they would have to rebuild. Before he left, he instructed the desk sergeant to wake me before dawn, so that I could catch the truck before it pulled out. He then closed the armor-plated shutters over the barred windows. The only way to see out was through the narrow slits in the steel plating. My house for the night was hardly vulnerable to small arms attack. Though the bench was narrow, but it was better than sleeping on the earthen floor.

When I returned to the truck in the morning, the driver and his assistant were sipping tea in the cafe. Apparently the other two men that had been in the truck the day before were passengers and had reached their destination. They beckoned me to join them. I knew they were wondering what had happened to me last night. So in the way of an explanation I pointed to the stockade- or fort- where I had slept. It was hard to tell which of the two it really was.

I rinsed out a teacup, filled it with tea, and started to munch on a piece of breakfast cake. Just then, a bare bottomed boy of about six years of age entered the café. He walked up to the serving counter next to us, took one look at the rice and vegetables on it, turned around and squatted on his haunches. Offal coiled onto the floor from his rectum. His chore complete the boy stood up and wiped his hindquarters with his shirttail. Immediately, a hungry looking hound greedily devoured the boy's handiwork. So as not to miss a tasty morsel the dog licked the earthen floor with his tongue. I had been about to take another mouthful of cake, but paused to gather my appetite. Guess I'm too finicky, I thought, as I pocketed the rest of my food for a more suitable dining environment.

I bought a handful of cheroots and hopped into the truck. The assistant driver gave the old jitney a couple of cranks and the motor roared. We were off again, barreling along at a pretty good clip on the open stretches, but slowing to a snail's pace every time we entered a village to avoid mowing down nonchalant pedestrians in no hurry to get wherever they were going. Graceful, multi-colored peacocks strolled among the crowds on the streets. Blackheaded vultures as large as turkeys were pecking away at the carcass of a calf with their sharp beaks when our truck scared them for an instant. They flapped the massive wings and lifted the calf off the ground, flying away with it in their talons.

We stopped in Pyinmana, a logging town and sugar cane refinery center, for lunch. Our meal consisted of tea and rice covered with a greasy curry of goat meat. Two live white goats wandered up to our table to get the scraps that we spit on the floor. The proprietor did not approve of their actions so he grabbed them by the ears and led them out to the street. A boy was crapping in front of the restaurant. This public defecation was taking some getting used to! Sometime during the afternoon the truck's motor went kaput: the gas line had come loose from the carburetor. While the driver was fixing it, a flock of scraggly red head vultures lodged in a tree near us. They were mean looking creatures. They surveyed our predicament and flew clumsily away in search of more vulnerable prey. Buses passed us, loaded to the brim with cargo and passengers clinging to the roof rail.

As the sun was setting our truck rumbled into the village of Yamethin, and stopped at a cafe for the night. The driver bought a bottle of a local favorite, "toddy" (fermented milk), to share. The three of us killed the abominable contents before eating our normal meal of rice and curry. The toddy did not affect me until I got up from the table and was wandering down the dusty street in search of the police where I was supposed to register. I wove my way down towards the railway station where my chance of finding an English speaking person was the most probable. The tracks were lined with battered, bullet-ridden freight cars, dating back to World War II attacks, and others were apparent victims of the current insurgent activities. The stationmaster directed me to the police compound on the far side of the village.

I found the compound, more of a military establishment than a police headquarters, just as darkness closed fell. A young Burmese officer, dressed in a lungi opened the gate and allowed me to enter. His knowledge of English was limited, but his friendliness more than compensated for his inability to converse. I spent the night sleeping on a mat on the floor of his hut. The sentries rang a gong every 15 minutes during the night to insure any insurgents that that they were still awake. Other than the gong and the occasional yelping of dogs, the night was quiet.

We reached our destination, the bustling village of Meiktila, by noon the next day. I thanked the driver and his assistant for the long lift, gave them a handful of cheroots, tossed my heavy pack on my back and trudged into the town. The road forked in the heart of the village, so I asked passing pedestrians which of the two routes led to Mandalay. Unfortunately none of the people could understand English. Suddenly I espied three white people in a shop across the dusty main street. I dropped my gear and ran over to them. The first white people I had seen since Rangoon, what a relief! It was not that I liked white people any better than green people. I was so jubilant to see them because I figured they would speak English. It would be a relief to be able to talk with someone for a change without having to speak baby talk to be understood, if you were lucky enough to find someone whom could speak English at all. I dropped my gear on the spot and ran over to them, two men and one woman wearing a western skirt. As I entered the shop they looked at me in surprise. They were as curious to learn who and what I was, as I was to learn of them. Now that I was inside the shop next to them I realized that they would not be likely to speak English. The woman was large and looked more like a German or Scandinavian, and her companions, two tall heavy set men, were swarthy enough to be southern Europeans.

"Sind sie, Deustch", I blurted in poor German.

"No, we are not German, who are you?" asked the woman in perfect English.

"I'm an American. Where are you from?"

"Where do you think we are from?" She asked.

"Are you English?"

"No".

"Danish".

"No, we are Russians!"

"Well I'll be damned, you're the first live Russians I have ever seen! We exchanged hearty sincere handshakes, for it was indeed strange that members of the world's two greatest powers should meet in an isolated village in Burma. The fact that the U.S.A. and Russians were currently engaged in heated "cold war" seemed very remote: these people appeared friendly and human and intelligent. That was all that mattered for the moment.

"What are you doing here in Meiktila?" queried the woman, an obvious interpreter for the two men.

"I'm trying to get back to the States by an overland route where possible. I am just about broke, but at least I'm getting a first hand look at some of the world."

"Will you join us for some tea?"

"Be glad to, it's about the only thing you can drink without getting sick around here."

The four of us and Chin were the only customers at this open air teashop. The Russians got a big kick out of Chin's antics. One of the men gave me a pack of Chesterfield cigarettes, which he had just purchased for eighty cents on the black market. Chin demolished a tomato while we ate spice cake and sipped tea. The woman explained to me that they had flown from Moscow to Peking in a new jet airliner and from Peking they continued on by plane to Rangoon. From Rangoon they had flown to Mandalay and then come by jeep to Maithili only this morning. They were on an agricultural mission to Burma. They would remain here with the latest Russian improvements in agriculture. They hoped that the Burmese would learn the ways of progressive farming by working with and studying the methods they employed. Naturally all the expenses would be borne by the Russians and the profits would be given to Burma. I could not help but think how much good could come of their model farm as far as the Burmese people were concerned, if the Russians were sincerely trying to teach the natives modern methods.

The U.S.A. has been trying to help underdeveloped countries for many years and including Burma. For some reason, many of our aid programs tend to create more ill will than friends. It was the opinion of the majority of the English speaking Burmese that the U.S. A. was trying to buy friends with our vast wealth. Even though this is not what we are in fact trying to do, it is what many of the countries think we are doing, and it is what they think, rather than what is, that determines their attitudes toward us. It is common knowledge that Burma is backward and underdeveloped, with present production even below that of twenty years prior. To alleviate the situation, the U.S.A sent a trio of economic experts to Rangoon. After their arrival at the Rangoon airport, they took on a train and spent the next three days making a survey of the economic status of Burma. When these experts returned to the states, they advised on the basis of their "thorough survey" that we send Burma so many millions for the purpose of erecting a rolling mill, a textile mill or some other enterprise. What the experts have failed to realize is that Burma does not produce enough iron to support a rolling mill. A weaving plant had recently been erected near Rangoon by foreign aid, but the sad thing was that the mill could not handle the type of cotton raised in Burma. They not only had to import all their raw materials but also had to export their own raw cotton to be processed.

In addition to these inadequacies of American aid, by the time the appropriated money (which the American taxpayers provided) got past all the graft and corruption, there was little left to help the economy of Burma, even if it were put to a logical use, which so rarely happened. This type of aid only tends to aggravate the average Burmese who lives a simple life by working the land. The American taxpayer may consider himself as noble for all the money spent on foreign aid, yet if the taxpayer could see how often this money is squandered, perhaps would not feel so magnanimous, and be riled to the point of seeing to it that money is spent to better advantage for not only himself, but for the countries that are receiving our aid.

"Our country has recently realized the importance of understanding the peoples of Asia. It is necessary that we speak their language, and understand their cultures and aspirations if we are to gain their respect. It is only when they accept us that Russia will be able to alleviate the suffering that exists there today. Without the confidence of the masses our model farm and future projects will fail. The world is so small now, nations are so dependent on each other today, and yet intolerance and ignorance between nations seems to be stronger than ever," Natasha explained in a serious tone. Looking me directly in the eyes she continued, "You are extremely brave and courageous to be seeing the world as you are. You should forget your little business in Alaska. You have more important things to do! The world needs men like you, who are seeing the truth regardless of the dangers involved. You will be one of the few who are truly enlightened as to the ways of the world. You should write and tell the whole world what you have seen and learned! For you to return to Alaska would be a complete waste of your talent! Would not the American government black-ball you if they were to find you speaking to us?"

"No, not that I know of," I replied, laughing. "When our government has so little confidence in its people that it prohibits them from talking with others for fears of being tainted, then I no longer want to be a subject of such a government. How are we to break down the propaganda barriers of our countries unless we have a chance to converse with each other?"

As we were finishing our third pot of tea, five more Russians joined us. There were all well dressed and well fed. None of them spoke English besides Natasha. She had traveled extensively on her own before working for the government, and she wished that she could accompany me. It was with great reluctance that I parted from the Russians that afternoon. I would have liked to have had the opportunity to know them better. They seemed every bit as human and friendly as any other people I had encountered.

Continuing on our way to Mandalay having obtained directions, Chin and I kicked up clouds of dust for the next two hours trodding to the northern outskirts of the village- without a single vehicle passing us. The sun was melting us when a truck packed with riders finally stopped for us. We clambered aboard and took a seat on a sack of rice. As bus service is rare, most cargo trucks pick up passengers for a small fee, making progress forward rather slow. The cargo consisted of bagged rice and over thirty passengers, many of them clinging to chickens and goats. We made it to Mandalay shortly after sundown. I climbed down from the truck when it stopped in what I assumed to be the center of the town. The streets were cluttered with beggars, stray dogs, chickens and holy cows, let alone the usual scurrying pedestrians: Burmese in their lungis, Hindus in their native dress and Chinese in their billowing slacks. A jeep equipped with a loudspeaker was creeping down the street blaring out an advertisement for some fifteen year-old movie that was the latest release in Mandalay. I stopped in at a local printing shop with the intention of seeking advice as to where we might spend the night. The owner rounded up two boys who tossed my gear into a jeep in front of the shop and signaled for me to join them. The jeep bounced through potholes, turned up a side street, and came to a hold on someone's front lawn. "This is the Y.M.C. A. You remain here," said the driver.

And so we did.

Chapter 15:

Mandalay: Baptists and Acrobats

I GATHERED UP my junk and walked over to the two story structure. A middle-aged Burman introduced himself as Chit Pe, a Baptist minister, as well as his young, attractive wife who had only recently become a Christian and spoke no English. I asked him if this was the Y.M.C.A. He replied that the "Y" had no hotel in Mandalay, but that strangers such as I are more than welcome to use his house as a hotel. He then invited me to dine with him in town, so the two of us pedaled bicycles through dimly lit streets to a Hindu restaurant where we had an edible meal followed by a quart of Mandalay beer, brewed and owned by the government. Chit Pe refused to drink, so I set about the pleasant task of consuming the cool liquid on my own. Chit Pe refused to let me foot the bill by saying, "It is Burmese custom to furnish guests and strangers with life's necessities, in fact rude for the stranger to even offer to pay for anything."

I found this custom could often be embarrassing. The humble people of Burma seem to anticipate your every wish, and will do things for you at great sacrifice to themselves. It must indeed be a shock to them if they ever have the opportunity to visit western countries only to find that their custom is not followed. We returned to Chit Pe's dwelling where he fixed up a bed complete with mosquito netting for me. It was luxury to sleep on a bed for a change, even though it did sag miserably. Chit Pe was eager to show me the massive church next to his house. It was a concrete structure and had been so badly shaken by bombing raids during the last war; its once smooth surface was badly cracked.

Chit Pe's dog seemed fascinated with Chin, so I tried to introduce the monk to the mutt, but the mutt lunged at Chin and tugged at his head until I thought he had killed the helpless monk. When I did get Chin's head out of the dog's mouth, it was still in one piece. To play it safe, I tied Chin high up in a tree for the remainder of the day.

Chit Pe took me to a Burmese high society wedding. The bride was the daughter of one of the town wealthiest merchants. We were too late for the ceremony, but we did get there in time for the reception which took place in a gaudy cardboard affair shed that had been hastily constructed in the front yard of the bride's mansion-like home. The table was lined with flowers and tea sandwiches. I sipped tea till I could hear the liquid washing up against the walls of my stomach. Cows were roaming disconcertedly in the street in front of the reception hall. On the way out, one of the ushers gave us each a bunch of flowers and a foot long cigar.

During the afternoon I changed five dollars for fifty kyats on the black market, which was double the official rate- in my favor. That way I could pay for any permits I might need to proceed in my travel. I chased around Mandalay on a borrowed bike trying to locate the Deputy Commissioner whose permission I needed before I could head either north or west out of Mandalay. My request to cross through the jungles to India only bewildered the officials I encountered.

Through the efforts of Chit Pe and his wife, Chin and I were invited by his colleague, Reverend Crain and his family for supper. Reverend Crain is an American Baptist missionary, originally from Rochester, New York. He is a bespectacled, quiet spoken man, sporting a tuft of beard. His family has spent the last seventeen years doing mission work in Burma. The Japanese used the mission school he administers during the war as their headquarters and supply depot. The archways between the buildings as originally designed have been gouged by the Jap trucks that were a bit too large to pass through them. Given the buildings and arches are made from brick, the damage to the Jap trucks must have been considerable.

We tied Chin to a tree and gave him a banana to eat while the Chit Pe's, the Crain's, and I ate a delicious dinner in the Crain's substantial living quarters. It was the first wholesome meal I had eaten since leaving Bangkok, and a welcome relief to know that I could eat all I wanted of everything- and not get sick as a result.

Mary Jean, the Crain's seventeen year-old daughter, was home on leave from her last year of high school in India. She had never been to America, even though she was a citizen, but she was leaving for the states within a few months to study at Oberlin College in Ohio. Mary was a petite, attractive girl who loved the people of Asia because she had lived with them, and understood their culture. And yet, despite her not having lived in the States, she would undoubtedly adjust to our way of life with little difficulty, perhaps a bit less ignorant than the average American. It was obvious that Chit Pe's wife was ill at ease while dinning with us. Even though she had recently become a Christian, she could not accustom herself to eating with men folk at the table. Burmese custom dictates that the men should be served- and eat- first. Also the manipulation of the knife, fork, and spoon must have presented quite a challenge after spending her life eating with her fingers. After dinner we chatted and listened to American records, the first I had heard since leaving Australia.

Early the next morning I pedaled down to the outskirts of Mandalay to the Irrawaddy River. Reverend Crain had advised me to try to get a ferry up the Chindwin River to Sittaung where I could trek through the jungles on a mule trail, at least according to the map in my possession. It would be by far the shortest route to Calcutta. I checked along the banks of the broad, meandering Irrawaddy for the I.W.T. (Inland Water Transport) office. Antiquated paddle wheel ferries were being relieved of their cargo on a nearby wharf. Ten water buffalo, hitched together in five pairs, were pulling a gigantic teak log along the riverbed several feet from shore. On top of the log stood a stick-wielding Hindu directing the cattle's movement. The buffalo were up to their necks in water making them nearly buoyant and difficult to get traction. At one point, five buffalo on one side dropped completely out of sight as they fell into a depression in the river bottom. The beast ahead of it in turn pulled each out, only to have the following buffalo dragged into the same hole.

In my search for the I.W.T., I mistakenly entered the local jail where a black-toothed woman was being reprimanded for her excessive use of opium. One of the guards gave me accurate directions to the I.W.T. after I had spent most of the morning on a wild goose chase. When I finally did locate the I.W.T. one of its officials informed me that it would be two weeks before I could get a ferry up the river, and that the trip would take an unpredictable number of days to get the two hundred odd miles to Sittaung because the river was unusually low, and ferries were frequently running aground on sandbars. Whenever this happened the passengers would have to get out to push the ferry back into the river. The I.W.T. official warned me that *if* I succeeded in getting to Sittaung, I would then have to trek over seventy miles through dense jungles before I would find any kind of road suitable for vehicles. In addition to the time element and the rigors involved in taking that route, I would first have to produce evidence that I had the Deputy Commissioner's permission to cross the border, officially closed due to local strife in that area.

I felt I had little choice but to retrace my route back to Rangoon and go by ship or plane from there to Calcutta as the Indian official had insisted and arrive in India nearly broke, or else try to cross the border illegally further north. According to the map there was a road to Myitkyina which lay some four hundred miles north, and from there to Ledo, India was roughly another 250 miles. The map did not even indicate that as much as a mule path existed between Myitkyina and Ledo. I decided to take the latter route. If I lived I would have at least fifty dollars when I reached India. There would be little expense involved in passing through the teeming jungles which lay ahead and there was the faint prospect that the famed Stilwell Road, which was hastily built from Ledo through Myitkyina to China, would not be so overgrown that I could not follow it. However, the fact that the map did not acknowledge its existence was not too encouraging at the moment.

I returned to Chit Pe's house in rather dim spirits to find that he was officiating at a Christian wedding that afternoon in his church, and I was invited to attend. I washed my khakis by pounding them on a slab of concrete after having saturated them with cold soapy water. The stains faded somewhat, and within an hour the blazing sun had dried them.

I was the last one to enter the plainly decorated church before the ceremony began. To avoid distracting anyone, I took a seat in the first vacant seat I found. Much to my embarrassment I realized that the men were all sitting in the left side of the sanctuary and I was sitting with the women folk on the right side. I hastily moved over to the male section, but as I did so, the five year-old ring bearer was coming down the aisle. When he saw me scoot from the female section to the male section, he stopped dead in his tracks, apparently afraid of my beard. He turned around as if to run out of the church. Luckily one of the attendants saw his actions and promptly forced him along toward the altar. The groom was a Christian Burman widower and the father of the little ring bearer and the flower girl. The bride was a non-Christian Koran; her face deeply pocked from small pox epidemics of the past, as so many in this part of the world. It was not the norm for a Christian to marry a non-Christian so when Chit Pe said "If anyone objects to this marriage, speak now or forever hold your peace," a visiting Burmese minister from Lashio, jumped up, turned to the audience, and bellowed: "On behalf of this happy gathering I wish to announce that not only do none of us object; we are all heartily in favor of this union- so let's get on with the show!"

My last night in Mandalay was a night to remember. I met a young English chap at the reception, which followed the ceremony on the church lawn. He had recently been stationed in Mandalay as a tea-taster for a Burmese firm. It was his opinion that even though the English were frowned upon for their colonization of much of Asia in the past, English men were often appointed to responsible positions with Asian-owned firms. The fact that Asians produced businessmen capable of handling these positions still left many vacancies open to the English. Quite often a firm would trust the integrity of a foreigner rather than appoint one of its own countrymen who were so often suspected of being unscrupulous.

That evening the tea-taster and I went to the outskirts of Mandalay to see a troupe of Russian acrobats who were performing in a small show. He did not want to put money in the hands of the Russians, so we attempted to sneak. We climbed over a fence and waded through an irrigation ditch only to be turned away by guards as we reached the rear of the show ground. Giving up, I returned to Chit Pe's for the night only to find the door locked. Rather than awaken him, I fetched Chin from the tree where he had been tethered and headed back into town, prowling for a place to sleep. Holy cows were comfortably bedded down on the streets throughout town. No less than thirteen dogs chased me before I reached an area with minimal streetlights. I could hear the bewitching sounds of a putt-waing (circle of tuned drums) off in the distance which indicated nightlife somewhere. I followed the trail of sound until I reached a scene of the live music. It was a zat pwe (all night performance of marionettes, dance, music, and slap stick), which is very common in Burma. There is no nation on the face of the earth so fond of fun and laughter and theatrical entertainment as Burma. The street was blocked with people who were sitting or lying in the road. A few had brought their beds along to sleep in the event that any of the stage performances should be dull. It was motley crowd transfixed with the dancing and antics of the performers. The music was unreasonably loud, which made it difficult for the tired to sleep. The monk and I took a place on the edge of someone's mat. It was very late and sleep was foremost on my mind, yet I could not sleep in a sitting position. Dressed only in a short-sleeved poplin shirt and khaki trousers, I was shivering from the cool night air. Nearby, a bearded Hindu was sitting on the edge of his dilapidated bed, watching the show. What a waste to have a bed and not use it! I brazenly climbed into it, making myself comfortable, and tugged at the base of his shawl in an effort to cover at least part of my chilled body. My intrusion was met with a glare from his penetrating glassy eyes. He then stretched out on the bed and rolled towards me, forcing me out onto the road. I was too tired to protest and picked myself up, staggering to the rear of the actors' stage where peeping toms were shoving each other to get a better view of the actors changing costumes.

One dark, sinister-looking Mongolian character asked me what I was doing with a monkey. I told him that I was looking for a place to sleep, and where I would be warm. He grabbed me by the arm and dragged me across the street to a wooden structure full of Chinese men who were playing some sort of gambling game around numerous tables. Suddenly, one of the players came over to us and waved us out of the building, shouting that it was a private club. My escort, whoever he was, snatched up a banana and an orange from one of the tables on the way out which he gave to me once we were on the street.

The two of us forced our way through the mob back to our former position at dressing rooms. Before long the very man that had kicked us out of the restaurant wormed his way through the crowd and told me to follow him, leading me back to the Chinese club or cafe, whatever it was into a room, which overlooked the zat pwe in the street. A couple of elderly Chinese were sipping tea at a small table in one corner of the room. My Chinese escort said that it would be permissible for me to sit on the bench along one wall. I asked him if it was a hotel, but he answered in the negative. The bench resembled a wooden small love seat, far from being comfortable. However, as soon as my escort left the room I took off my boots and curled up on the bench. I stuffed Chin under my shirt so as not to alarm any onlookers and turned my face to the wall, and tried to sleep, but the blaring incongruous noises emanating from the zat pwe made rest intermittent at best. I awoke several hours later to find that the sun was shining upon me, the street music had stopped, the two old gentlemen at the corner table now bent over in sleep. I tiptoed out of the room and down the stairs to the street before I put on my boots. I did not want to awaken anyone and possibly be charged for sleeping there.

The streets were empty of people at such an early hour. Only listless cows and Buddhist monks in their billowing orange robes moved about the quiet town. The monks were carrying shiny black begging bowls from door to door where the woman of the house would donate her share of their daily rations, mostly rice. When each monk had collected what he considered a sufficient amount, he would devour the contents of the bowl before noon, and not eat food again until after sunrise the following day. I returned to Chit Pe's house and gathered up my gear to head north and hope to cross the border into Assam, not far from Tibet. This roundabout route to Calcutta would be over fifteen hundred miles, but my chances of crossing the border undetected would be better up in the remote and primitive northern region. Chit Pe wished me luck, and warned me to avoid the dacoits as Chin and I headed out of Mandalay on foot under the gathering steam of the morning sun.

Chapter 16:

Maymyo: Opium and Dacoits

I HAD GONE but a couple of miles when a young Burman dressed in a clean, white shirt pulled up alongside me on a bike. He did not say a word at first, merely dismounting and walking silently beside me. His presence annoyed me because I was sweating and weary under the unforgiving sun, now pressing into my head and back like an iron. Then he started to question me as to where I was going, and where I had come from. His curiosity made me impatient. The least he could have done is to have tied some of my junk to his bike to save me the extra weight! I gave short, vague answers to his questions and finally flopped down under a tree in front of a home for lepers. The young man with the bike then revealed that he was a detective, and that they had to be very careful of strangers in light of all the insurgent activities. When I told him that I was trying to get a lift north, he seemed relieved and stopped the first truck headed in that direction to order the driver to give me a lift. The detective assured me that the truck would be going at least as far as Maymyo, some forty miles ahead.

The interior cab was overcrowded, so we clambered on top of the cargo- salt, flour, and fresh tomatoes- and the truck rolled forward. Chin and I feasted on the latter, their juice perfectly thirst quenching under the punishing midday sun. Within the first hour the truck started to climb into the rugged Shan Mountains, the road twisting and turning with one blind curve after another. Native huts were few and far between. Occasionally we would pass smoldering pits where logs were being burned into charcoal. Military lookout posts were perched on the highest points where one could see as far as Mandalay and beyond.

Our truck crawled at a snail's pace on the steeper grades, its motor roaring laboriously. Every time another truck approached us, the vehicle on the downgrade would stop to yield to the climbing vehicle. Over ninety-five percent of the vehicles I had seen in Burma were American built relics of World War II. It was miraculous to me that they were still functioning.

Flames from a pungent, widespread brush fire licked up from the shoulder of the road toward the truck's tires, but were not potent enough to do damage. We passed a bullet-ridden bus in the ditch, ambushed by dacoits two days previously. The truck developed a radiator leak, which our driver quickly realized when plumes of steam started to hiss from under the hood. From that point on, we stopped at every stream and tea hut to top it off. The forty-mile trip from Mandalay to Maymyo took six grueling hours.

We reached the scenic hill town village of Maymyo just before dusk. It was much cooler here high in the hills and was widely known as a haven from the heat of Mandalay by the more fortunate who could afford to retreat. As I disembarked from our truck in a crowded street, a soldier came over and beckoned for me to follow. I did so without question since we didn't share a common language. He continued to lead me out of town, across fields and to the top of a hill to a military compound. The barracks were of thatch, and more than one was sadly in need of an overhaul. It must have been after duty hours as we entered the encampment because we were suddenly inundated with scores of soldiers descending upon us from all directions. They stared at Chin and I and while jabbering among themselves.

Finally a tall, slim soldier broke through the human barricade, which surrounded us. The others became silent. He spoke English clearly as he asked me to identify myself and prove my intentions. When he seemed satisfied that I was harmless, he shook my hand and introduced himself as Tun Lin, the only officer presently in the small encampment. He ordered me to make his camp my home for the night. Tun Lin had learned to speak English as a result of working with the American forces on the Stilwell Road, a backbreaking project at ten thousand feet and plagued with constant monsoon conditions during construction in the last war. I tried desperately to glean as much information about Stilwell Road's present condition as possible, but Tun, like all the others I had questioned, doubted that it could even be found, let alone followed. In addition to constant torrential rains washing out huge sections, the rest would have been reclaimed by jungle growth after twelve years of disuse.

Tun assigned me to a room with one of the other soldiers and invited me to the mess hall for supper where I was the source of great entertainment for thirty soldiers who sat watching me eat clumsily with my fingers. Tun produced a bottle of rice whiskey from under his coat. The soldiers had their own pet monkey running loose about the compound. We could hear her pawing on the roof, trying to get at little Chin. By the time the whiskey bottle was half empty, I was completely at ease, almost senseless.

As Tun Lin had been a former MP, he boasted that he knew where he could find some opium in Maymyo. He selected one soldier to accompany us, and before we left for town, swore us to secrecy. If he were to get caught in an opium den, he would be in serious trouble. Opium smoking is illegal in Burma proper, unless you are already addicted, in which case you are allowed to have your own special pipe and an adequate supply of the dope to smoke. When Tun was convinced that we would not betray his confidence, we proceeded to grope through the dark fields behind Maymyo toward the slums. Only once did we stumble into an irrigation ditch as we were walking three abreast. When we reached a certain dimly lit alleyway, Tun posted us as lookouts. Once we gave the all clear, Tun rapped on a heavy wooden door. It opened, and I could make out a small Chinaman within, silhouetted against the dim light. Acrid smoke billowed out of the door. The three of us entered and the Chinaman immediately bolted the door behind us. The air was thick and musty with smoke from candles and two opium pipes. The room was no larger than an American bathroom, yet there were twelve of us crowded into it. A bamboo platform covered two-thirds of the crammed floor space, covered with five men who lay smoking special opium pipes, heads resting on little individual wooden pillow-benches. We waited while two of the reclining men finished their smoking, then crawled in between the other men on the platform and rested our heads on the little stools. I gave the den keeper fifty pyas, (ten cents) for a small bowl of opium tar. It looked like coagulated molasses, or tar. The den keeper gathered a bit of the opium on a match stick and deftly shaped it into a small sphere by rolling it about on the brim of the pipe bowl. The opium pipe is no ordinary pipe; it is thick stemmed, about a foot and a half long, with the bowl placed about a foot from the smoker's mouth. The den keeper then placed the opium ball over the tiny sixteenth inch opening in the pipe bowl and placed a candle near the pipe to allow the opium ball to soften and boil. As soon as it began to bubble the den keeper nodded and motioned for me to inhale deeply. The fumes gagged me at first because I inhaled too sharply.

After three inhalations, the ball of opium was consumed, so while the den keeper prepared another pipeful, his assistant offered a Burmese cigarette and tea in a cruddy cup. I doubt if it had been washed for years, thick with a dark substance much the way the bowl of a well-used pipe is encrusted with tobacco tars. When I finished with the tea and cigarette, the den keeper repeated the procedure two more times. I felt completely relaxed, as did Tun who was obviously familiar with opium smoking. At his suggestion, we left the den before we had too much of a good thing.

The frosty mountain air seemed unusually brisk in comparison to the musty den. We walked through town as Tun pointed out the various establishments to me. I was beginning to get the sense that Tun was a man of influence, or authority. First, he stopped a taxi-jeep and told the driver to take us to a combination bazaar-carnival on the northern outskirts of Maymyo. Tun refused to pay the driver when we got out, and the driver did not protest. The carnival ground was cluttered with a series of thatched lean-tos and one holy canvas tent. There were no rides, or popcorn stands. Most of the spectators were too poor to purchase the trinkets that were being sold in the booths. Then a woman running a food concession recognized Tun and offered us a bowl of rice and bits of boiled chicken. After consuming the slimy morsels, we walked over to the tent and entered- free of charge. Inside, a wild looking lad was caretaker of a number of weak and unusual animals. A live three-legged chicken and an infant bottled in a solution drew most of the attention. The miniature human had but one head, four legs, and four arms. Another jar held a two-headed, three-eared, legless monster that some unfortunate woman had birthed. They were a gruesome sight to say the least and something not likely to be on display in the U.S.A.

The night air was extremely cold as we stepped out of the tent and headed back to camp for the night. I found that my warmest clothes were far from adequate of keep me warm in the event of cool weather. I had not expected to run into cold days until I had reached Europe. The lesson for me was about "elevation".

Tun Lin offered to give me a lift to the border of Shan States on his motorcycle before he had to go on duty. The early morning air was frigid as I crawled out of my miserable cotton sleeping bag to put on my warmest clothes. I noticed that Tun was sporting a pistol. He explained that the road ahead was often ambushed by

Dacoits, and that only the foolhardy- or the unauthorized- went without protection. Tun's military motorcycle shined in its fresh coat of OD (olive drab) paint. Tun boasted about his cycle, saying that it was originally a Harley from the last war, but since then it contained parts from numerous vehicles of every description. We hopped onto the cycle. I clung to Tun with Chin on my shoulder and we roared off toward the Shan border. The old cycle had plenty of spunk to climb the steep inclines. We had to lean almost horizontally as we raced around the series of hairpin curves that wound up and down the mountainside.

By the time we reached the distant border, our hands were numb. We stopped in at a dumpy café in a two hut village on the side of a heavily vegetated mountain for a cup of tea to warm our insides. As Tun Lin was preparing to return to Maymyo, a rattletrap bus pulled into the cafe. The driver ran over to us and started jabbering excitedly with Tun. The bus had just been robbed by Dacoits four miles back on the road we had just come over. Had I taken the bus, I would undoubtedly have been relieved of not only my money, but camera and passport as well. Since one of the Dacoits recognized a passenger, none of the passengers were shot, as often happens when the Dacoits run into the opposition.

In a way, I wished that I had been robbed by the Dacoits because then I would have an excuse for being so broke. Perhaps then I could appeal to the American embassy to help me out- if I ever reached another American embassy -which was dubious since as far as I knew, the closest one was back in Rangoon.

Tun took off on his cycle back toward Maymyo, and I listened as the rattletrap bus, now far less a target having been stripped for the day, continued on without me for lack of a fare.

Chapter 17:

Myo, Khin and Lessons of Patience

ONCE THE BUS disappeared to the north, the fading engine's moans gave way to natural sounds: a flock of pigeons roosting on the roof of the store; a little spring trickling down to the road between the village's only two buildings; a mutt's plaintive howls from somewhere out of sight. There were simply no sounds to indicate that this was the modern twentieth century.

A tiny, hunched back Chinaman was scurrying about scooping up buffalo dung with his bare hands. Some of the deposits were so soupy that they slipped through his fingers before he could get them into his basket. To counteract this drawback he would gather up dust and mix it with the dung so as to thicken and enable pick up. He kept glancing furtively about as if afraid someone else might beat him to the precious few piles. He went about his task with an air of greedy delight. The farmer eventually wiped his hands on his frock to join me at the table in front of the cafe for a pot of tea. He spoke no English, but merely stared at me out of curiosity as thousands had done before him since my arrival in southeast Asia all the way back in Singapore.

I waited three hours in the increasingly hot noonday sun before a single vehicle stopped at the cafe. It was a 1942 GMC 6x6 truck, loaded three times as high as normal. The load of salt and mammoth bags of packed cotton hung far over the tailgate. Pointing north, I asked the driver and his assistant if they were going to Lashio, the largest town in Shan State. They did not understand my question, but seemed so friendly that I took the liberty of tossing my backpack on top of their cab and tied Chin to one of the bags of cotton. So as not to antagonize the driver, I climbed on top with Chin and made a seat among the baskets of chickens and two bed rolls stashed up there. The mid-day sun was high in the sky and this would be the most comfortable place on the truck by far, not to mention having a much better view of the countryside from such a lofty perch.

Within a few minutes the two drivers came out of the cafe, and quickly understood that they had a passenger. They said a few words pointing to themselves, which I deciphered to mean: Myo, the driver and Khin, his assistant. Myo cranked the engine while Khin got in the cab. After five cranks, the engine chugged and sputtered to life and we started moving. Within the first half hour we had already passed three military checkpoints. We only had to stop at the third one because the first two were manned by sleeping soldiers.

A few miles north of the last check point, our engine sputtered and died. Once we had blocked the rear wheel of the truck to keep it from rolling, I helped Khin fetch water from the nearest stream. There were so many different streams within sight we did not have to go far for water. We returned to the truck a few minutes later to find Myo fumbling with the generator on the road in front of the truck. There was far too much play between the armature shaft and the housing so he cut a bushing from a tin can and worked it to the proper size, inserting his masterpiece and replacing the generator. We poured five gallons of water into the radiator, but much of it had leaked out by the time Khin got the engine started.

The truck rolled on, but broke down three times within the following hour. Each time Myo and Khin would block the wheels and tear the generator out. But the third time the truck would not start up no matter how much we cranked. Myo and I bummed a lift into the next village with the first truck that came along. We combed through the village looking for a machine shop and found a hut with a heap of rusty automotive parts piled in front. The owner of the hut invited us into his combination living room and repair shop. Greasy engines were on the earthen floor. He happened to have a well-worn spare bushing for the generator, and Myo thought it would serve our purpose.

I was to wait in town until the truck was repaired and then they would pick me up on their way through, I hoped. My money and all other earthly possessions were left with their truck.

There were three dumpy cafes in the village and I was dueling with my old friend, Hunger. I had no food since the previous evening and walked into the first cafe, pointed to the food I wanted, and sat down at a table. The Chinese couple running it started to tremble with laughter. Unless I served myself, it was evident that I would not get any food. I walked to the next dump, which was run by a chubby Shan woman. She, too, only laughed at me, showing her black teeth, covered with betel tar. She spat a stream of the reddish liquid on the floor. In desperation, I marched down the dusty unpaved road to the last option, a Hindu teashop. The proprietor spoke some English, so I asked him for rice and pointed to some green stuff that looked like spinach, but was pickled and spicy- much to my disappointment.

I barely had enough small change to pay him, and when he saw how carefully I doled out my scant coins, he asked me all sorts of questions regarding what I was doing in that particular part of Burma. I was very tired after the miserable meal, more from being undernourished than from lack of sleep. I did not want to fall asleep in the hot sun and possibly miss the truck. As it was, I had no guarantee that the truck would want to stop for me, for the drivers could put my money and other belongings to good use. They could even sell my passport to the Chinese for we were not much more than a hundred miles from China at this point. And then I began to wonder if Myo could bypass the town altogether by taking a back road. I had no way of checking: my map was back on the truck.

Rather than sit and fret about the things that could happen I walked down the road to the edge of the village where five soldiers were stationed at a road check. If the truck came through town it would first have to pass through this gate, so I fell asleep on the bamboo platform that had been erected to keep the soldiers out of the mud when it rained, covered by a thatched roof which served to keep the penetrating sun off of me. A couple of hours later, I was awakened by the noise of the dilapidated truck. It was indeed a welcome sight despite its frailties. Myo motioned for me to join them in the cab so I did. Chin was still clinging on to the side of the truck and looked no worse for the dust and wind he had endured.

As we continued northward, the terrain became more rugged and we began a long decent of several miles into a river gorge. The road was barely wide enough for a single vehicle, and further degraded to nothing but a series of hairpin turns. The curves in three instances were so sharp that the two and a half ton truck would not maneuver around them in a single pass. We had to creep up to such curves slowly so that Khin could grab a wooden block we carried with us, jump out of the truck, and place it in front of the wheel. Then Myo would back the truck up and make another bite at it. I realized that the truck had absolutely no emergency brake and that the regular foot brakes were damn near worthless, and could only slow the truck down a bit, but not keep it from rolling. If Khin misplaced the block, then the truck would roll over the precipice and freefall hundreds of feet through the air. As we had been taught in paratroops, it is not the fall that hurts you in case your parachute fails, but the sudden stop that does the damage.

We crept down the treacherous decline in low gear, the motor whining and groaning in complaint as it held the weight of the truck from gaining too much momentum. Looking over the precipice, we could see two other trucks that had been less fortunate in the days gone by, lying in twisted heaps in the shallow river far below. When we finally reached the river at the bottom, Myo pulled the truck over to the side and sighed with relief, the sweat dripping from his brow. He pointed to the equally treacherous road ahead which looked more like a terraced cliff than a roadbed.

The engine raced, sputtered, and seemed to lack power. Myo shoved the gearshift into low and we crept up the first stretch. Khin walked behind to be ready to shove the block under the wheel when necessary. We could not make the first four curves on a single pass. Through anguishing moments, Myo and Khin coordinated chucking the block under the wheel and trying to get the truck around the acute angled bends in the road. On one occasion the truck lurched, and the top-heavy load shifted to the downhill side. The load was so cockeyed that we expected it too tip the whole truck over. I got out and walked with Khin. The motor was losing compression, its spark getting weaker by the foot, probably from the faulty generator. Before we had advanced another hundred yards, the truck jerked to a halt. The sudden stop jarred two of the huge bundles of cotton onto the road. Khin hurriedly chucked the block under the wheel but the incline was so steep the truck began to creep backwards over the block. We frantically gathered large rocks and jammed them behind all the tires.

We had a hell of a time trying to get the heavy cotton bundles back onto the truck. They were each the size and weight of a cow. We finally had to drag them to the front of the truck and push them up onto the hood, then onto the top of the cab, and finally force them onto the load where they belonged. Myo surveyed the lopsided load. To untie the ropes on such an incline meant all the bundles would topple off, and we would be unable to get them back in place with the truck at such an angle. I guess that is what Myo concluded as well, for he forgot about the load and opened the hood once again. He tore the generator out and dissembled it, made a few adjustments, put it together again, hooked it into place- only to have the engine refuse to start. He repeated this same process three times in a row. I would have been at my wits end had it been my misfortune to be the driver of such a fouled up wreck and undoubtedly would have taken the block out from the wheels and let the whole shebang roll over the cliff!

I think most Americans would have done the same. But Myo and Khin dressed in their lungis merely laughed each time the truck quit on them. Although this time Khin ran his hand through his unruly hair and shook his head from side too side as he looked at the parts of the goddamned generator that were all over the road. Myo, like his fellow countrymen could not afford to get riled with his truck, for it would undoubtedly be the only truck he would ever own, and he was mighty lucky to have it, even if it was pieced together from a military graveyard of vehicles back in 1945. The first new truck to reach Burma would probably be in the museum in Rangoon. But this truck would not run, and darkness was closing in around us. Another, more able bodied truck chugged up the hill behind us. We stopped it and Myo indicated for me to take it to the next town for the night. Myo and Khin would stay behind with their truck. By now I trusted them completely but nevertheless, grabbed my possessions and frisky monkey and hopped into the waiting truck.

Chapter 18:

Kyaukme and the Mighty Mongols

LESS THAN AN hour later we rumbled into the mountain village of Kyaukme and rattled to a half. The town seemed mysterious and foreboding as I sat on the side of the main street and put on my boots to avoid the oozing mud. The air was miserably cold, and a sharp wind cut through my flimsy clothes. A strange crowd gathered about me. If I had not known better I would have sworn that I was in Tibet, or back in some Mongolian town of a thousand years ago. The people were the mighty Shans, who yet owe their allegiance to Sawbas (kings of little kingdoms) rather than to the central government of Burma. The Shan men looked like monsters, large and beastly, as they swarmed about me with their heads covered in fur caps, and bodies layered in rags. I had felt weak and sick for weeks now, possibly from fear- or altitude as well- as I forced my way through the milling crowds. The unappealing street was slimy with rain and garbage.

I had no destination in mind as I plodded down through the town with Chin on my shoulder. I wondered if it was all just a bad dream that I was alone in such an unknown village. The straps from my heavy backpack dug deep into my shoulders. I was about at my wits end. Everyone turned to stare at me, and hundreds of them followed at my heels as I stumbled for traction through the slime trying to keep my footing. Once I reached the end of the town, I then turned around and headed back. I passed by the bazaar where the poor were eating scraps of food. I knew that I should eat and yet I could not bear the thought of devouring the rancid slop whose smell alone nauseated me. I stooped down at an open sewer and splashed some cold water on my grimy face. The water was ice cold, and looked clear in the dusk. But I was not surprised when a human feces turd floated by as I was standing up to leave. Nothing seemed to alarm me anymore. I just did not seem to care.

Without warning, two armed soldiers suddenly grabbed hold of me from behind. They were dressed in slovenly uniforms that must have been issued in another era from some unfamiliar country. I produced my passport without question. They looked, and let me go but continued to follow me, as did a mob of others. Even the mangy village dogs singled me out of all them, snarling and barking as I passed. I did not care whether the omnipotent people following me were going to attack. Then I would go down fighting, or maybe I wouldn't. What did it matter? I'd be dead anyway!

I trudged up what started as a deserted side street. Until my faithful followers and I entered it! I passed a cafe that had a real floor in it, and though it was rough lumber, it was cleaner than the earthen-floored holes I had been frequenting. It was empty of customers and looked too expensive but I was so weary and in need of escape, I walked through the excited crowd, dropped the heavy sack to the floor, and tied Chin to a post. I was sick of having him shit on my shoulder while I ate. Not a single one of the people entered behind me, probably too poor to set foot in the restaurant. Two men were in the kitchen at the back of the cafe. I took a seat and rested for a few minutes. The proprietor did not come to wait on me, so I got up and staggered weakly into the kitchen.

The cook was hacking away at what was obviously a goat. I pointed to a dish of green saucy stuff, and to some rice and then to my mouth indicating that I wanted to eat. The tiny Chinese proprietor shook his head in bewilderment. He led me over to the warm wood burning stove and indicated I should wait. Then he said something to the cook and they both darted out the back door. I was wondering what the score was when the two of them returned a few minutes later lugging a rusty water-filled basin the size of a bathtub. In the process of setting it down, some of the water sloshed out and quickly vanished through gaping cracks in the floor. The cook tossed a bar of soap into the tub, and pointed as if to say, "It's all yours." I would be the last to deny that I was in need of a bath, but in an open air café? It was not only too damn cold, but I lacked the strength to do so. How they ever happened to think I wanted to bathe in the first place is beyond me. I dished out a bowl of rice and picked up a pot of tea from the stove and took a seat at a table. The proprietor ran out the back door again.

I held the rice bowl to my lips and scooped the rice into my mouth with the chopsticks, Chinese fashion. I was nearly finished when the proprietor returned with a tall dark Shan who did not look mean like the others. In fact, he smiled, and addressed me in English.

"Do you speak English," he asked in a firm but pleasant voice.

"Yeah," I answered, saying no more so as not to confuse him.

"What is it that you wish in this establishment?"

"I just wanted something to eat, but I guess the owner did not understand me."

"So! You wanted something to eat, but the man thought you wanted a bath. I am Kahn. It is very cold tonight so I will go home and get my coat. I will be back in a few minutes to talk with you."

"Okay Kahn, I'm an American, just call me Thill."

"Oh, you're an American- even better! I thought you were British- I do not care for British," he said, and left to get his coat.

No sooner had Kahn departed than I heard heavy footsteps banging on the wooden floor. I looked up to see seven Shans advancing toward me through the front door of the cafe. A more fearsome bunch I had never seen. They spread out and stopped when they were ten feet from my table. They jeered at me, and I felt like I was facing a pack of hungry wolves waiting to attack. My heart sank. I knew they had wanted me as soon as they entered the cafe. I thought the proprietor might intervene in my behalf, but I could see that he and the cook were cowering in a far corner in the rear of the dark kitchen. I was scared.

They encircled and stood their ground while an excited jabbering audience accrued at the front of the cafe. The seven Mighty Mongolians edged their way toward me. They were hunched down and swinging their arms like apes. I thought of throwing the table at them and trying to escape through the rear door. It seems to work in Hollywood movies, but I realized it would be futile. Even if I got out the door, they would catch me in the street. I was the only white man within a hundred mile radius. I was the minority, the exception, the odd one, and the *hunted*! I sensed the end was near.

In the following split seconds the proverbial whole life passed in review. Death seemed like an anti-climax. I remembered vividly the time I made my sixth parachute jump. (see photo 2) I had made too vigorous an exit, the chute whipped across my body as it was caught by the prop blast. I did not get much of an opening shock and when I forced my head back to look up all I could see were the entangled risers and shroud line. I started to laugh hysterically as I plummeted toward earth. "Wallace, you fouled up," I said to myself. I zoomed past the other chutes that were drifting to earth. "Wallace, you goofed, ha, ha, ha, ha, haaaaaa." I had brought it upon myself: I was my own murderer! And then from the loudspeaker I was jarred to my senses by the terrified shouts of the drop zone officer. The planes were off in the distance and all else was tranquil. Then cries from the bullhorn brought me back to reality.

"You've got a malfunction…"

"Who, me?"

"Yaas, you…."

"No kidding!"

"Pull your reserve…Pull your reserve!" the voice shouted. I could detect the trembling desperation in his voice as the officer begged and pleaded with me to pull my reserve; he was frantic, half crying. He was directly below me. My guts would have splashed all over him from the impact. I yanked the reserve handle, and the chute popped out and jerked as it filled with air. I heard the racing whine of the medical jeep as it bounced through the sand to where I would land. No sooner had my reserve chute blossomed than the earth rushed up to meet me with a mighty SMACK.

That was all in the past, but maybe the delayed head concussion had affected my brain, as the doctor feared. Maybe I really was insane! I could not escape my present predicament. I lowered my head and stared at the greasy tabletop, oblivious to the Mighty Mongolians surrounding me. The largest, undoubtedly the leader, was a two hundred pounder with hot, foul breath that I could feel on my sweating neck as he stood directly behind me. Two of his henchmen flanked my chair. The other four leaned across the table and glared at me. I was a fly in their web. The stench of rotgut whiskey was overwhelming. The towering beast to my right bashed his burly fist on the table, sending my rice bowl and chop sticks clattering to the floor. It was the signal for the cats to play with their mouse. The Mongol on my left swung his arm sideways into my shoulder. My body rocketed to the right, only to be knocked back by the bully on my right. The man to my rear wrapped his arms around my head in a bear hug. It served to stabilize my body as the others rammed their fists into my sides, shoulders and back. But I could barely feel their punches. I was beyond caring, or physical pain. Between punches I tossed my passport on the table for them to have. I wouldn't need it much longer, and they would find it anyway.

The leader released his bear hug, uncovering my eyes in time to see him pounce on my passport. The others stopped mauling me and merely kept their hands on my shoulders. He held my passport before his face as if he was near sighted. "You are American?" he half asked, half commanded in a loud guttural roar. He leaned over on the table on his elbows and stared me straight in the eyes waiting for an answer. His face was not more than six inches from mine, his eyes penetrating right through my head. The pily pores on his nose were virtual craters. His dangling oriental mustache twitched as he bared his large betel-stained teeth. His face would have given nightmares to an ape.

"Yeah, I'm an American," I answered in a half-hearted voice, not particularly pleased with the fact at the moment.

"Why you in Kyaukme?" he blurted.

"I am only passing through on my way to India."

"Why you go to India?"

"I am trying to get to America"

"Why?"

"Because I live there, I went to Australia to work, and now I am trying to get back to my home in America."

"You look like a soldier to me. You are soldier." He thumbed through the passport and found the news clipping from Singapore Tiger Standard that told about my trip.

"You are killer of communists," he shouted! He pointed to the inch high letters: *ANTI-RED Pledged to Wipe Out Communists*, which was the title of the article adjacent to the story and the picture of Chin and me. He jabbered something to his henchmen and they pushed me down in the seat and held me firmly in place. He pretended to read the article, but I knew he could not understand it for he would surely have gotten riled if he had read the line, "Wallace sneaked into a security patrol and went out jungle bashing." Reverting to baby talk so that there would be no misunderstanding I said, "Me no soldier."

"You bad man, you kill communists, paper say so. Maybe you are spy too, ugh."

"No, No! You make mistake, I am this man." I drew my finger around the article about myself. "Anti-Red is different man." I drew an arrow to the other article, trying to indicate that I was not the anti-communist that had so valiantly pledged to wipe out all communists. I only wished he could be in my place at the moment.

The head Mongol squinted, and drew his arm and hand across his cavernous mouth, partly to wipe the saliva from his lips, partly to fondle and smooth his mustache. "Me Major in Burma Army, but me good communist, blow up bridges and men, we make bad time for Burma government. I think you tell lie, we make bad time for you when you tell lie."

Whatever they planned to do, I was sure relived to see Kahn re-enter the restaurant with his coat. He spoke fluent English so I was able to explain the predicament to him. I told him about the confusion over the newspaper article. He listened attentively, but kept a respectful eye on the seven brutes. He then translated what I had said. They shook their heads in disbelief. It took Kahn more than fifteen minutes to quiet them down and talk some sense into their heads. I noticed that now the Chinese proprietor and his cook had the courage to come out and listen to the conversation. When the Mongols finally quieted down, Kahn advised me to destroy the article, saying I was lucky to be alive. When I asked him to explain why they should want to kill me just for being a non-communist, he said that he dared not talk about the subject any further.

The Mongols drew stools over to the table, and one of them produced a bottle of beer from under his coat, and then three more bottles appeared. The man who called himself a Major drew a pistol from his shoulder holster and placed it on the table. He pushed a bottle of beer over towards me. "You drink beer!?" I didn't know whether it was a command or a question, but I was in no position to argue.

"Yeah, drink beer," and I pulled the cork out of the bottle and gulped down a third of the quart bottle. I passed it on to one of the other men and he killed the remainder. It was strong stuff, but not strong enough to cause the bastard to slobber all over the table. They had obviously been saturated when they arrived. The leader passed me another bottle of beer and handed me a cigar. Kahn explained that the cigar was made of ganja, a drug smuggled in from India. It seemed strange that it would have to be smuggled into the Shan States where smoking and raising poppies for opium were legal. But I had learned not to be alarmed by such paradoxes: I was beginning to believe that life was full of them.

"I want your fur coat," the top Shan said as he looked admiringly at my army surplus field jacket lining. The fur the Shan referred to was only imitation.

"I can't give it to you- it is only coat I have. I have no money to buy other coat." I said in a slow distinct voice so that he could understand me. The burly Shan reached across the table and felt the imitation fur with his dirty, rough hand. His eyes lit up as he thought of the envy such a coat would create among his friends. "I give you good hat for coat," and he handed his lambskin hat to me to appraise.

"Hat is okay, but will not keep my body warm."

"I give you hat and belt for fur coat, is good Chinese communist belt. I like to keep belt but you can have." He reminded me of a big baby now as he continued to beg for my "fur" coat. I was eager to part with my coat for it amounted to nothing but a vest with sleeves, nor did it cover enough of me to make it very useful, but I was not about to part with it unless I could get a better deal in exchange. The bartering went on until after midnight. By this time Kahn and four of the others had departed leaving only the head Shan and his two right-hand men. When we finished the last of the beer, he said, "Come, we go now." He indicated that he meant for me to follow him. "We take care of you. I want fur coat," he mumbled as the two of them scuffled their feet to the street.

I got my pack onto my back. Poor Chin was shivering from the cold and I put him under my famous "fur" coat. I was wondering just what he had meant by, "We take care of you. I want fur coat." They could take care of me all right- in more ways than one. But being desperate for a place to sleep, I tossed my chances with their lot and followed them like a zombie into the deserted street. Except for the occasional flicker of a candle flame that could be seen through the gaping holes in huts, the town was covered in blackness. There was not a sound except for our feet squashing through the muddy street and the gurgling of open sewers teeming from the recent rains. I followed the Mongols to the outskirts of town until they pushed through the front door of a nondescript hut. He lit a candle and placed it on a shelf. I could make out the shadowy figures of three other bodies sleeping on a platform that stretched across one end of the room.

"You sleep here," he said pointing to the platform. Then he led in a German police dog, the largest I had ever seen. The dog growled at me until the Mongol kicked him in the side and chained him to a post. I was reluctant to spend the night in the hut; it looked as if I had fallen like a fool into their trap. I put my pack up near my head and climbed into my sleeping bag wearing my boots and fur coat. If I should have the good fortune to awaken alive, I did not want to be told in the morning that they had mysteriously vanished. This, and plenty of other unsettling thoughts, passed through my mind.

I was wedged in between two of the other sleepers whose faces were covered with shawls. The big Mongol blew out the candle and entered a side room. The dog barked a few times and all was serene, with the exception of my pulse and thoughts. Certain I would be eliminated before dawn, I felt in my present numbness that to die while asleep would not be painful. Finally sheer weariness and weakness overtook my anxiety and I succumbed to sleep.

To my surprise I awoke to sun shining through the door and an empty room, other than the big Mongol sitting cross-legged in its center, staring at me. I felt better now because I had slept reasonably well and since the Mongol was alone, I knew I could crash through wall if he came towards me. Across his lap lay another coat, a faded, but clean trench coat. "I have coat for you, give me fur coat." Gone was his ferocious affect and he looked more like a shaggy dog bringing slippers to his master. My own indifference to fate had vanished as well, re-routed by sleep and a shiny new day.

I got out of the sleeping bag and tossed the lumps of monkey shit onto the floor. Chin tugged at his chain to get at some food scraps that he spied. I laid the Mongol's coat on the platform and examined it carefully. It was lined with wool cloth and had a high collar. It was just what I needed, but I pretended that it would not be warm enough and that it was far too heavy. "Give me your Chinese belt to boot, and I will swap coats." He was reluctant to part with his belt, but as additional compensation, I gave him mine. He ceremoniously handed me a banana on my way out and bid me farewell with a boisterous clap on the back.

Chapter 19:

Unexpected but Welcome Reunion

THE EARLY MORNING air was chilly, but the sun was rising. For the time being, I was warm in my new coat, and damned thankful to be alive. I headed down the main street to get back to the road to Lashio. When I got near the bazaar, I noticed a familiar-looking truck off in the distance, grinding its way to a halt. It was none other than the one I had ridden on the previous day. It was nearly impossible to believe I had been riding on that vehicle a mere fifteen hours prior: I had lived a lifetime since yesterday!

Myo and Khin were all smiles when they saw me. They were installing a rebuilt generator they had just purchased which looked even worse than the original. It had undoubtedly been rebuilt scores of times in the last ten years since it was manufactured, but Myo was adept at replacing the generator. It was wonderful to be back with the two friendly Burman, even though they did have an untrustworthy truck. I felt embarrassed that I was unable to converse with these men whom I had shared much and would have had much to tell. On the other hand, perhaps it was a blessing in disguise. I could spare the re-telling of the tale of my night with the Mighty Mongols, and in the process, bury my traumatic experience a little deeper for myself.

After we shared a pot of tea, I cranked the engine and was happily surprised that it actually turned over on the first try. While the motor was warming up we rearranged the top bundles of cotton, tightened the ropes, and refilled the jerry cans with water for the radiator and gas for the truck. Myo led me to the engine and pointing at the generator, counted out fifty kyats, the equivalent of ten dollars indicating that amount he had paid for the rebuilt generator. He shook his head and mumbled, undoubtedly swearing in Burmese. I felt sorry for him and cursed for him in English, sharing a hearty laugh. It was a piece of junk, but it was the *only* piece of junk we could find to use.

We were but a few miles out of Kyaukme when the generator in question failed, bringing the truck to a halt. This happened at least twenty-five times during the day. Each time we would disassemble the generator, add a shim to the shaft seating, or adjust the brushes-whatever it took to make it work. Virtual paragons of patience, not once did the two men show signs of despair, nor did they raise their voices. But by nightfall when pulled into the village of Mansan to rest, we had only covered about fifty-five miles, an average of six miles per hour for the day. When we unloaded our bedrolls from the top of the cab, Myo stood looking at the truck and running his hand through his hair, no doubt pondering how long it would take him to get to his final destination.

We entered a ramshackle cafe and huddled about the charcoal stove because the air was even colder than it had been the previous night. A large cat tried repeatedly to get hold of Chin's tail, and their antics entertained us while we awaited our meals. A beady-eyed Hindu cook blew his nose into his left hand and wiped the contents on his already greasy shirt. Without washing his hands, he began kneading the rice dough into patties for our evening meal. I did not feel too hungry, but it did not seem to affect Myo or Khin.

From the café's window, I had spotted a bullock cart pulled by two oxen as it creaked to a halt across the road. A woman clothed in rags gathered brambles and lit a campfire in front of the oxen. A tiny girl climbed out from under the cart canopy and crouched by the fire for warmth. She was barefooted and her shoulders were covered with a shawl made from a burlap sack. When I saw the woman's husband squat by the fire, I excused myself from our completed meal to walk over and join their cheery fire. I took Chin along to play with the little girl.

The three poverty stricken creatures looked frightened when I took a seat on the damp ground beside them. I offered the man a Cheroot cigar and his wife reached out her thin arm as well. They were less apprehensive of me after that and we even sang a bit together, although I could only hum. Chin made the mistake of getting his tail to close to the hot coals. Fortunately, the smell of singed hair and the sound of his screams were but momentary interruptions in an otherwise peaceful encounter.

Their bullock cart contained rice. It was also home for this family. How they managed to survive is beyond me. Yet they seemed quite content, probably because they had never known another existence. Dressed as I was in filthy, patched khakis and muddy boots, with a beard, grimy face, and a trench coat splattered with monkey dung I would have been looked upon as a poor man by most people in America. Yet, sitting with a homeless family clothed in layers of rags, I felt highly conspicuous of the "fineness" of my wardrobe. The barefooted man placed his feet closer to the fire and leaned over and caressed my leather boots. His eyes gleamed as he ran his fingers over my thin soles. The bottoms of his feet were tough as leather and deeply crevassed through the years of walking barefooted. When the fire died down, they nestled into their bed of rice bags for the night.

I crossed back over to the cafe where Myo and Khin were gathering up their bedrolls. From the light of the single candle I found my way onto the bamboo platform that was to serve as my bed for the night. The damp, freezing air had numbed my hands before I could get comfortably situated. Chin had a case of diarrhea. I hated to let him crawl into the sack with me, but it was not his fault that he had been dragged into such miserable weather, so I let the little creature snuggle up to my beard. Now that it was so cold he relied on me for warmth and it was the least I could give him in return for the companionship he had offered me on so many lonely occasions.

Rain fell during the night, and droplets of ice water splashed onto the platform about my head in what turned out to be a restless, cold and uncomfortable sleep. By morning I was saturated from water that had come through the flimsy thatched roof. When daylight finally came, I could bear it no longer, and got quickly out of the sack to find that my sleeping bag was stiff with ice. Fortunately I did not have to dress because I had slept in my clothes.

I walked outdoors and jumped up and down to get warm. The surrounding landscape was a veritable fairyland in the early morning sun, the jungle greenery glittering with frost. Beautiful as it was, I was colder than the fat sow rooting in the frozen earth by my side. She did not seem to realize that rooting in the frozen ground had caused her snout to bleed. Before long the cafe began to come to life as the eight year-old cook's helper, sporting a cigar, lit a fire in the stove. Myo and Khin looked as if they had an equally miserable night, shivering while we breakfasted on tea and tough chapattis.

No matter how many times we cranked the engine on this frozen morning, the truck would just not start. We had no choice but to huddle around the stove in the cafe until we heard an approaching truck break the early morning silence. Myo and I ran out to the road and flagged it to a stop. He explained our predicament to the driver and then the two of us hopped on top of his load. I had brought all my gear along just in case the truck should never run again.

Within an hour we reached Lashio, an ancient city located on a spur of a low mountain, overlooking the valley of the Nam Yao River and with population of about five thousand (today the population is over one hundred thousand). The narrow streets were crowded with heavily laden merchants bound for the bazaar to sell their wares. Early morning Lashio reminded me of what it must have been like as a medieval town of centuries past. The plastered buildings were crumbling. The walls still standing were thick with street scum that had splashed and accumulated on them through the years. Myo left to try to locate another generator. Perhaps I would meet them again if they got their truck fixed. Natives from the surrounding countryside were dressed in their colorful tribal dress. I noticed an unusual amount of cheap tin ware, such as teapots, most of which came from nearby China which bordered the Shan states to the north and east.

Most of the natives, whether Shan, Chinese or Burman, dropped what they were doing to stare at the monk and me. Scores of them followed me from booth to booth, tittering among themselves. I guess I was just as fascinating to them as they were to me. Chin always presented a problem when in bazaars: he could not keep his hands out of mischief. Luckily, most of the merchants merely laughed when Chin would dart out and steal a tomato or a fist full of beans.

As I trekked down the hill on the road that led north out of Lashio, I spied a slow moving bullock cart up ahead. It was difficult to run very fast or far with sixty pounds of junk on my back, but I hustled, and finally caught up to the cart. The Chinese peasant was guiding the oxen with a long slender stick from his perch at the front of the cart. To simplify matters, I did not confuse him by trying to ask for a lift in English, which I doubted he could understand. Instead, I tossed my pack onto the back of his cart and crawled onto the crude plank flooring. He turned in alarm when I tapped him on the shoulder to let him know that he had a rider. He halted the oxen, but when I offered him a cigar he sensed that I meant no harm and the cartwheels turned once more. The creaking, vibrating, bumpy cart moved no faster than I could have walked, but it took much less effort to ride. The bullock cart turned off the road as we neared Old Lashio so I jumped out without interrupting the oxen's gait.

Chin had an annoying habit of leaning against my perspiring neck when he rode along on my shoulder, so I made him get down and walk in the dust for the next few miles. We soon reached a cargo checkpoint where four sluggish soldiers held post. All they had to do was to stop each vehicle, write down its license number and compare the bill of lading against the actual cargo. If everything were in order, they would lift the draw gate and wave the vehicle through. This appeared to happen less than once an hour. Rather than wander aimlessly up the seemingly endless dirt road, I put my faith in the thought that Myo and Khin would get their truck rolling before the day was over. I fell asleep in one of the guard huts next to the gate while the soldiers played with Chin. The soldiers were highly amused.

The hot sun had shifted while I slept and had beat directly upon me, so that I was now sapped of strength to the extent that I could not laugh at Chin's antics. I was almost in a semi-stupor when I saw Myo's truck off in the distance to the south. He was barreling along at a good clip leaving a cloud of dust in his wake. He geared the truck down as he neared the gate and came to a halt. They did not seem surprised to see me, and just shook their heads and smiled. I secured my junk over the cab.

The truck engine purred smoothly for the remainder of the afternoon. We would have made good time except that we were stopped every few miles by soldiers who checked our cargo. (see photo 13) At one point the official came out of a hut and said something to Myo that made him throw his hands up in despair. He was on the verge of tears when he explained the circumstances to Khin who obviously could not understand the officer's dialect. Addressing me in English, the official told me to follow him. I was relegated to a chair inside his hut while he examined my passport. Through the window, I could see two soldiers probing the loaded truck with long steel rods.

"Sir, why is it that this particular truck has been detained so long at all of the check points this afternoon." I asked, curious to understand the trouble.

"My men are searching the truck because it is bound for the China border, and we have reason to believe that it contains smuggled goods. Why else would it be nearly three days since it left Mandalay which is not much more than one hundred fifty miles from here!"

"But sir--" but he cut me short. "The drivers have had ample time to smuggle additional goods into their load of cotton," he said, as if satisfied with his logic.

"But sir, I have been riding with this same truck ever since Maymyo. The only reason it has taken us three days to get this far is that their truck has broken down about fifty times," I said in a pleading voice. The official must have been well-educated if his fluency in English was any indication. He thought a moment of what I had said.

"I was going to make them unload their cargo, but in as much as you are an American, I can safely assume you are not a communist. So I will take your word. I noticed glancing through your passport that your country has no diplomatic relations with several of the communist countries." Then he walked to the door and shouted something to the soldiers. Obviously he had told them not to unload the truck.

With that I ran out to the truck. There is one word that Myo and Khin knew in English, as did many of the people I had encountered. That one little four-lettered American slang word was more descriptive than the most eloquent speech so I shouted it:

"OKAY!"

"OKAY! OKAY! OKAY!" chorused Myo and Khin. We wiped the sweat from our brows and our smiles broke into boisterous laughter, as we roared away from the military checkpoint. Myo and Khin slapped me on the back in their ecstasy. There was something wonderful about being with these two characters, even though we only had one word in common. Their race, religion, dress, and custom were all foreign to me. They may well have been ardent communists, and for all I knew, their truck might be carrying smuggled goods to Red China, which was not more than fifty miles north. Yet, it was inspiring to know that such a deeply rooted fellowship could thrive between us despite all those differences. Together we had conquered a common enemy, in this case the governmental official who had threatened to detain us, and yet we had become bonafide brothers in the process. Although I could never communicate to him my experiences of the night before, it did not matter, for I no longer felt like the odd one, the hunted stranger in a hostile land.

As the truck ground forward I could not help but ponder how the world could be in such a state of tension. The geographic elements of the earth could surely not be blamed. It has to be because ignorance by its two billion human inhabitants has bred intolerance, not because of national, religious, or political blocks, as we are so prone to believe. I was beginning to realize that I- along my own country- was as ignorant and intolerant as the others. We had been taught to believe that we, and we alone hold the key, and that our way is the *only* way. I had been blinded for twenty-four years, by unenlightened policy makers who righteously shielded themselves behind the veils of specific ideologies designed to make us appear as saviors of the world. At least the outer shell had been broken in my particular case, and perhaps I would find the answer sometime...

More important matters at hand suddenly interrupted my philosophical musings: the truck had chugged to a halt. Generator failure. We fixed and proceeded. Again and again and again. As darkness fell, Khin and I were wrestling with two bundles of cotton that had fallen off while Myo was making repairs by candle light. The truck was blocked in the middle of the narrow road on a steep mountain incline, and on a blind curve to boot!

The sun had set long before we got the generator in place. The night was black as coal between the mountain peaks. The truck started after a few cranks, but the lights would not work. Trucks seldom need light in Burma; they do not drive at night as Dacoits are at the peak of their activity from sunset to dawn. As Myo pulled slowly forward, one of us stood on either side of the running board to try to direct him through the opaque air. Even creeping along in the low gear was a strain on our nerves; to leave the road would have meant a plunge of hundreds of feet into the bottom of a peaceful valley. We did not want to trespass! The only solution was to walk along in front of the truck, one of us on either side of the meandering mountain road.

It took us two hours to trek the remaining five miles to the nearest village of Kutkai. Even though the air was frosty, we were soaked with sweat from the rigors of the jaunt. We plopped our weary bodies into a cafe. By the time we finished eating it was late and miserably cold. Myo and Khin sacked out in a lean-to. For some reason the cook led me in to a small cell like room with no windows barely large enough to accommodate the bamboo platform that severed as a bed. By no means luxurious, the room stunk of urine and I could not see the floor but the blackness felt spongy and slippery under my weight. The bamboo walls were thick with moisture. My bedroom was a dungeon above the ground. All through the night the coughing proprietor awakened me. He sounded as if he had a case of double pneumonia. Living in such dampness surely was a life of hazards.

I was shivering in the early morning. Ice covered the landscape as it had on the previous morning. Out behind the café, a litter of pigs was snuggled against their mother's belly for warmth. Purple men were common in Kutkai. Their entire bodies had been tattooed a solid purple, including their heads, with the exception of their faces, hands, and feet. It gave the impression that their torsos were covered in a tight fitting purple shirt, even though they were actually nude from the waist up. Colorfully dressed native women and girls moving in a group stopped at each shop along the main street in an effort to sell their wares of firewood and yarn. They were all barefooted, carrying heavy baskets of split wood on their backs, the weight supported by trump lines rather than shoulder straps. Some of the girls were so small they staggered under their loads. All of them were either smoking a cigar or chewing betel nut. Besides carrying their heavy loads of wood, they were deftly spinning yarn from balls to spindles, which they carried in opposing hands. But even with two jobs at once, they did not make enough to buy sandals.

Chapter 20:

Kurt Weiss & Dr. Silgardo

MYO AND KHIN tried to get the truck started but gave up and waited for a passing vehicle to give them a push. A Volkswagen car, piled high with luggage, raced into town and pulled up in front of a shop down the road. It was the first car of any kind I had seen since Maymyo. A car in upper Burma usually is synonymous with Caucasian foreigners so I dashed down the road to where it was parked. Sure enough, a white man stepped out of the car, accompanied by a bony middle-aged Indian and a wiry young Burman, all three dressed in western clothes. The white man's complexion was abnormally fair, almost bluish-white. His medium build hung on a fine boned frame, giving him an air of frailty. Blond, blue-eyed and poker-faced, he could still be described as handsome. Just above his thin, colorless lips was a mustache to match. I managed a faint smile when he noticed me. "Howdy, you wouldn't be headed up north by any chance would you?" I asked.

"Yes, as a matter of fact we are, why?" he answered coldly.

"Well, I'm trying to get to India, and the truck I have been riding in for the past three days has broken down again. I'm bound for Europe and in a bit of a hurry."

"Are you able to prove your identity?" he asked.

"Yeah, here's my passport." He looked at it carefully and handed it back.

"So you're an American. I'm from Switzerland, my name is Mr. Weiss, but you can call me Kurt if you wish." He extended his hand which was chilly and lifeless in my own. He did not introduce me to his Indian interpreter, nor to his Burman chauffer, but continued to ignore their presence. "I suppose we have room to take you along," he said, as if sorry he had opened his mouth. I ran back to get my gear and say goodbye to Myo and Khin.

During the next hour, Kurt's driver wheeled the little Volkswagen for all it was worth along the winding, rolling road to Muse, a peaceful village situated on the Shweli River, connected by a bridge to Yunnan Province, China. Kurt was constantly telling the driver to go faster, lest we should fall into the ambush of communists or dacoits. He felt he was living dangerously by taking this business trip into upper Burma. He had been appointed to manage a firm in Rangoon some four years back. He had been reluctant to leave Switzerland, but the fact that he could lead a sheltered life in Rangoon at the company's expense helped to compensate for the hardships he had to endure.

Money was no object; he dined and moved with only the elite foreign element in Rangoon. There are such elements in all the larger cities of Asia. Foreign whites live like lords within local societies compared to a mediocre existence in their homelands-on the same income. But after four years of business in Rangoon, Kurt was compelled to take a business trip to upper Burma. It was the first time he had been out of Rangoon proper, believing the country was too dangerous. After four years of postponing the trip, his mother company back in Switzerland had ordered him to leave his little "shell" in Rangoon and tend to a few transactions up north. It was amusing to observe a grown "man" who wielded such power for his age, and yet was helpless to prevent ambush. He had each of us in the car keeping a lookout for insurgents while he curled up in the back seat so as not to form a target for any stray bullets. I was laughing inside at Kurt who, with a lash of words, could command his two escorts to do anything- except allay his fear of being ambushed. He would be a nervous wreck by the time we reached Muse.

The road cut to the west along the Shweli River, which vaguely constitutes the border between Burma and China in this particular area. It seemed odd that as the river meandered, China could be on the southerly side of the river and that parts Burma would still be on the same side. The dirt road we traversed crossed intermittently from one country to the other. When it was built it was supposed to generally form the border between the two countries. A single concrete marker, similar to a tombstone, was the only barrier that separated the two countries at that point. There was no China wall, no military barricade, not even a bamboo curtain to signify that this was the actual border between the communist oppression and a socialist Democracy. Despite the government of China, its topography is this area was equally as peaceful and serene as Burma's. The broad Shweli River water drifted lazily to the southwest, where it would join with the Irrawaddy and later flow into the Bay of Bengal. The mountains of China were thick with dense forests, unbroken with the exception of an occasional cart trail. The broad flat Shweli Basin yields great harvests. The surrounding hills are terraced with rice paddies. For the most part, the native huts are hidden by healthy vegetation. Rumors circulated that the Chinese were building up forces in this area for an invasion of the adjoining section of Burma, but this was hardly necessary: the Chinese have been infiltrating Burma at the rate of a thousand a month without bloodshed. In fact, the number of Chinese in this area of Burma was probably outnumbering the Burman at this time.

Some twenty miles beyond Muse, we pulled into Namkam, a fairly large town that was once an opium growing center. Kurt and his obedient interpreter stopped in a couple of the shops to transact some type of business. About half an hour later he returned to the car and asked me to join him for a meal. We finally found an open hut where food was served, clean but with an earthen floor. Kurt looked completely out of place with his pressed trousers and starched white shirt.

Everyone looked at him when he shouted at his humble Indian interpreter. First, he insisted that a white tablecloth be procured to cover the greasy table. The cook sent a boy running into a nearby shop to buy a cloth. Before Kurt would sit down on a stool, he ordered it be cleaned. I could sense that that the cook was getting riled and that the interpreter was highly embarrassed at having to ask so many favors from the cook. I, too, was embarrassed for being associated with Kurt, who carried on as if the natives were only there to serve at his beck and call.

By the time Kurt sat down on the stool, I could bear his arrogance no longer and joined the crowd who was watching the escalating scenario. Kurt ordered the cook to rewash the dishes, and to pour boiling water over them. When the cook placed a pot of tea on the table, Kurt dumped it on the floor and told his interpreter: to have a fresh pot of tea brewed; demanded to see his eggs before they were cracked which the cook obliged; nearly gagged when he saw the manure on the fresh eggs; ordered them to be washed and soft boiled. The cook began to realize that he had a first rate snob for a customer. Had the eggs been from a virgin hen, Kurt would not have thanked the cook for his efforts. Kurt himself walked back to the stove while the cook was preparing some noodles, and vegetables, and insisted that the cook wash his frying pan before he cooked his food. Then Kurt personally supervised the washing and rewashing of the cook's vegetables.

The whole process took well over an hour. By the time Kurt was satisfied with what lay before him, the cook was about ready to blow his top. Kurt's interpreter had practically begged Kurt not to embarrass him any further by asking the cook for additional favors. Kurt was unable to eat the food in the end for he still did not think it was sanitary, so I had the dubious pleasure of eating the bastardly pimp's food for him. There was no doubt that it was delicious and sanitary, but it made me sick to think of a white man making such an ass out of his interpreter, the cook, and making the natives think that what they normally ate was shit, and last of all that he, Kurt felt no qualms about his little display of what money can do for one. The bill came to four times the normal rate, but it did not faze Kurt: the firm he worked for would foot the bill in the end.

As I finished eating, Kurt was telling his interpreter to find a decent place to spend the night. The interpreter threw up his arms, "Mr. Weiss, I know of many places but I doubt that you would find them suitable. Doctor Segrave's hospital is not far from here. He is the well-known American surgeon that you have undoubtedly heard of back in Rangoon. Perhaps you could spend the night there, Mr. Weiss." With that Kurt ordered the driver to take him to the hospital. It was back toward Muse, between the small village of Nawng Sand and Kawn Nawng Sang. The little car climbed up the long drive leading to the hospital which was perched on a foothill, overlooking the Shweli River, with its fertile basin- and beyond to the mountains of China.

The hospital was larger than I had expected for such a remote area. The main buildings were constructed of large cobblestones, which had been gathered from the river banks. The roofs were corrugated tin. It was indeed a beautiful setting for a hospital. A Shan lad directed us to Doctor Seagrave's dwelling; a humble frame house located several hundred feet from the main building.

Doctor Seagrave's associate, Dr. Delgado, a dark haired, mustached, average sized man welcomed us into his quarters. He explained that he seldom had the opportunity to speak with outsiders and welcomed every opportunity to do so. His devoted efforts to help the sick and needy were readily apparent. When

Kurt asked the doctor if he could spare us a room Delgado said we would be welcome to spend the night if a room was vacant, and led us over to the hospital. The interior was plain and drab, but very clean. Delgado found an empty room with two real beds on the second floor. The room was spacious and full of light, which entered through two large windows. As soon as Delgado left the room, Kurt went to the bath to take a shower. Running water in this part of the world is out of the ordinary, but Kurt returned to complain that there was no *hot* water. I could hardly sympathize with him. Without hesitating, he stopped the first nurse he encountered in the hall and told her to bring him hot water so that he could take a bath with the comforts due a man of his importance. While the busy nurse was having water heated for abominable Kurt, I took a cold shower and went out for some fresh air. I was ashamed to be associated with him among the overworked nurses who would obey his orders.

I sat under a tree to watch the sun set. A dark tan Town and Country car pulled up beside me. The car was several years old with dented fenders and driven by an elderly, heavily framed man casually dressed in a bright checkered mackinaw, and rumpled gabardine trousers. His skin and hair were white, but he shook hands with the firmness of Gibraltar and introduced himself as "Doctor Seagrave". He spoke slowly, mentioning the hardships facing the natives of the area. Even in this day and age when he is in dire need of basic medical implements, or a wheel chair, he is unable to get them through Rangoon for various political and bureaucratic reasons. It was a pity to see a man with his strength and goodness be handicapped by red tape. Doctor Seagrave is indeed a humanitarian. He treats sick people regardless of their race, creed or political affiliations. Many of his patients are from nearby China. He often travels hundreds of miles to operate on the needy. Where there were no roads he has taken mules or gone on foot. He has devoted his life to the medical needs of the people of Burma, not only operating on them, but also training nurses and young doctors in the art of medicine. He finished our conversation and entered the hospital where he was to perform an operation on a goiter.

I returned to the room to find that Kurt's driver was unrolling his plush bed roll on top of the bed for him. Kurt then ordered one of the nurses to bring him a couple of extra blankets for he did not want to get chilled during his sleep. None of the other patients had any more blankets than I did which would suffice, yet Kurt's comfort was of tantamount importance.

I awoke in the morning to hear Kurt shouting at his driver, telling him to get his (Kurt's) bedroll packed. Kurt lamented to me that he had spent an uncomfortable night on the bed that had been provided for him free of charge, not to mention the hot water and numerous other things the hospital attendants had done for him. I thanked the floor nurse and headed into Namkam on foot. Anything to get away from that Swiss "god." By the time I reached the village bazaar, it was teeming with colorful natives from the surrounding villages. A number of Chinese women with their broad pointed straw hats shielding them from the sun were squatting on the ground in a row behind their baskets holding rice for sale. The colorful and interesting gathering consisted of Kachin women with their goiters, Shan women with their betel nut and black teeth, and occasional elderly Chinese women who walked with stiff legs because of tiny feet bound from childhood. Chin busied himself by snatching the towels from heads of women as I moved along through the crowd. One small girl was selling glasses of pink water, probably colored to hide its natural dirt. It was cool and the girl seemed pleased to have made a purchase. Chin and I shared a bowl of cooked rice and then started walking out of the town on the northbound road.

The crowds in the street ahead of us parted to let a truck pass through. It was none other than Myo and Khin whom I had left the day before in Kutkai when their truck had refused to start. They pulled off the road as soon as they saw me, all smiles. Namkam was their destination so we shared a last tea and departed after much friendly backslapping, a crude but sincere way for us to express our gratitude, lacking any other form of communication. Right after leaving Myo and Khin, I ran into Doctor Silgardo who arranged for me to get a lift to Bahmo, about forty-five miles north. I helped two Chinese coolies unload the rice sacks from the truck and piled my gear, myself, and Chin into the back, along with seventeen natives of various walks of life. Among the ragged coolies, chickens, and goitered women were three skin headed monks in their traditional orange robes.

The road began to climb skyward, up and around the mountains until we came to a sudden halt, tossing the passengers all over each other. We were about to cross a river using a precarious bridge. The driver and his assistant got out and placed the layers of sheet steel over the holes blown in the bridge by insurgents. To travel the road after dark would be sheer folly; one could end up at the bottom of an abysmal gorge. The truck proceeded at a snail's pace over the damaged bridge while the assistant driver directed its movement by waving his arms from his position on the north side of the bridge. Safely across, the truck continued to climb until we were riding within reach of the clouds. The road was another narrow, dusty, endless series of blind curves and right angle bends. The landscape consisted of lumps of bamboo, vine covered trees, and an occasional terraced rice paddy; the more distant view of valleys and corrugated mountainsides. It was an untamed paradise. Seldom did we see signs of human life beyond an occasional simple shelter of bamboo.

At one point, where the road leveled off for a stretch, the truck swung off the main trail across a meadow to a peaceful village of seven huts by the bank of a lazy river. Water buffalo were wading in the water and sunning their backs. A primitive water wheel lay idle. A man came out of a house, handed a small pig to one of the passengers, and climbed aboard himself. The truck then pulled down along the grassy riverbank. Two golden tan women were finishing their bathing where the river rippled over stones covered in bright green moss. The women's wet bodies glistened in the sunlight, as they gracefully let their colorful lungis slip into the water and wiggled their bodies to allow the dry lungis to shimmy into place. The two women then drifted toward our truck as if weightless. In their simplicity and natural grace they would far surpass western women educated to be charming. The two young ladies boarded our overloaded vehicle and we rolled northward again.

By early afternoon we reached Bahmo, which was the truck's destination. It is a rather dumpy village on the banks for the Irrawaddy River, Burma's main line of transportation. In the center of the village where four dirt trails converge, was a sign in English. On it were listed the names of the outlying villages with separate schedules for incoming and outgoing vehicles; the roads were too narrow to allow two-way traffic even though not more than a few vehicles a week that traversed all of the roads combined.

I washed my feet in the river and then found a quiet hut of a cafe. It was broad daylight yet so dark inside that I could not even see the cook until my eyes became accustomed to the blackness. When the cook did make her appearance, it was well worth the wait. Petite, barefooted and perfectly proportioned, her fine black hair lay lightly on her bare back. Her lungi was taught by her natural feminine curves, which were exotic and an intriguing masterpiece: only God could have created such a natural beauty.

No western woman with her falsies, girdles, high heels, makeup, perfume, custom cut and padded clothes or expensive hairstyles could possibly be as alluring as this seemingly innocent beauty. My tired body rested on the stool while my eyes rested on her. She did not make a move, but stood motionless with awe at my unexpected presence in her village.

Her spell was broken when I got up and crossed over to the charcoal stove to see what I would find to eat. I meant no malice, but her eyes filled with fear and she backed into a corner. I filled a bowl with rice and curry and retreated to a table to devour the food. As I was forcing down the meal a greasy pot bellied old man waddled into the hut. He took one look at the cowering girl and then at me. The two of them exchanged a few hurried words. He came over to the table and addressed me in English. "Girl is very nice."

"Yes, very, very nice. " I sighed.

"She say you look hungry when you see her."

"She gave me quite an appetite, the food is very good." I said.

"Me lucky man, she my number three wife," he said proudly but in broken English. I nearly choked at learning that the old "tub of guts" counted this girl among his wives. He was undoubtedly thrice her age. To make me feel like a complete heel he refused to accept any payment for the meal. I walked out of the cafe bewildered.

On the way through town, my body was suddenly racked by fever. I dropped my bag onto the ground and collapsed beside it. Chin was anchored to my backpack. I lay there for more than an hour. A young Kachin who had been observing me from across the road worked up the courage to come over and talk to me. He invited me to have the evening meal with him and his parents. It was a kind offer, but I did not want to accept. When I ate in a native's hut I would eat whatever was put before me rather than offend by refusing. One of these days it might prove fatal. He insisted that I not spend the night sleeping next to the ditch, which was sensible, but I lacked the strength to go on when there was no definite place to go. He left saying he would find me a place to sleep.

I was asleep on the ground when he returned. It was dark when he woke me and led me out of town to the government bungalows. These bungalows were built to serve as guesthouses for traveling government officials. There is a small fee for the use of them. Although they are not elaborate, they are far superior to the average native hut. The Kachin lad led me into one of the sleeping rooms and introduced me to an elderly official from Mandalay. The Kachin explained that I was not feeling well, excused himself and told me that I could ride out of town with him the following morning. There were two beds in the room, neither of them had mattresses, and one of them was occupied with a sleeping body. The elderly official left the room. While he was out I laboriously rolled my sleeping bag out on the floor, and then tied Chin to a tree just outside the hut. I returned to the room to find the official had brewed me a cup of tea. He pushed back one of my eye lids with his thumb and exclaimed that I looked very sick. I had not looked in a mirror for weeks so I did not realize that I looked sick. All I knew was the I ached all over, felt faint, and did not have the strength to fight my way out of a paper bag. The official insisted that I not sleep on the floor, but rather on a bed. I answered that I was used to sleeping on floor, that a wooden one like this was indeed a luxury. He would not hear of it, it just was not decent in his mind to let the sick sleep on the floor when there is a bed. I tried to refuse on the grounds that it would do him more harm to sleep on the floor than me.

"No, it will not affect me if you sleep in the bed," he said as if he meant every word of it. He then crossed the room and shook the sleeping body, and forced him out of the bed. The sleeping beauty must have been a lesser official for he did not argue with the old man. "There, now we each have a bed," he said, as if he had performed magic. The lesser official did not seem upset or particularly angry at having been roused from a sound sleep and forced to sleep on the floor. Nonetheless I felt embarrassed to be taking another's bed.

I slept soundly only to wake up feeling worse than I had before going to bed. I tiptoed outside the hut to put on my boots. The sky was overcast and the day seemed unusually muggy in spite of being overcast. The Kachin lad's sputtering government motorcycle broke the early morning silence. I was covered with sticky sweat, yet chilled. The trees were motionless, the air so humid, still and dense it seemed to press on me.

With much effort I got my pack on, and Chin on top of it, and then managed to swing my leg over the cycle and take a seat. The Kachin informed me he was an engineer and had to make the trip to check on the road gangs that were repairing washouts. He handled the cycle carefully and drove slowly; obviously he had not had much experience. The road was no more than a sandy trail and he had a great deal of trouble steering the cycle. I had all I could do to hang on.

The Kachin stopped twice to check with the foreman of road gangs. The foreman carried his work roster rolled up inside a bamboo cylinder to keep it dry in the event of rain. The laborers had not a single machine. They dug the earth from just off the road with the aid of a mattock and hoed the earth into baskets, which a coolie would put on his shoulder and carry to the roadbed to dump. This process went on all through Asia. I had not seen a single piece of heavy earthmoving equipment since Singapore. In all cases the man who does the original digging makes certain that he makes a defined rectangular. In the middle of each of these pits, a column of earth remains to mark the average depth of progress by the foreman, the supervisor, and so on up the ladder. Little did I know at the time that I was taking mental notes that would be useful one day in the future.

The Kachin dropped me off at a hut twenty-five miles north of Bahmo, and still eighty-five miles to Myitkyina. Once he'd left, I moved down to the edge of the road and sprawled out on the ground to rest. When I finally heard the roar of an oncoming vehicle, I forced myself to a standing position and waved my arm feebly at the approaching truck.

I ran as best I could dragging my sack by one of the straps behind me and Chin's chain in the other hand. One of the native passengers lifted my bag onto the back of the truck and then I crawled over the side of it using the tire as a step. The truck was piled high with bags of rice, chickens, and parts salvaged from disabled world war two vehicles, three young puppies, and no less than thirty-three humans. There was standing room only so I clung to the back of the truck. I was so weak that I lost my footing several times as the truck bounced along the irregular surface. Luckily I had a good grip on the steel canopy bracing with my hands which prevented me from falling off. A score of men were sitting on top of the canvas tarpaulin, but when the driver stopped to pick up some Kachin women he chased the men down from their relatively comfortable positions.

The truck was delayed at a customs checkpoint in a small village in the early afternoon. I counted five Kachin women out of the group of nine that had grotesquely swollen necks containing goiters. Due to the official delay most of the passengers scrambled to the ground to exercise their legs. I wandered off on a nature call. To my astonishment in the clearing just beyond the road were more than seventy abandoned American tanks, in varying stages of completeness. The big white stars on their sides had not been obliterated through the years since the war. The tanks had been dragged there at the close of the war to disintegrate. At the rate they are weathering it will be centuries before the last trace of them has vanished. Unfortunately the Burmese are not equipped to salvage them, and hence convert their metal into something constructive. The money that those tanks had originally cost to build would have undoubtedly far surpassed the yearly income of thousands upon thousands of natives.

By late afternoon we pulled up to the edge of the Irrawaddy River and waited for the small ferry to cross over to us. The interlude gave me time to dunk my throbbing head into the frigid water to try to cool it off. The ferry consisted of a crude platform strung between two pontoons that had originally been part of an American pontoon bridge. The ferry's motor was so weak that it could not counteract the swift current and hence we drifted way down stream and then had to chug up along the shore on the opposite side of the river until the ferry reached the existing unloading dock.

Soon we were laboring slowly along the crowded streets of Myitkyina. The truck came to a halt at an intersection where two dirt roads met. The Kachins climbed down off the truck and paid the Hindu driver for the ride. When it came my turn to pay I was embarrassed for I did not have but half the fare in Burmese currency. Unlike the other generous natives, the young Hindu driver became highly indignant at my lack of funds. A crowd gathered as I tried to explain to him that I had no more Burmese money. Finally someone intervened in my behalf, and explained to me in English that the driver was charging me double fare. He was a kindly old man and reprimanded the driver for trying to cheat me. I dragged my sack across the street and leaned against a tree wondering what I would do for food. Somehow I would have to convert some American money, but there were no banks in Upper Burma. Most of the natives would not possess the equivalent of five American dollars, and they would not be willing to change their money for money they would not trust to be real. A crowd of Chinese, Kachins, and Hindus formed a semi circle around me as darkness descended. They did not come near me, but merely stood about ten feet away murmuring among themselves. I just looked back at them, sick of being viewed as a freak. I held up a hand and pointed at them to count their numbers. There were seventy-three in all. I just wanted to be alone. I was too exhausted and beat to carry my bags, or the monkey.

To hell with everything.

I chained Chin to a branch in the tree and walked off leaving all of my possessions by the tree to stumble along one of the town's crowded streets in the black night. I don't know where I thought I was going; I just wanted to get away from the world in my misery. I did not worry about my bags and monkey being stolen; in fact I almost wished they would be stolen so that I would not be burdened with their weight anymore.

Chapter 21:

Tin & Myitkyina: Friends Indeed

SOMETIME LATER I realized that a young man dressed in a lungi was following me. He continued to follow as I plodded up one street and down another and back again. Finally he worked up the courage and shouted "Hello, Mister…Hello, Mister!" and ran up to my side. "I am Tin, your friend, may I help you?" he asked in a youthful voice, his use of English easily understood. For some reason I regarded his friendliness as an intrusion. I was so damn fed up with answering the same old questions: Who are you? Where are you going? How much did the monkey cost? Where did you get him? And usually I could not converse with the people at all: they did not speak English, or if they spoke pidgin English, it usually created misunderstandings, and if I spoke to someone who spoke English fluently, then I would be besieged with questions. The Burmese were undoubtedly the friendliest people I had ever encountered; yet it would have made things simpler if they had been hostile. At least I would not have to be pleasant in return. I simply did not have the strength to talk and just wanted to curl up someplace alone and sleep forever.

Hence, my answer to the friendly Tin was short. "Thanks, but I don't need any help, I just want to be left alone." I felt like a bastard for not returning his friendliness, and I blamed him for striking up the conversation. If one tries hard enough we can always blame our shortcomings on others. Tin was a persistent cuss, and would not take no for an answer.

"But sir, I would like you to be my guest. It is a rare opportunity for me to be able to practice my English with a stranger. My uncle would be very happy to have you spend the night with him. Please, sir, be our guest."

"Don't sir, me Tin. I know it is meant in respect, but I do not like to be referred to as sir. We are all equal; none of us are any better than the rest. I am no exception. Just call me Thill. I'm sorry Tin. It is nice of you to want me to be your guest, but I'm very sick and I just want to be alone."

"Mr. Thill, you can be alone, I will take you to a hut where you can be by yourself, no one will bother you. Follow me, please!" I had nothing to lose, so I told Tin of my monkey and sack and we picked them up, all intact. Tin realized how weak I was and carried our pack. Chin seemed glad to see me, and chirped to show his gratitude. I dragged my feet along behind Tin until he pushed his way through a clump of bushes and entered a darkened hut of woven bamboo. The leaf roof had gaping holes in it but it was better than nothing and I was surprised to find that the hut had an electric light bulb. There were no windows, and for a door, merely a single hole in the wall covered with a bamboo door. The most essential piece of furniture was a home made bed, and though it had boards instead of a mattress, at least it would be better than sleeping on the earthen floor which was muddy from the rain that had come through the roof. There was even a mosquito netting to go with the bed. I could not have asked for a more ample provider and sincerely thanked Tin.

He was jubilant that I was an American, the third he had seen in his entire lifetime. I told him of my plans to hitchhike to Europe and then cross the Atlantic to America and Alaska. This was Myitkyina, the last large settlement I would encounter until I reached Assam, some two hundred thirty miles away. The map showed nothing, not even a mule trail connected Myitkyina with the Pangsau Pass, which I hoped to cross. Before Tin left, I asked him if it would be possible to get to Ledo in India over the old but famous Stilwell Road, used during the last war. Tin was unable to answer the question; he had never been but a few miles from his village. He said he would take me to the local army official in the morning who would be able to advise me on my chances of getting through to Assam. With that plan, he excused himself, aware that I was in dire need of rest. The air in the hut was extremely damp, but it did not seem to daunt Chin who was gingerly pawing through my beard in search of bugs. My mind was heavy with disconnected thoughts as I lay awake in the darkness wondering where I would get the strength to continue the journey. I was well past the "point of no return" with no choice but to try to push forward. Buzzing mosquitoes and the sounds of a rat scurrying up and down the walls accompanied my dark thoughts.

I was awakened by Tin early the next morning. It was black inside the hut, but I could see daylight through the cracks in the wall so I forced myself out of bed to face another day. I noticed in the daylight that my new home had a couple of banana trees, devoid of fruit for lack of sun. Behind the hut was the usual large clay vase, which contained the water supply for the premises. Official water bearers from the village wells to the homes about town hauled water. The hut was located on the corner of a busy intersection just a few hundred yards east of the broad Irrawaddy River. Across the street the two of us shared a pot of tea in a cafe, and ate a few English cookies that were imported, and therefore presumed safe to eat. Tin did not drink his tea from the cup, but poured it into his saucer and slurped, explaining that it cooled the tea much faster, and I could not argue with him. Tin explained that he was a Mohammedan, and hoped to someday get out and see the world.

A heavy set Sikh, his black beard braided and wearing a pink turban atop his head, entered the cafe. Tin called him over to our table and introduced him as Chowdbury who owned a shop, which sold everything from food to spare automotive parts. When Chowdbury learned that Tin was going to take me out to the military base, he insisted that we take his dilapidated jeep the few miles to the camp. Moments later Tin and I were wheeling out of town in the battered grey jeep with tires so worn that the tubes protruded through two of them.

The most striking thing about Myitkyina is the countless hulks of rusting vehicles that had been left behind by the Americans at the close of the last war. They are scattered all over the town. It seems that just after the war, jeeps sold for as little as ten dollars because there were so many of them. As the years passed by and parts were impossible to get, the price rose until now a jeep, assembled from numerous others, went for as high as a thousand dollars! No one can afford them except the very well-to-do. As the relics became more valuable the natives began dragging the bodies of the abandoned vehicles- and their assorted parts- to their homes in the hopes that someday they may be able to salvage them and sell the parts for a fair amount of profit. This resulted in turning the town of Myitkyina into a huge salvage yard. Tin told me that Chowdbury and his associates had formed a big company after the war and purchased most of the abandoned equipment for next to nothing. Through the years they had made a fortune selling them piecemeal to all parts of Burma as far south as Rangoon.

We passed the airport, with its one hangar that was built by American engineers during the last war. It was far from bustling with activity as it had been near the close of the war with only one plane a week. The military camp was close by with its spacious parade grounds surrounded by bamboo barracks and the homes of the officers.

A guard halted us at the gate, and then escorted me to the commanding officer, Major Saw Tan, a plump, healthy looking specimen, with excellent usage of the English language. I told him of my desire to get across the Stilwell Road into India, and he seemed to respect my "courage and determination". His orderly served us tea, while Major Saw Tan informed me that the old Stilwell road was closed to all civilian traffic, and was impassable, even by elephant, seven months a year, due to the monsoons which created swollen rivers. During the dry season it was sometimes possible to get to Assam by jeep or all-wheel drive trucks. Besides that, the road had not been maintained since the war, bridges had washed out, and jungle growth had enveloped the road where it had not been severely gouged out by landslides and washouts. But there was a Burmese outpost near the Pangsau Pass that depended on occasional supplies from Myitkyina. Legally, the road was open only to military trucks, which would try to supply the Pangsau outpost during the dry season. Even they had not been successful this year. He lamented that a supply convoy of three trucks had left only yesterday for the outpost. If all went well, they would return in three days and try to make one last trip. However, the monsoons were already starting in the mountains to the northwest so he could promise nothing. He assured me that I would be welcome to get a lift with the convoy if it did make another run to Pangsau. Since the outpost was very low on supplies and it would be isolated for the next several months, they would do their utmost to get one more convoy through. "It is dangerous route at best, Mr. Wallace, but if you've come this far, I guess you are willing to accept the risks involved. I will contact you when the convoy is ready to leave again, if they return safely."

I thanked Major Saw Tan for his interest and concern on my behalf and returned to Myitkyina in the jeep with Tin and we returned it to Chowdbury. He invited us into his shop for tea, and wondered how else he could help me. I asked him if he knew where I could exchange a five dollar bill for Burmese money and he said that he could do it himself. He gave me no more than the official rate of five to one, when I could have received double that from a free-market peddler back in Rangoon or Bangkok. I was thinking to myself that he was really a cheapskate for not giving me more, when he made me feel like a complete ass by not accepting my offered bill. I insisted that he take it, for as long as I had any money at all, I did not want to accept handouts. But he became highly angered at my reluctance to accept his gift. His bold glassy eyes opened wide and he shouted, "Keep your American money, I do not need it!" I accepted his money, realizing that to refuse it would only further anger him. "You must visit me again, before you leave our village," insisted Chowdbury as we left his shop.

Against my better judgment I accompanied Tin to the home of his uncle, Sein Ko. It was one of the finest homes in Myitkyina, high above the ground on stilts, new and made of wood, and very clean. Just behind was a levee that kept the powerful Irrawaddy within its banks during flood time. Across the river the snowcapped mountains of China glistened like white jewels against the green of the jungle draped hills. Beneath Sein Ko's house was a pile of salvaged scrap, which contained radiators, truck rims, truck bodies, and a few engines. His uncle, Sien Ko welcomed me with open arms. He was quiet spoken and sincere. His wife had passed away only a month previously, and he seemed to bear an air of mourning and shell shock. Sein Ko introduced me to his two charming daughters, neither of whom spoke English. One of them was married, and was nursing her baby from one of her full breasts as she sat on the floor. In one corner of the large main room was the usual Buddhist altar (shrine) where they religiously gave their daily offerings of rice, and decorated with fresh, beautiful flowers.

Sein Ko was well-to-do, in part because he owned one of the two movie theatres in town, a ramshackle theater that presented an occasional American film, westerns from the early thirties. Despite his comparative wealth he was one of the most humble persons I had ever encountered. His hospitality could not be outdone. He insisted that I eat all of my meals at his home, and tried to give me money, but I refused by telling him that I had more than enough.

The cooking was done over charcoal pots, and we ate in a small cubicle at the rear of the house. It was so small that there was not enough room to get around the table without disturbing the people who were already eating. We tossed the bones and scraps onto the floor, to be washed down by the cook later, through a hole in the corner to drop to the ground below. As kind as it was of Tin and his uncle to supply me with free meals, I would rather have gone hungry than to have to eat with them. Most of the things they ate were so strange that I could not make out what I was eating. I did not recognize mashed minnow, and chunks of goat, fish heads and other tidbits, and when I did not eat as much as they thought I should eat, they would remark about it, causing me much embarrassment. Due to my illness, it was a chore for me to look at it let, alone eat it. All of the meals we ate with our hands, and not being very adept at this style of dining, proved to be a greasy task. They would reach into the common bowl and grab a fish, or rice-and then place it on their own plate. Often they would bite a chunk of something off and then replace the remainder of it back into the common bowl for someone else to eat. I was queasy enough to begin with and this ritual almost was almost too much to bear.

I was no stronger than I had been the previous day, so I returned to my private hut after lunch to get some peace and sleep. The air in the hut was musty and damp, but at least I would be able to conserve what little energy I possessed by lying down. Burmese music in the form of unfamiliar tones and instruments, felt more like a torture of maddening noise than music. The gongs and cymbals and drums made my head throb. My body was weak with fever; I had not been so weak since I had had bronchial pneumonia as a teen-ager, only this time I had no idea what was wrong – malaria, insanity, paralysis? I thrashed and rolled, unable to sleep. Sometime during the night when the streets were deserted I felt half my head was paralyzed; it was numb to my touch, except for the tremendous pressure and pain in the right side of my head. I could not believe that my head could be partially paralyzed, so to prove to myself that I had only had a nightmare, I rolled out of bed and left the damp hut to pace the quiet streets. I learned that I was not dreaming – my head actually felt numb. I became scared; there was no one to run to for help, no one to whom I could tell my troubles. I was totally deaf in my right ear, and by stumbling around in the dark, I had disproved that it was only a dream, and felt even worse knowing that my sickness was a reality. I returned to the hut where I spent the long hours of darkness twisting and moaning in agony, with nothing but an unsympathetic monkey for companionship.

By morning I could put up with my condition no longer and decided to see a doctor regardless of the expense. I could not go any further in my present state, so it seemed more sensible to spend what little money I had to regain my health and be stuck in Burma, rather than to continue forward only to die of sickness in the stifling jungle. When Tin came to the hut in the morning I asked him where I could find a doctor. His reply was not audible, and it angered me to have to keep telling him to speak louder. I simply could not hear properly.

Tin led me to a man who considered himself a doctor. I was hardly impressed by his medical wisdom when he did nothing but handed me a pipe and indicated for me to inhale the vapors. To cure my hearing trouble he poked around in my ear with a cotton covered stick, but it proved nothing. I left feeling as miserable as I had entered, my only consolation being that he did not charge for his "services". I returned to the hut to get Chin and then went down to the river to lie in the sun, hoping that its penetrating rays would cure my ailments. I stripped to a pair of shorts and waded into the chilly water to submerge my head in an effort to quell the throbbing and lower my fever to a normal temperature.

Scores of native women were doing their laundry along the riverbank. They would beat their clothes on the stones, pound them with clubs and wade into the river to rinse them in clean water. Many of them did not use soap, yet got their garments surprisingly clean, and somehow managed to avoid beating them to shreds after repeated washings. When they finished with their laundry, the women themselves would wade into the deeper water to bathe. They would rub their bodies with a small dark object, probably a stone, which they used in place of soap. The results were commendable, for their bodies could not have been cleaner. Once cleaned, the women would gather their laundry to spread on the ground to dry, gossiping with their friends while it dried.

An antiquated river barge was lying on its side with only its steel ribs remaining, looking like the skeleton of a whale. Natives were skimming across the surface of the swift moving river in their dugout canoes. The opposite bank looked much more appealing to me because it was devoid of people, with a sandy beach where I could lie in peace and regain my health without being disturbed by holy cows which cluttered the stony embankment. I spotted a small dugout a few hundred feet upstream, which was anchored, near the shore. Chin and I plodded around dung piles and waded out to the primitive canoe. The bottom of it was covered with stagnant water, greenish and teeming with wiggling insects. There was a long narrow crack in the one-piece hull, but it looked sea worthy so laboriously I worked the anchor chain free from under a pile of rocks and hopped in.

It was difficult to keep the boat headed in the right direction after I got a couple of hundred feet from shore; the current was much more powerful than my exhausted body. For this reason I drifted downstream several hundred yards before I managed to cut through the main current into the slower moving water near the opposite bank. I was too beat to pole the canoe upstream. It kept turning in circles, so I got out and pushed it in the shallow water, stumbling over slimy moss covered stones. I pushed the dugout near shore, dropped its anchor, and trekked off through the sand to a nearby clump of palms where I dropped onto the hot sand. For the next several hours I lay there swatting at bugs, unable to sleep. As the sun was setting, I mustered enough strength to pole back to the Myitkyina side of the Irrawaddy and retreated to my hut for the night. The same old rat, the splashing of rain drops on the floor, and the mystical noise of Burmese music were hardly co nsoling in my agony. Yielding to overwhelming exhaustion, I slept intermittently until daylight.

Tin came around in the morning with bad news. The Pangsau outpost had radioed back to Major Saw Tan that the rains had started, thereby making the road much more precarious than usual. The army convoy had not yet reached its first destination. Each day I waited to learn that the trucks had returned, but only disappointment awaited me. When they did return a couple of days later, they were in such a broken down condition that it took the mechanics a three more days to get them back into working order. After nine days of despair and sickness in Myitkyina word reached me that the trucks were ready to pull out. I did not feel up to moving on, but I was only deteriorating more-mentally and physically- with each passing day. Perhaps I would la st a little longer and be somewhat nearer to home before I expired altogether.

The news that I would finally be leaving reached the Sikh Chowdbury and to my surprise, he came to the hut with a gift for me. From his shop he had brought me a vacuum packed ti n of Quakers oats, a can of grapes, and a box of English biscuits, all imported and sanitary. I carefully packed these delicacies in my backpack, keeping them for the day when I would run out of money. Tin gave me a handy woven Kachin shoulder bag, and a native girl gave me a unique handbag of monkey skin, complete with its long grey-black haired tail, which formed the shoulder strap. Chin eyed that latter suspiciously. A young petite girl gave me a bracelet of jade. I felt like a hypocrite accepting these tokens of their devotion to me, when I had been too miserable to repay their kindness. I accepted their gifts nonetheless, knowing that to refuse would only humiliate them. The Major's personal command car, a battered, unreliable ¾ ton truck came into Myitkyina to fetch me. During my nine days in this last link with civilization, most of the town's people had learned of my presence, and now that I was leaving, scores of them came to see me off. Despite their poverty, they had tried their best to be good to me, although for the most part I had shunned them for I wanted to be alone in my condition. I sincerely thanked the natives of Myitkyina who had been such wonderful hosts, in spite of my hostile attitude. Perhaps someday I may be able to repay them in some small way, for actions speak louder than words. If we so called Christians were as kind to strangers as the people of Myitkyina, there would undoubtedly be a worldwide depression: military budgets which seem to uphold our economies would no longer be necessary and wars would be a thing of the past.

I took a last good look at the village as we rumbled through town to the military camp. We passed a hand operated brick factory (outdoor) much like what I had seen earlier with the addition of oxen walking in circles which generated the power to grind the clay and make it pliable. Then this clay would be carried by coolies and dumped into a pile behind four molders, working from a platform. Women would gouge chunks of clay from the pile and knead them into the proper sized balls and then place them on the molder's table. The molders would then dump the clay into a wood mold and make three bricks at a time. From there a child-like boy would carry them on pallets to the drying area, and once properly dried they would be packed into a huge underground pit over a fire built to bake them. I noted the final results were fairly professional looking, despite their primitive methods.

Chapter 22:

On the Road to Pangsau with Kogi: Machetes and Big American Footprints in the Jungle

MAJOR SAW TAN met us at the camp and introduced me to Kogi, a healthy looking Indian who would be the driver for the truck I would ride on to Pangsau. Kogi spoke about ten words in English, so it was evident that our conversation throughout the trip would be limited. The convoy consisted of three trucks with ten wheels each, but due to the lack of tires each truck was minus two wheels on the back. The trucks were 1942 GMC's, without doors, and without tops for the cabs. I helped Kogi and his tiny assistant roll forty-four gallon drums of gasoline into our truck, eighteen in all. The drums as well as the truck were badly dented and rusted as they had been used continuously for the past twelve years since abandonment by the Americans. The drums did not look solid enough to hold a solid, let alone a liquid. (see photo 14) We packed them carefully in hay so as to lessen the danger of sparks, and any resulting explosion. From what I had seen of the roads in Burma, I took my seat on top of the drums with great reluctance. I felt it was safer to sit on top of them than to sit in the driver's seat: I would be able to jump off at the first sign of fire, if there was a chance- before it was too late. When the three trucks were loaded and the motors checked over a final time, the Major wished us luck, and waved us farewell as the dilapidated convoy pulled out of the camp.

We bounced along at a fair clip to the village of Mogaung some thirty miles to the southwest of Myitkyina without incident. The road was level and there were no rivers to ford. We stopped in Mogaung to pick up two native women carrying chickens. A holy cow was eating off of table in the cafe a few feet away. Although our cargo consisted of gasoline, Kogi and his assistant had been smoking cheroots, their ashes blowing back to where I was sitting. As the native women clambered aboard, I noticed with alarm that about two inches of gasoline swashed about the steel bed of the truck. Kogi wiped his brow, indicating that he would be glad when we reached our destination. If we got through at all, this would be the last convoy of the season. He backed the truck over a ditch and allowed the gas to drain out. The undernourished villagers came running out of their huts with coconut shells, bamboo cups, and whiskey bottles to catch the gas as it poured out, apparently familiar with this routine. One wrinkled old woman came running up with a large battered can and managed to get more than all the other combined. Most of it had already run off on the ground before any of them had time to salvage it. But Kogi was in no hurry and the natives seemed eager to catch the single drips of the precious fuel, so we waited until they had gotten every last drop. We rearranged all of the barrels looking for the leaky ones, which we turned upside down. One of them had a small leak on both ends, so it did not leave us much choice. We would just have to pray that an explosion would not put an end to our journey.

Kogi drove with less haste after that, while I kept checking for more leaks. We forded a couple of rivers that afternoon, and as predicted, the Stilwell Road was not what it used to be. It was considered impossible to build a road through the rugged jungle covered mountains and swamplands of Northern Burma prior to its construction. The Americans had done it within a few months with the strain of wartime needs upon them. The original roadbed went up to the river's banks, where it once continued across the waters on pontoon bridges. Now the bridges were no longer to be seen, long since washed away in the flood season.

We continued until after dark. Kogi wanted to reach Namtu where we unfolded banana leaves and ate a meal of rice and fish, squatting around a candle for warmth and light. Electricity ended in Myitkyina, and from there to India we would find little to remind us that this was not the thirteenth century. Kogi swore when rain began to leak through the roof of our overnight accommodations, not because we would get wet, but because it meant the roads would be muddier, and rivers swell to the point of being impassable.

A cold damp mist greeted us with dawn. We dumped the gas from the leaky drum into jerry canes, filled the truck's gas tank, and tossed the useless can into the ditch. We smoked a cheroot for breakfast and then piled into the truck, roaring but few hundred yards down the trail till we lurched over a bank into the riverbed. We drove for half a mile upstream along the shore in a couple of feet of water and then slowly Kogi worked the truck out into the river. His assistant sat up on the hood of the truck, navigating a sand bar for Kogi; to go off its edge would be the end of our journey. The river was several hundred feet wide, but at no point did the water get our feet wet. We passed through a banana grove once we got to the west bank, and then rolled on. We passed some natives carving a huge dugout from a massive tree near the road, far from any stream. How they planned to get the boat to water is beyond me, although with an annual rainfall of two hundred inches, perhaps the road becomes a river?

About noon we passed clearings in the jungle that were piled high with abandoned war vehicles, mostly American. There were acres and acres of them. In front of each clearing was a sign with the letters IDC, which stands for Industrial Development Commission (of Burma), recent claimant of all scrap metal not in the hands of private citizens. The government was building a mill near Rangoon to process this scrap since it would not pay to ship it a thousand miles south. When the road had first been built, the natives of this area had never seen a vehicle, yet when the war abruptly ended, countless thousands had been left behind. The Americans destroyed most of them to some extent. The Burman would have to salvage parts from several vehicles to get one in operating condition. While they realized these vehicles were of some value, but they had no inkling or understanding of how to make them operate. Therefore they went about the jungles dragging bits and pieces of equipment off to their bamboo huts in hopes that one day someone might give them money in exchange for their salvage. Shrewd businessmen formed a few large corporations at the close of the war. They bought up all the pipelines, as well as vehicles by the gross, that stretched from Ledo, India to China- for a song. They would then repair them and ship them to southern Burma where they would get a good price.

In contrast, the average illiterate native would merely collect motley and assorted parts, having no essential functions as far as making a vehicle run. They might collect hundreds of door handles, headlights, gearshift knobs, or other ridiculous parts. Others collected generators, timing gears, tires, or windshields. Very few of them had the sense to collect the necessary assortment of parts to make a complete vehicle. The generators and other essential parts were left lying in the mud to rust and corrode. Surprisingly, many natives had made enough from selling their meager findings to the large corporations to keep them from starving. Now that the IDC has taken over all large deposits of scrap, the natives were deprived of their very livelihood, even though their wants were simple: just enough rice, a little opium and whiskey to keep alive, a few fish, a bamboo hut- and that about covers it.

Kogi whipped the truck to the left through some jungle growth that formed an arch of bamboo overhead. We were crossing an airstrip completely overgrown with the thriving jungle vegetation, finally coming to Shinbwiyan, a village of huts, one cafe and a couple of stores. The town looked more like a salvage yard than a village and I learned that it had been a supply depot and airstrip for the Allies during the war. Rather than move the large, heavy scrapped vehicles several miles to their huts, the natives moved and rebuilt among the scrap. Under and around each hut were oil drums, steel truck bodies, airplane wing tanks, motors, axels, bulldozers, and so on.

We turned off the road and pulled up before the customs station. The customs official checked through my gear, and passport. He asked to see my currency and declaration papers, but I had misplaced them somewhere along the line. I found that paper was much more luxurious to use on certain occasions than were tropical leaves which were often prickly, or rough, and lacked the fibrous strength of declaration paper. While likely illegal, at least it had been put to good use. The customs officer was broadminded enough to overlook this slight irregularity. Once he was satisfied that none of us were smuggling goods into India, he released us to spend the night.

Our host this night was the proprietor of a windowless one room home was an attractive native woman smoking a cigar who was cutting goat meat into small chunks, its bloodstained goatskin just outside the entrance. The cook area and furnace were one and the same, a section of floor in the center of the room covered with sand with a crackling fire upon it. Two small candles dimly illuminated the interior, and smoke from the fire billowed up toward the upper half of the room where it eventually sifted through the thatched roof. We squatted on the floor around a low bench from which we shoved questionable rice and curry into our mouths with our fingers.

After the meal Kogi communicated to me that he was going to check the truck over before taking off for the next village later in the afternoon, indicated by pointing to the sun's arc, so I went down to the river to clean up. Partially nude native women were bathing, and washing their clothes at the same time, so I followed suit. From the way they stared at me, I guess I was the first white man they had seen in a good many years- or perhaps I was the first man to do his own laundry!

When I returned to the hut to see if Kogi was ready to leave only to find the men had taken the motor out of the truck, along with the radiator and fenders. They had done all this in less than an hour, but I later learned that they tore vehicles down so often that they could nearly do it blindfolded. I would not have been so upset over the delay except for the fact that I had four days to get to India before my entry permit expired. There was no alternative but to wait until they fixed the truck.

An amicable native addressed me in English, and introduced himself as Singh. He was of medium build, dark and did not seem to have a care in the world.

"My woman, she work in my poppy field. Me no like so hard work. Her make money for me when she sell opium. Truck no good, no go Pangsau today. Maybe me and you go fish, okay?" suggested Singh.

There was nothing better to do, so I cut down a couple of green bamboo stalks with my machete and made us a couple of poles. I still had some green twine left over and some cheap Australian fishhooks from my days on Rottnest Island a couple of months before. Singh led the way to the fish. Thousands of them were swimming lazily about in the water near the suspension bridge. We used rice for bait, but the fish were not interested.

"Me know how to get fish, you got some dynamite?" he asked.

When I apologized for not carrying dynamite on my person, he said, "Is okay, last time my friend dynamite fish they all die, but is sad my friend was died long ago same as fish. Dynamite make my friend in many parts. Boss of Shinbwiyan say is no more okay to get fish by dynamite. How you say – too danjarus."

An aged woman with large empty breasts looked at my fishhooks as if they were jewels. I gave her several of them, and tried to warn her to not get hooked by them. Singh and I spent the remainder of the afternoon trying to catch the disinterested fish. As the sun began to go down, Singh came up with another brilliant suggestion.

"Maybe we shoot tiger soon as dark. Tiger take walk on road after night comes. Is gun at my house, we get, okay?"

With that I followed Singh to his hut. He showed me his hairless diseased monkey which was tied to a tree, and then we climbed up his front steps was no more than a log with notches. Molting chickens greeted us as we entered the shack. Singh chased them out and lit a candle and added some wood to the hot coals to the fire in the center of the room. After putting some rice on to cook, he left to fetch a bottle of rice whiskey and returned with the alcohol in one hand and a peacock under arm. He handed me the bottle and told me to drink. "Is very nice bird, maybe you like to have – it not cost too much, me want only five kyats. Bird is good friend for you to take to America. She is no trouble to you, she does not eat too much."

Singh had quite a sales pitch, but it was not convincing. I had more than enough worry keeping myself and a monkey out of trouble, let alone leading a peacock along behind us by a string tied to its leg.

When the rice had cooked, Singh drained and dumped it into a couple of leaves for us. Besides the rice, we ate a spicy long stemmed plant, resembling mustard weed. Singh consumed whisky until he was unable to walk without faltering. He picked up his gun, a rusty .45 pistol and rummaged around in an ammo box and drew out a handful of corroded, rusty shells. We stalked out of the hut and down the road, but after the first effects of the whisky wore off I realized that if we did encounter a tiger and Singh fired, the gun would undoubtedly explode. He was in no condition to listen to reason, but I finally managed to get him to give up the idea of tiger hunting and we returned to the village.

Kogi was still working on the truck-by candlelight. Upon seeing me, he stopped what he was doing and beckoned to follow him into the hut. Our host dished out some rice and goat meat and passed us more rice whiskey. We smoked cigars and conversed in pidgin English after the meal until we had exhausted our limited subject matter.

Chin had an acute case of the "runs" so rather than let him sleep with me, I tied him to the foot of the bed. But Chin did not like the idea of sleeping alone on the floor and tried to climb over the end of the bed. No matter how many times I pushed him back, he did not give up so I placed six small candles on the bedstead and lit them, forming a barricade of flames. But the little monkey was not so dumb; he would knock over the candles and climb through the gap. I finally gave up when the room was in total blackness. It was a bit crowded with four of us sleeping in the small room, but it was much better than sleeping out in the open where it was damp and cold.

Kogi had started to put the truck together in the morning, but found that he needed some essential parts so the two of us hopped into a wrecked ¾ ton truck and took off to the nearest IDC salvage yard. Now that the government had claimed possession of all salvage dumps it was risky business to be caught trespassing in the IDC areas, but this did not seem to bother Kogi. Armed with a handful of wrenches, we climbed over abandoned ambulances, trucks, jeeps, and airplanes, which had been piled high by bulldozers at the close of the war. All the equipment was American made, and the nicknames were still legible on many of the trucks doors: "Donna Sue", "Betty Jean", and numerous others that the GI's had painted on their own vehicles for morale boosting purposes.

We absconded a couple of generators, a timing gear, nuts, bolts, and metal screws and then jumped back into the truck and proceeded up the road a few more miles. We followed a stream through the jungle until we came to a village of three huts in a small clearing. The village leader did not seem too pleased with what Kogi had to say and pointed up river to a couple of jeeps that had been abandoned in the river bed. Kogi inspected them, but everything was rusted beyond salvage value. When he returned, he scrounged around under the native's hut and found another generator and timing gear, both badly pitted from rust. Kogi paid the man a pittance and we left for our truck. Kogi did not seem satisfied with his timing gear, so he turned up yet another narrow jungle trail which led us to a clearing lined with heavy earthmoving equipment, and a few smaller GMC's. Kogi was determined to get a decent timing gear so the two of us looked through a heap of discarded motors until we found two that were not stripped, and with much effort we managed to get them into the back of his truck. He covered them with a piece of burlap so the IDC officials would not be able to easily spot them and roared back to Shinbwiyang.

Kogi had no intention of leaving for Pangsau until the following day so I wandered off into the jungle to take a closer look at the equipment that had so hurriedly been abandoned after the war. There were eight D-8 bulldozer blades in one clearing. They were just like new except for superficial rust and the fact that one arm of each of them been cut off with a torch. There were road graders, cranes, and power shovels. Each one of them had disabled drive shafts, cut in two, or other strategic parts damaged, parts, which the natives of Burma would not be able to replace or correct because they lacked the proper tools. When the war ended so abruptly the American government was mainly concerned with getting their soldiers home quickly. It would not have been financially practical to ship all of the heavy equipment back to the states. Not only would shipment have been costly in money and personnel, but would have greatly undermined the postwar economy of our country to flood it with surplus army equipment. But for some reason we did not give this potentially useful equipment to the Burmese, or other underdeveloped countries which did not have the money to buy it, nor will they ever have it at the rate they are going. Incomprehensively, millions and millions of dollars' worth of heavy equipment were deliberately destroyed by our government rather than be put to the useful task of helping the Burmese and others rebuild their war torn countries to a state where they would be self-sufficient. Instead we now grant economic aid to these same countries even though the war ended decades ago. The American taxpayer pays through the nose for what little "friendliness" his money creates abroad.

I spent the whole day mulling through the wasteful, abandoned equipment, wishing that it could come to life again. I helped one native pry the steel plate from the floor of a half-buried bulldozer. When we finally got it loose, we found the original clean oil in the gear housing and a fresh coat of red paint on its interior. It made me sick thinking that there was such senseless waste of equipment, which could have made a significant difference today, improving the lives of the very people we tromped over during our occupation.

Our hut was a beehive of activity at the break of dawn. As we grabbed a bit of rice and tea, our host packed some bowls of food for the journey, and the trucks were given a last minute checkup. Besides the three original trucks, the ¾ ton truck was to accompany the convoy just in case one of the other trucks failed to run at all. As soon as we had left the village we started to climb up and around the rugged mountains that had once cost so many lives during the war. The road narrowed until the vegetation on either side of the road formed an arch overhead where they met and interlocked. On one side rose a precipitous slide with water dripping off plants, running in rivulets to drip down onto the roadbed, forming large puddles and eventually eating away the very roadbed. On the other side of the road was the precipitous drop that would mean certain death if the truck ever had the misfortune to slip.

We forded streams and crossed washed out culverts with caution. One bridge was still in place, but Kogi stopped the truck and looked underneath before attempting to cross. He shook his head, and we drove down into the stream. As we bypassed the bridge I could see that all of the vertical supports had rotted. What had once been the lifeline to China was now no more than a mule trail. Every few hundred feet we came to a culvert that had ruptured through the years, the corrugated pipe disconnected and hanging in grotesque shapes. Usually not more than a quarter of the original roadbed remained. Everyone would get off the truck except Kogi and he would follow his assistant's directions as he guided him across the worst stretches so narrow that only the inside dual tires on the truck would be on the road while the others hung precariously in the air. The rains had started early this season, and the road turned into a quagmire with numerous landslides.

As was feared it wasn't long until the truck conked out. There was no telling how long it would take to get it running again so I walked up the road to sleep, away from the hubbub of chatter that accompanied the truck repairs. The ants and bugs feasted on me, until Chin got around to devouring them. I slept until rain awakened me much later in the day. When I walked back to the truck, the radiator, fenders, and grill were off on the ground and Kogi was once again patiently replacing the timing gear. By now the rain was coming down in torrents, we were all drenched, and unless the rain let up, the trucks might not be able to go any further. It was already next to impossible for the trucks to climb the steep inclines.

The ¾ ton truck was loaded as high as possible with gas drums and rice from Kogi's truck, and six of us climbed on top of the cargo to chug on to the nearest village of Nam Lep. Kogi remained behind with the disabled truck and the other drivers to complete the repair work. We were drenched as we huddled together in the rear of the truck, half buried by cargo. We dumped the gas drums off in front of the military outpost, a large building perched on a hill overlooking the few usual smattering of huts that composed the town. Gas spewed from one of the drums as the top split open when it hit the ground. Three of us righted it before the drum was half empty. Even though this would be the last petrol the soldiers of Nam Lep would see until the following six months, they did not seemed alarmed at the waste of gas.

By the time we finally stopped, we were dripping wet and our boots caked heavy with mud. We fled for cover under a shelter down near the river, next to a comforting fire. We had been on the road thirteen hours and had only progressed twenty-five miles: two miles an hour was not a very good average.

I headed closer toward the river to clean up, passing through a large poppy patch where the native women who tended them did not seem to mind the mud or rain. Suddenly, a Chinese lad came running up to me. He was friendly and his English was easily understood. He had migrated to Burma during the last war with several mules, which he loaned to the American forces for use in packing supplies over the mountains. Wong was my age, and so eager to practice his English he invited me to be his guest for the night. He led me up the hill to his little open-air shop where he sold food, salt, cloth, and assorted odds and ends. Wong was doing okay for a young man; he had a good business head and kept a neat shop. He offered me some Chinese food for supper, but I refused telling him that I preferred to treat him to an American delicacy: oatmeal.

I hated oatmeal as a child, but the important thing now was that the cereal Chowdbury had given me was vacuum packed, clean and sanitary, in contrast to the native rice, which, particularly in this area, was full of rat dung. Wong lit a candle in the dark lean-to where he did his cooking. The earthen floor had a stream of water running across it from the heavy rains falling. I may be the world's worst cook, and normally abhor oatmeal, but the pot I prepared that night was undoubtedly the most welcome and nourishing meal I had had since Mandalay. It was a wonderful feeling to be able to eat food for a change without having to worry about it weakening me. I had had diarrhea for weeks on end. I offered Wong some, but he did not like the looks of it. It was the first time I had eaten oatmeal with chopsticks, but I managed. When I had finished the succulent meal, I carefully packed the tin of oatmeal away for future savoring.

A group of about ten Nagga natives from the surrounding hills had come in to Nam Lep on a buying spree, or for a look-see-I wasn't exactly sure. They did not possess money, but did bring things to swap for salt and other essentials. It was obvious that I was an oddity to them: they caressed my clothing and could not take their eyes off me. The most intriguing thing about them was the long knife each carried, about two feet in length overall, with a handmade sheath which hung on a bamboo strap across the chest. They were decorated with tiger teeth, and other ornamental pieces. The men were colorfully dressed in bright red and blue though ragged lungi, with equally ragged jackets. I asked Wong if it were possible to buy a knife like the proud Naggas carried, but he explained that these knives are handmade by the Naggas themselves, and that they cherish them more than they do their women. I pulled out my Army surplus machete, which looked pretty dull by comparison with its OD colored handle. I passed it around to all the Naggas who looked it over carefully, but shook their heads as if to say that it was not on a par with theirs. Then the chief himself looked it over. Wong interpreted for me and asked him if he would be willing to swap his knife for mine. The chief finally consented and reluctantly parted with his beloved knife. I shook his outstretched hand and thanked him, followed by all the Naggas extending their hands, which I shook in turn. The Naggas are among the most primitive peoples of Asia, yet this little bartering proposition revealed how sentimental the "uncivilized" can be, perhaps even more so than we who consider ourselves as the standard of civilization.

The chief placed his knife across my chest, showing me how the Naggas carry theirs, then beckoned for me to follow him and three of his men. Wong told me that they were going to smoke opium and that they wanted to bestow their sincerity by inviting me to join them. The chief held my hand and led me out into the blackness and up the slippery hill to a cozy looking shelter on top. The glow of fire illuminated the room with a reddish tint. We climbed up the log ladder and removed our foot wear before walking across the spring bamboo floor to the fireside where we squatted on our haunches. There were six of us in all, excluding Chin, a dog, and three chickens that had also come in to escape the rain. Except for Wong and me, the other men were elderly sages of their village tribes who spoke slowly, with much deliberation. Each of us was either smoking a cigar or chewing betel nut, and sipping tea from a common bamboo cup, which we passed around while our host, prepared the opium with much ritual.

First, he shredded a dried banana leaf until it resembled tobacco; then he heated the opium tar over the fire until it turned to a liquid in a small bronze colored cup. With grand ceremonial gestures, he held another metal cup to his mouth, breathed into it, placed a bit of the banana tobacco inside, and finally, poured a portion of the opium over it. Next, he worked the opium into the banana leaf with his fingers, the result being a ball of tobacco cemented together with the tarry pitch. He passed the bamboo pipe to me first as a sign of respect. About a foot long, it was similar to a conventional pipe except that it had a much larger mouthpiece, and the area between the bowl and the stem was filled with water to filter the smoke. Finally, he handed me a ball of the tobacco which I placed in the bowl, followed by a red hot coal from the fire delivered with a simple set of wooden tongs to give a light.

It was a mild, relaxing smoke. When the ball of tobacco had turned to ashes I passed it on to the next man. The pipe went around the circle many times during the next few hours. The Nagga who had invited me to the gathering stood up and began rambling on as if filibustering. The other men were silent, except for an occasional grunt. The Nagga talked continuously for a long time, waving his arms to stress a point. I asked Wong what the Nagga was so excited about, and Wong explained that once this man had gone from the hills and become a Christian and that it was against his beliefs to be smoking opium. The others were not Christians, and he was trying to convert them. It seemed like an odd place to find converts. The men continued to pass the pipe around, but the chief was the only one who did not partake of either the pipe, or the whiskey brought out later.

I could easily understand why the Naggas, and other mountain tribes were so inclined to smoke opium and drink whiskey to forget their troubles. Jungle rats usually ruined much of their meager rice crop, and there was not much incentive to work in what was mostly a cashless society. Our friendly gathering broke up about midnight at which time Wong led me back to his shop. He rounded up an extra cot and the two of us slept comfortably among the stacks of merchandise, the rain falling steadily throughout the night.

By morning, the village streets were deep with mud and pools of water. The gunky mud stuck to my boots, making them feel like they were made of lead, as I stumbled and slid down the hill to where Kogi had parked his truck. Kogi stood cursing at both the truck and the condition of the road. He had spent the night working on it and managed to get it running only a few hours earlier. As bad as the road appeared, he said that we would pull out in a few minutes for the Pangsau outpost: conditions would only get worse with the passing of each day.

One of the other trucks had broken down completely and hopelessly, so the ¾ ton remained behind to shuttle the goods from the disabled truck into Nam Lep which was the planned destination for its cargo. Kogi led our two truck convoy as we pulled out of Nam Lep. A dense fog made low clouds, cutting the visibility to the point that Kogi may as well have been blind, but the truck could go no faster than a creep anyway so it did not matter. The night's rain had raised hell with the road. On several occasions we had to cut bamboo shoots and lay them across the mud so the truck would not sink out of site. Kogi was forced to drive through stream beds, over boulders and through deep water more often than not because the road was washed out completely.

About noon we came to a remote village of five simple huts. The smaller children hid behind their parents upon seeing me. To my utter amazement, a woman came up and asked me to accompany her to her hut for a cup of tea. It was the last place I had expected to find a native girl who spoke such understandable English. It was much easier to go barefoot in the mud than to have to bother to unlace my boots and take them off each time I entered a hut. It is Asiatic custom to remove the shoes rather than the hat when entering a hut, and I did not want to infringe upon their customs. The beguiling woman told me that she had been trained by Doctor Seagrave as a nurse back in Namkam, and that now she cared for the needy of this area.

The whole village turned out to welcome me and crowded into her humble home. She apologized for not having eating utensils and a cup for the tea, but her bamboo cups were just as practical. She insisted that I eat something but I refused saying that I had just eaten. She told me how undernourished and poor the people of her village were and that meat and eggs were a luxury, but the chickens of the village had laid three eggs that day, and she wanted to make a present of them to me. The natives crowded around with hungry expressions as she handed me the eggs apologizing for having nothing more lavish to give me as a token of friendship from her village. I was most embarrassed to accept the eggs when it meant that the natives would not only have to go hungry, but that they would have to stand by to see a total stranger eat them. I told her that I could not possibly eat all three eggs and tried to give them back to the natives, but they shook their heads and insistently motioned for me to eat them. I did so, having no alternative.

The two trucks wound through the treacherous jungle road, carved from the side of the mountains, like snakes for the remainder of the day. When our truck bogged down in a mud hole on the edge of a washout, the roadbed under us started to give way from the weight. We hurriedly hooked the winch cable to a tree and pulled the truck out.

My entry visa for India would expire at dark, but I was crossing the border illegally in the first place so it did not matter. I would not be able to go back to Rangoon and get another one since my Burmese visa was due to expire in a few days as well, not to mention it would take another month to get back to Rangoon. I may as well be stranded in India as Burma. We reached Pangsau outpost just before dark, which is a mile from the Pangsau Pass, the official border between Bu rma and In dia. The outpost was one of the most isolated in all of Burma. It consisted of a mule shed, a cookhouse, briefing room, and a couple of private quarters for officers and two long shabby thatched huts for the enlisted men. The view was magnificent from any place in the small compound set nearly a mile above the Patkai Hills and its beautiful valley, which stretched out below a light layer of low clouds.

Kogi wiped his brow as he stepped down from the truck, happy with the accomplishment that we had made it with the much needed rations, and glad that he would be making the return trip empty. The outpost would be isolated from the rest of the world for the following six months until the rains ended and the trucks could make the trek again. Even with an expired visa in my pocket, I still felt immense gratitude. Had I not been able to get out of Myitkyina with the military convoy, I would have had to spend weeks retracing my route back to Rangoon for nothing. I would have been broke- or dead- before I had gotten there.

The soldiers hastily carried the heavy drums behind the supply hut where they stacked them. One of the soldiers who approached me had a fair command of English. He introduced himself as Maung and led me to his residence on top of the hill overlooking the camp. He introduced his wife, his helper, his little monkey, and the monkey's playmate, which was a young chicken. His monk was female, and Chin a male, but for some reason they ignored each other. Maung handed me a cigar and then fetched out the whiskey bottle. I tried to refuse, but he insisted that it would be an insult to do so. His wife spread the table with fish, rice, and jungle plants, which I had not seen before. The whiskey was as strong and putrid as only rice whisky can be. As much as the sight of the food sickened me, I forced it down so that it would deaden the effects of the whiskey.

Maung was fascinated by the thought of making a journey such as mine, but he did not like the idea of having to go through India. He showed me his transmitter, the only contact they had with the outside world during the monsoon season. He tried to raise Myitkyina to show me how effective the radio was, but we heard nothing but static. The radio had been made in America, a relic of the last war. I was surprised to learn that the Burmese Army does not use the International Morse code but instead uses a code all its own. Maung showed me some of the monkey skins he had collected during his tour of duty at Pangsau. He gave me two that were sewn together forming an eighteen by thirty-six inch rug. I assured him that I could put it to good use as a mattress.

He ushered me down to a small hut there I was to spend the night. The hut was unusually clean, but the bamboo walls and floor had gaping holes, which allowed the chilly wind to blow through the tiny cubicle. A bamboo platform provided the bed, and the bottom of an oilcan served as the stove. I lit a fire and invited Maung to partake of some of my western food. He found the dry oatmeal stuck to his teeth, so he tried the canned grapes, which he really enjoyed. We ate English biscuits till we were stuffed and then Maung left the hut to retire for the night.

It was a wonderful sensation to be in a clean little cubicle of my own for a change, the fire giving a cheerful glow to the environment as I snuggled down in the cotton sleeping bag, fully dressed per usual. Chin gave me no trouble for he was shivering and quickly curled up by my beard and fell asleep. I did not sleep much for the chilly wind sifted easily through my sleeping bag, and lay awake well past the fire's dying embers, wondering what the morrow would bring: I was going to attempt to cross into India illegally. I had no choice.

Chapter 23:

India and the Misery Train

MAUNG CAME DOWN to my sleeping abode a few moments after dawn. The other troops were already going about their early morning chores. Kogi was loaded with engine chugging, ready to head back to Myitkyina. I thanked him for all he had done and followed Maung to the border a mile distant. A weathered sign, no doubt also a war relic, gave the elevation as 4,125 feet above sea level which is not high as far as mountains go, but with nearly impenetrable jungle growth and heavy rainfall, more difficult to traverse than other similar sized mountains. The tropical vegetation and ever present chatter of monkeys made the view across Assam to the snowcapped Himalayas of Tibet incongruous. A mere one hundred miles to the north, the majestic mountains towered in their whiteness against a brilliant blue bird sky.

I had eight miles to trek to the first Indian outpost, the town of Nampong, formerly known as Hell's Gate by the allies who created the famed Stilwell Road. Hundreds of Americans had died of disease in Hell's Gate, and authorities had been unable to determine the exact cause. The mosquitoes of the area were noted for their potency to give humans cerebral malaria. A few educated people had warned me that it was folly for an unadapted white man to traverse the territory. I did not know how malaria presented. Other than being constantly plagued with dysentery and weakness, and the occasional chills and intermittent sweating which I blamed on that weakness- I felt healthy.

I soaked up the beauty of the three countries, Burma, India and Tibet from my elevated perch, which made me feel as if I were in heaven looking down at the world. It was impossible to imagine such a grand vista could be hiding so much potential trouble ranging from terrorists to disease and wild animals. I waved goodbye to Maung and began the descent down the mountain. Monkeys screeched continually, but I never saw one. As soon as we neared their sounds, they would become silent and other monkeys in the distance would pick up the chatter.

My sixty-pound backpack seemed to grow heavier as the day went on, forcing me to stop for rest. When I had first started the trek to Nampong I was glad that it was downhill all the way, but legs tired greatly lumbering down the mountainside. One's weight hits the earth with each step. Chin had been riding on my shoulder, but he insisted on resting his hot body against my sweating neck, which was like wearing a fur collar. By the time I reached the lower slopes, my legs were like rubber, my entire body was trembling, and I was sweating profusely.

Water was running along the trail in a bamboo aqueduct that the natives had ingeniously constructed a few feet off the ground. I was gasping for breath, my mouth thick with heavy saliva. As I stopped to scoop some of the water into my mouth I could hear the pounding of my heart and the throbbing of my head. To hell with everything, I didn't care if I was entering India illegally: I just wanted to get home. They could jail me- or anything they liked. I just wanted to rest. I stumbled weakly into the Assam military outpost, past the surprised soldiers and collapsed in the shade of a tree. I lay on my stomach, too exhausted to take off my backpack.

An English speaking nom-com broke through the circle. He squatted on his haunches to talk to me. The neatness of his uniform was the first thing to strike me. His skin was nearly black, much darker than the golden tan of the average Burman. After I had recuperated somewhat, the amicable nom-com led me across the drill field to a circular hut on stilts. The camp was constructed of bamboo and thatch, similar to the Burmese outpost, but there was a vast difference in appearance between the two; the Assam outpost was immaculate, and the buildings in good repair. The sharply dressed troops were beating stalks of green bamboo with clubs to splinter them so they could be used to weave into the walls of a new barracks that was under construction.

An orderly served us tea and chapattis as we sat in the shade, cooled by a gentle breeze. The nom-com eyed my Nagga sword suspiciously but said nothing. I was surprised that he did not attempt to check my passport, but he informed me that he was not the customs and immigrations official. I would encounter them a half mile down the trail. I left the camp with a wonderful first impression of India and its people, the opposite of my entry into Burma where my first impression had been of filth and poverty, which I later overlooked because the Burmese people had been so wonderful to me in general. I would soon learn that my first impression of India was also misleading.

As soon as I crossed the bridge going away from the outpost, an armed Indian guard apprehended me. He led me into the nearby whitewashed customs house where he took my sword, confiscated my backpack, and led me into an office to be scrutinized by a petty officer who looked me up and down suspiciously. I handed him my passport.

"We heard that you were coming through five days ago. This is the Tirap Frontier District. It is restricted. What are you doing here?"

"How could you have known that I was headed this way, sir, there are no communications for two hundred miles to the east!" I asked, astonished that they knew of my arrival in advance.

"The natives have their own communication system. The jungle telegraph is very effective. We have our informers." The guard brought in my Nagga sword and handed it to the official. "So you have been collaborating with the Naggas, just as I suspected."

"That knife was given to me in exchange for my machete by a friendly Nagga."

"I suppose you expect me to believe that you did not know that our government has been waging war against the Naggas? You are a gunrunner like the other Europeans we have caught. Why else would you be in this area?" He checked through my passport carefully and when he noticed that my entry visa had expired the day before, he shouted. "You have no right to be in this country, your visa is outdated!"

By rights I had three counts against me, but the most important one he had not mentioned: the entire India–Burma border was closed to overland traffic, by his own government. I could readily understand how a remote outpost would not have received the latest word, so naturally I did not bring the subject up. My chief worries were: my expired visa; the fact that I was in a restricted area; and how to prove I had not collaborated with the warring Naggas.

"But sir, how was I to know that this is a restricted area? When your embassy issued me my visa in Rangoon they told me nothing about this being a restricted area. I do not mean to imply that your government agencies lack coordination, but surely the Embassy of

India in Rangoon should be up on the latest restrictions." He did not want to admit that his command was so distant and minute that he would not be cognizant of the latest regulations. He got out a book of regulations, and pointed to the regulation which made Triap a restricted area.

I laughed aloud when I noticed that it dated back nearly a hundred years! The cause for the original restriction of the area was obscure. The reason for its existence now was purely ridiculous- the legislature had failed to void its application when the reason for its instigation had long since vanished. He admitted that it was a foolish regulation, and said that possibly it could be overlooked.

The guard dumped the contents of my backpack on the floor and held up my tattered clothing to the light, as if he expected to find secret documents sewed into the lining. To prove I could not have been fighting with the Naggas, I showed him the regulation on the back cover of my passport, which prohibits Americans from joining foreign armies legally. He asked to see my money, so I placed my wealth in a pile on his desk: all forty-five dollars in American bills and traveler's checks, plus a five kyat bill worth nothing in India. Had I been a mercenary gun-runner I would have had a lot more than this paltry pile. I tried to tell him that my visa did not expire until midnight of this day. The entry visa had been issued to me in Rangoon on the 8th of February and was valid for one month. It was now the 8th of March.

"I am aware that it is only a technicality, but our government would soon collapse if we did not abide by the regulations. I will let you speak with the Director of Nampong when he comes back this evening."

I argued with him telling him that I could not afford to wait, but the guard raised his rifle to port arms when I raised my voice. I would be waiting for the senior official. I briefly considered escaping down the streambed when I went to bathe behind the official's domain, but it was thirty miles to Ledo, the beginning of the railway and a semblance of civilization. A white adult male would stand little chance of going undetected for long in Assam. I would be picked up for certain.

The junior official's attitude seemed to change when I emerged from the stream wearing wet clothing. As I lay in the sun letting myself dry, he told me that according to their records, I was the first American to come through the Pangsau Pass since the last war. He found it hard to believe that I had not collaborated with the Naggas, and yet been allowed to journey through their domain unharmed. I told him that the Naggas had been most hospitable. He was indeed a frustrated official. He had been educated in Calcutta, only to be stationed in what he termed the country's "most abandoned point of exit". It did seem like the end of the world in many respects. The only people who passed through his gates were the illiterate natives who often had no identification, yet were allowed to go undisturbed, except when they were caught with opium or other illegal contraband.

The junior official invited me to his quarters for a mid-day meal. He was dressed in white western style clothing, in contrast to his house boy, who wore a dhoti, a traditional men's garment of unstitched cloth wrapped around the waist and legs and knotted, resembling a skirt. The lunch consisted of rice, a greasy goat curry and chapattis. His superior, the senior official arrived late in the afternoon.

Before showing him my passport, I explained the technical difficulty, and told him it was a matter of interpretation. I was certain I was within the time limit. At first, he refused to see my viewpoint. Then he asked me about America, and told me that he had a good friend living in Tennessee who was a former associate of his during the Burma campaign and the building of the Stilwell Road. Since they had been such loyal friends in years gone by, he determined it would not be proper to detain one of his friend's own countrymen.

He invited me to ride back to Ledo with him, so Chin and I piled into the back of his pickup with five scrawny coolies and were on our way. On three occasions military road blocks stopped us, but the official spoke for me and we were allowed to pass without delay. We passed pedestrians by the thousands, walking slowly to their humble bamboo abodes at the end of yet another day's work. They were by far the most undernourished people I had even seen. The majority of them looked like living skeletons, their bones covered only with skin. Their elbows and knees stuck out like burls on a tree. I avoided eye contact with my host as I didn't know how he felt about such matters of humanity, but I was deeply touched by the indelible images of hunger manifested on such a massive scale.

We reached Ledo, and its busy railroad, well after dark. The truck stopped in front of a jail house, of all places. I wondered if I was being lead into some sort of trap, but the police chief needed to double check that I was not a spy, saboteur, or thief for which he would have to assume full responsibility of allowing to immigrate. I was surprised that I had not received a currency declaration form upon my entry into Nampong. It is an essential document in most countries where a foreigner lists all valuables and currency, which he brings into the country. This safeguards both the foreigner and the country. The country is protected from him changing his money at usurious rates, whereas the foreigner is protected from having his valuables or money confiscated when he leaves the country by officials who declare that he has come upon those commodities through fraudulent means. It is also necessary to have the form stamped each time you convert money by the official bank, as well as the rate of exchange. I would lose nothing by not having such a form with my limited resources, so I felt relatively free as I left the jailhouse and climbed back into the truck.

I was driven to a spacious government bungalow where a room had been ordered for me. I had noticed on the thirty-mile drive from Nampong to Ledo a large number of government projects under construction and this appeared to be one of them. It was part of India's five-year modernization and industrialization scheme. Modern kerosene lamps instead of candles lighted the bungalow. My room was spacious room with a double bed and a real mattress, my first since Bangkok. There was even an American toilet with a seat, but without running water. The shiny white pail under the seat had to be emptied manually, but there was a servant to do that.

The official bid my good night saying he would return in the morning to take me to the train station. I had not told him that I was too broke to afford the luxury of commercial transportation, but I would wait until morning to disillusion him: in Asia all white men are suspected of being men of relative wealth. I stowed my pack and left in pursuit of a meal.

The dogs began to bark at Chin as he walked along, so I shoved him into the large pocket of my coat. The village streets were jammed with people. The stench of the open sewers struck me anew, having been fresh from the clean smelling jungles for the past weeks. I had to hand it to the Hindustanis for one sanitary innovation, at last. It was possible to buy tea from street vendors who served it to you in rust colored clay cups that were disposed of after a single use. Coolies were staggering through the town with huge sacks of coal on their backs. Women were moving along in their flowing saris, adorned with pierced ears, jewels in their noses and rings on their fingers and toes. They spat globs of reddish betel juice on the walls of buildings and streets, leaving wet stains in their wake. Beggars who could walk followed us holding out their hands for money, and those who were limbless, or too weak to follow, merely looked up from lying on their backs in the mire. The Hindus did not smile as much as the Burmese and seemed to move about with the air of doomed people who accepted their station in life. As I learned more of India, I would come to understand why they had such an attitude.

I asked around to find out what chance I had of hitchhiking to Calcutta, which was 1,000 miles away. I learned the people of India did not pick up riders, or there were so few vehicles and so many millions of poor people that they could not hope to get a lift. In addition to this, India does not possess many roads, and as a result, I would never be able to find my way to Calcutta. If I still had any doubts, he allayed them by telling me that there were few if any road bridges that had not been washed down the many rivers flowing through the area. Even with the train, it would take several days to reach Calcutta and then there was the issue of not being allowed to go through East Pakistan if I wanted to re-enter India. That required a special re-entry visa, which would not be granted except in one of the major cities, and probably not there either for the Hindustanis did not care much for the Moslem Pakistanis. I lay awake a long time wondering how I was going to find my way to Calcutta without a map, little money and an exhausted, weary body. So I did what has worked for me in the past: I waited until the morrow to think of a way to overcome it.

The official that had driven me from Ledo showed up early to take me to the train, where I secretly decided I would try to avoid the ticket collectors. I waited on the platform along with the multitudes of poor, and finally an antiquated train chugged into the station, black smoke billowing from its stack. The cars were very small and constructed of wood, much like the coaches of America were in the late 1800's, only these were black with soot and crowded with people by the time we got aboard. There was nowhere to sit, and I felt the bodies of strangers pressed against me as the train jerked along. I kept feeling my pockets to make sure some hand was not removing my wallet or passport.

After the first stop, enough of the passengers got off so that I found a vacant seat on the wooden bench. A young wench boarded the train at Bargolai, carrying her bare-bottomed infant son. She placed him on the floor and began to sing, more of a wailing chant than music. Tears came to her eyes as she made gestures to her baby during the show. Her lips and mouth were red with betel stains, her teeth black with tar. The colors of her tattered sari were indistinguishable because it was saturated with dirt and grease, but a single jewel hung from her pierced nose. When she finished her eerie chant, she began to make the rounds, pushing her tottering son ahead of her to collect any money that the passengers contribute to her cause.

The little boy, not more than two years old, had already been taught to hold out his arm to collect offerings for his mother. As soon as a couple of the more well-to-do passengers dropped a few annas into his tiny hand, his mother would quickly take it from him. She spied me at the end of the car and pushed her son toward me, forgetting the other passengers. Being white, she probably expected me to be worth a small fortune. I had encountered professional beggars before and rationalized that I could not help them all- not even a few at this point, or I would be forced to resort to begging for an existence myself. I did not relish the thought, therefore when her little boy held out his grimy hand before me I put my head down, embarrassed because I was too stingy to give him anything. The man next to me held out his hand to give the boy a couple of annas, without warning, Chin, who had been concealed under my coat, jumped out and began to growl at the child. For some reason, he hated women and children, perhaps because they were smaller than men, or they would scare more easily. At any rate, Chin was almost harmless, yet he could act so ferocious that he could bluff even the most toughened men when he bared his teeth and hissed. The boy jumped back, afraid to keep his hand near the monkey. When his mother pushed him toward the man with the money, the little boy broke into tears and cried, afraid that Chin would bite him. I forced Chin under my coat and the woman took the money from the man, while giving me a nasty look and mumbling something-probably condemning me for being so tight.

Chapter 24:

Digboi and The Class System

WE GOT OFF at Digboi, one of the most respectable looking towns I was to see in India. A great many foreigners lived here in plush homes, many connected with the local oil refinery. I had not gone far when I came to a British Oil Company warehouse. A large group of Hindustanis was following at my heels. I dropped my sack on the ground and walked into the warehouse where I met a tall, slim impeccably dressed Englishman. He was very much surprised to see me, a white man- dressed so shabbily. I told him I had come through Upper Burma, and his attitude changed for the better. I asked what the possibilities were of getting a lift on an oil truck to Calcutta, but he said that they shipped their oil by train. Getting a lift with a company official by car was out of the question: travel by land in India was much too slow; the only way to travel was by air.

The Englishman told me to hop in his little Austin car, and he took me out to his friend's house in a beautiful residential district to get more information. All the houses were two story stuccos with large balconies and spacious lawns and beautiful gardens. We turned up a circular driveway and parked in front of one such "mansion" where he led me inside the lavishly decorated home, complete with modern furniture. The man and woman of the house entered the living room wearing pajamas, covered by elegant robes. It was a real shock to see a western woman for the first time in a month. She was a youthful, vivacious lady of fragile dimensions. It was past noon so they poured us a drink. They bemoaned the fact that they had to get up at all, but it was Saturday and they had a golf engagement. They concurred that it would be impossible for me to get a lift to Calcutta by truck or car. They had never ridden a train in India, but imagined it would be a regretful experience. Most foreigners flew to their destinations throughout the country: it was the only respectable means of transport. They would have invited me to stay with them, except that they were tied up with social engagements for the weekend, tactfully admitting that I would feel out of place with them as currently dressed. However, they telephoned American acquaintances of theirs who had recently arrived in India, and asked the Englishman to deliver me to their residence, convinced they would appreciate my company.

Jim, the young American, was a chubby, bespectacled intelligent looking man. His pretty young wife, Betty, was awed to have an "explorer" for a guest. They had only arrived in India two weeks before, fresh from the States. It was the first time either of them had been outside the continental limits of the U.S.A. Their home was two and a half times as large as the average American home, and their lawn was at least an acre in size. Back in the states, Jim had been drawing a decent salary with the oil company, but here in India he could live like a king on the same salary, yet he got his house and many other essentials supplied at company expense. While his wife could not have afforded even a part-time maid in the United States, here she had five full-time servants, three of whom lived on the premises. Jim and his wife were casually dressed in American clothes, their conversation was light and interesting, and their hospitality included an invitation to spend the night.

They made me feel at home immediately and told me to take a bath if I wished. I reeked with an odor that can only come from not bathing daily in a sub-tropical climate. While I was taking a real bathtub, in an actual tub complete with running water, Jim knocked on the door to beg my forgiveness for not having hotter water. It was the first water I had bathed in over two months that was heated at all, indeed a luxury. My boots reeked so badly that I dared not carry them through the house so I tossed them out the back window into the yard. Jim had a servant bring me a scotch on the rocks while I was soaking in the tub. After what I had been through, this was really living.

It bothered me though, as I sipped the soothing drink. How could it be that in a country where the majority of the people lived in abject poverty, many of them dying from disease, malnutrition, and starvation, that a select few, and all foreigners, could live in such luxury? The wealthy did not seem to care that most of their fellow men were so destitute, or for that matter, lived or died. Their own happiness came first. The contrast between peoples was beyond common comprehension, making life itself nothing but a farce. All the things I had been taught about the Christian way of life *sounded* fine, but how many Christians were doing anything to aid the less fortunate? Most of us are nothing but hypocrites, myself included. Yet many of us hide ourselves behind a superficial shield of righteousness and convince ourselves that we are really interested in the plight of our fellow man. It is so easy for us to rationalize and convince ourselves that we need a new TV set, rather than give money to the needy. There seemed to be little logic in life, which seemed little more than a greedy game, a virtual free for all to see what we can accumulate for ourselves.

I washed all my musty clothes and hung them to dry. A neatly dressed servant waited on us in the dining room. Betty did not have to do a thing around her house with servants taking care of everything. Yet her mother had written to her, wondering how Betty could stand the rigors of jungle life! She must have been expecting her daughter to be living in a hovel like the majority of the country. As might be expected, Jim and Betty had already formed their opinions of what was wrong with India that made it so poverty-stricken. They meant well; it is easy for an outsider to enter any realm and come up with cure-all remedies. In my experience, they have only scratched the surface and do not understand the underlying reasons for the deep undying issues.

That night I slept in a luxurious double bed, covered with warm blankets and cooled by a fan. It was like sleeping in a four-poster with mosquito netting hanging down from the ceiling. I actually felt clean that night. When Betty awoke me early in the morning, it was like rousing from a dream to find myself in a luxurious bed being awakened by an elegant lady. She had gotten up early to see me off. It was still dark when I sat down in the dining room to eat breakfast.

I walked into the darkness away from their estate to the railway station to catch the first train to the west. When the train arrived, I pushed my way aboard, Chin clinging to my shoulder. I had not purchased a ticket; I could not afford to ride and eat, and eating was far more important. Six hours later, the train came to the end of the line at Dibrugarh Town, the 11th station from Digboi. I had no map, so I asked the trainmaster where I was and how I could get another train to Calcutta. I was disheartened when he told me that I was only sixty miles from Digboi, and that I should have changed trains thirty miles back at Tinsukia Junction. I was now at the end of the line, way out of the way, and at a dead end.

It would be impossible to get a train out of Tinsukia Junction until the next day, but the station master recommended that I take a bus for Jorhat, about 70 miles away to link back with the railroad, and which would leave later that afternoon. I had three hours to kill before the bus left so I set out on foot to try to find of a map of India since I really had no idea where Johhat- or Calcutta-were. It had been different in Burma, with so few roads, but India had villages every couple of miles, with railways crisscrossing the country and if I did not find a map, I could be end up going around in circles.

Chin and I walked the main thoroughfare until a policeman dressed in tan shorts and with a bright red high hat apprehended us. He led me onto a dingy brick building, which turned out to be another jailhouse where I was interrogated in fluent English. The policeman wondered what I was doing in this part of India with a beard, sword, and backpack. I explained that I was just passing through on my way to Calcutta but he told me I would have to remain in his custody until he could contact his superior officer. He could not afford to let a spy slip through his hands. I told him that I must go check on the bus, or I would not be able to get out of town that day. He let me go on the condition that I surrender my pack and passport. I was glad to be rid of the weight as I walked through the town fruitlessly pursuing a map.

Frustrated, I squatted against a building to eat the remainder of the English cookies that Chowdbury had so generously given to me back in Myitkyina. A pound and a half of sweet cookie filled my stomach cavity, and it would be a pound and a half less baggage for me to haul around. The odor of urine was strong in the street. The number of men I saw relieving their bladders exceeded the number of holy cows doing likewise. Peddlers were hawking their wares, and food vendors lined the streets- but no one sold maps.

I would just have to go from town to town by train, hoping that I would not get sidetracked again. I returned to the jailhouse to pick up my belongings. I became angered when the official informed me I would have to go to the Deputy Commissioner to obtain permission to leave Dibrugarh Town. The red-hatted policeman called a trishaw over to us, and ordered me aboard. I had but a few minutes to catch the bus to Jorhat, and if I missed it, I would not get out of town until the following day. The trishaw driver was in no hurry as he pedaled the bike the several blocks to the commissioner's house. I was raging mad, as I jumped to the ground and raced into the commissioner's office. Even if I had entered the country illegally, or sneaked on a train, I had not been noticed, they had no right to detain me now. It was an injustice. I pushed the door open with a bang and stepped up to the deputy commissioner's desk. Throwing my passport at him, I blurted out in no uncertain terms how I felt about their stupid regulations. The police guard said nothing as I filibustered in an outraged tone. The deputy looked flabbergasted. I grabbed the passport out of his hand and jumped into the trishaw and hollered at the driver to start pedaling. The guard came running up behind me and grabbed hold of the trishaw and hopped in. He did nothing to stop me. He just sat next to me with a bewildered expression.

We turned a corner and headed down a broad dusty street when a voice from our rear bellowed, "Stop! Stop! Get in here, get in here!"

My escort and I both turned our heads to see who was doing the shouting. Then I read the sign on the lawn of the house we had just passed. "COMMISSIONER OF POLICE, LAKIMPUR". The middle-aged commissioner was running out to the road waving his arms and shouting for the driver to stop. I told him to keep pedaling. He stopped.

By now the commissioner was beside us with a plainclothesman.

"Give me the knife, and get inside here. Where do you think you're going?" he shouted. I grabbed my pack and the cloth bag containing Chin. I had to put him into it to smuggle him on the bus. I dropped both bags by a tree, as the guard took hold of my arm and shoved me toward the commissioner's house. I was fighting mad, fed up with the stupid police. The commissioner and his aide took a seat on the veranda as the guard held me before him.

"What are you doing here, who are you, where are you going, where did you get the knife, what's in your bags?" And he noticed that the green cloth bag that Chin was in was hopping about the lawn. He was shocked. "You have something in the bag. What is it?" he jumped back as the bag moved closer.

"It's just a cobra I picked up in friendly Burma, I answered disconcertedly.

"A what?"

"I said 'it is just a friend of mine, a monkey'."

"You are also cruel, keeping a monkey in a bag – let him out now!"

"I would, but he bites. I wouldn't want him to hurt you, Officer," I said as sarcastically as possible.

"Give me your passport."

I tossed it on the table and asked "Sir, may I use your toilet?"

"How did you know I have a toilet?" he asked tersely.

"I assumed a man of your importance would certainly have a toilet, Sir."

"I have one, but why do you want to see it?"

"I don't care if I see it, I just want to use it," I said in desperation.

"Why do you want to use it?" he asked.

I was dumbfounded by his stupidity but I tried to explain the situation to him. "Look mate, I got some business to attend to. I gotta get to the toilet, outhouse, privy, john – I don't give a damn what you call it, but you better let me go now or you're going to have a messy porch."

He seemed to be convinced at last and sent me with the detective to a ramshackle privy behind his house. I walked in and started to shut the door, but the detective held it open, probably concerned I would jump through the hole.

I felt relieved when I returned to the commissioner. He was studying my passport and the visas from other countries as if he were boning up for an exam. I asked him what bearing my Australian visa had on his apprehending me. He seemed at a loss for an explanation, and after many more ridiculous questions, let me go and told the guard to direct me to the bus station.

The rickshaw driver was still waiting for his money. I was not about to pay for it, I did not order it, and besides how did I know the police department hadn't already reimbursed him by this time? When I left the guard and the rickshaw driver at the bus station, they were still quarreling over who would pay the fare.

I tossed my backpack on top of the bus, bought a ticket for a few rupees and piled aboard to be packed in like a sardine by the overflow of passengers. Chin was still in is bag, I did not want him to be seen for the border official at Nampong had informed me that animals are charged fares the same as humans and I did not want to take any chances.

Luckily, the bus was an hour late in leaving or I would have had to spend the night in Dibrugarh Town. The air in the bus was nauseating from the foul breath of the spice loving Hindus. They spat their betel nut juice on the floor or on the feet of standing passengers. The luggage racks were crammed with cardboard boxes and time-worn cloth sacks containing the passengers' belongings.

The bus rumbled down a narrow bumpy road along the broad Brahmaputra River valley. The land was very flat, broken only by occasional villages, or isolated huts. Coolies were rebuilding the roadbed and bridges that had been damaged by the most recent flood.

The rickety bus reached Jorhat sometime after dark. I was beat from the day's heat as I plodded wearily down the main street of the village. The train would not leave until past midnight. I wanted to sleep, but the streets were crowded with people, cows, traffic, and blaring Hindustani music. I did not think it would be wise to sleep on the streets along with the Hindus, for they looked so wretched and hungry that I would not blame them for trying to take my meager possessions if they had the opportunity. Some of the shops were closing up their fronts with steel grates. I went into a couple of them and through the use of pantomime asked the proprietors if I could spend the night on their floors, but they either did not understand me or they did not approve of my bedraggled appearance.

The food for sale on the streets did not appeal to me, and the decent food would be out of my reach, so I satisfied myself with a cup of tea. A crowd of Hindus gathered around to fondle my knife and poke into my pack making me uneasy. I made my way out of town to the train station. The station was fenced off so that it was impossible for me to sneak onto the train without a ticket. I purchased a ticket to the next town, just a few miles away. This would allow me to board the train and I would simply "forget" to get off at the next stop. The station platform was piled high with cargo, and hundreds of natives, many of them in rags, sleeping on the concrete platforms. Whole families would be crowded together; women in their saris with shawls over their heads, barefooted, or sandals because in addition to being too costly, conventional were not only too hot, but did not come off easily when entering a home.

I lay down on the concrete, and wrapped the straps of my sack and knife around my arm so I would be awakened if anyone tried to walk off with them. Chin snuggled up by my beard inside my coat: he presented no problems at night for he slept soundly as a rule. When the train finally did awake me, I was too late to find a seat. People were pushing and shoving their way aboard, through the windows, knocking old women around without preference. I stood all night long as the train crept along at a snail's pace. It would just get moving and it would start braking for the next station.

There was not enough room to allow me to sit on my backpack, or to squat on the floor. Even the filthy toilet was crowded with the standing. It was no more than a small cubicle with a hole in the concrete floor through which waste was supposed to drop, but more often than not, ended up on the floor. The barefooted peasants were left standing in offal, the stench proportionately sickening. The luggage racks were crowded with people, some hunched in between the racks and the low ceiling, while others had the arrogance to stretch out. They would spit down onto our heads, and those who were sitting would spit on our feet, or clean their nostrils with a violent exhalation through one nostril at a time. Bags of rice and chickens, sugar cane, and almost anything imaginable was wedged among us. There was but one consolation: the ticket inspector would not be able to work his way through the carriage, so I could spend the night without the possibility of detection. Some people clung to the outside of the carriage steps. At each stop a few people would climb out the windows while others would come in from the opposite side. The doors could not be opened inward: we were jammed up against them. Everyone in the car looked miserable.

When dawn came, the passengers thinned out. Those who had sneaked on the train during the night departed with daylight, for the inspectors would make the rounds frequently, looking for parasites such as myself. But with the dawn, also came those who could not see. Blind men, woman, and boys would stumble along the tracks at many of the stations, holding up their frail arms for money. Their faces were pitiful, some of them a mass of scars. In addition to them, there were the cripples, the limbless, the poor and above all the professional beggars. Many dogs walked along the tracks, heads low, looking for morsels to eat. Often the train would pull out before the vendor could collect his money. If he did not sell from a pushcart, then he would jump aboard the carriage to argue, or fight it out with a customer, and get off at the first station to catch the next train back.

I was exhausted having to keep awake all day and the previous night for lack of space to lie down. I dozed frequently in the sitting position, but the train jerked so much, and there were so many passengers coming and going that I could not sleep. At each stop, I would poke my head out the window to see what car the inspector was in. The car did not have doors running between them, so the inspector could not surprise us by entering our compartment when the train was in motion. At each station, when he got to the compartment next to ours, I would climb out of the compartment I was in and go into the one that he had just inspected.

By late afternoon, the train came to a halt and all the passengers disembarked. I had read in some informative tourist report that it was easy for a person to travel in India because English was so widely spoken. In fact, at least forty percent of the population was supposed to have a working knowledge of English. I would like whoever wrote that to take a ride on a third class train in Assam. I could not find a single person who could tell me why everyone was getting off, nor had I encountered anyone since I had boarded the train who had spoken to me in English. Instead, they just stared at me and made no bones about continuing to stare into my eyes when our glances should meet.

Everyone else got off the train, so I did. The station signboard said Pandu, which meant nothing to me. I hopped down from the train and walked along the platform behind the others. Then it dawned on me that we had come to the edge of the Brahmaputra River and there was no bridge crossing it. A river ferry was docked not far away. There was a mad scramble as the coolies grabbed the bags of the wealthy, put them atop their heads and rushed aboard. I was caught in the mob and pushed aboard by those behind me. A few minutes later, the ferry docked on the north side of the river and the mad scramble began for the waiting train. Those who were slow would not find standing room. I was too heavily loaded to run as fast as the empty handed, and by the time I reached the train, the only entrance was through the windows, so I tossed my pack and sack in and climbed through.

It was dark soon afterward, how I envied the lucky few who were sleeping luxuriously in the luggage racks, even though it was constructed of hard wood slats, it was relatively comfortable looking, and offered a semblance of privacy. This was my second consecutive night spent in misery. I was on the verge of collapse from the heat of the day, the smells, lack of food and sleep deprivation.

A score of sharply dressed Hindu soldiers were pushing their way into one of the carriages as the train came to a halt. They were a clean looking bunch next to their civilian counterparts, clean by any standards for that matter. I fell in behind them, but as soon as they got on the train they began tossing the civilians already there out the doors and windows to the platform. If anyone gave them any resistance, they would just toss the poor bloke's bags out the window, and when he went to retrieve them, they barred the doors and windows.

One of the soldiers took me for a foreign soldier in my khakis and his cohorts pulled me in through the window. There is a universal fellowship among soldiers regardless of their homelands, providing they are not officially at war with each other's countries. The spokesman for the group spoke English so I told him I was no longer a soldier, but had been, and he translated what I had said to his cohorts. They slapped me on the back, showing their approval of the monkey and me. He said they would take care of any trouble and they meant what they said. Each of us suddenly had a luggage rack or part of a bench to stretch out on from the point forward. There were just enough civilians allowed in the compartment to keep it from being too crowded. They unscrewed the lights and all was in darkness for the remainder of the night. In the morning they treated me to tea, and we exchanged smokes. I offered them some of my dry oatmeal, but they refused. I had eaten nothing substantial since leaving Digboi four days back, but my stomach was used to going without food by this time.

A ticket inspector got on our car about noon, all soldiers had travel papers, and when he came to check me he was so fascinated with Chin that he forgot to ask for my ticket. All he wanted to see was Chin's ticket. I shrugged my shoulders pretending that I did not understand what he meant, why would a monkey have a ticket? Ridiculous. I asked the soldier spokesman what the inspector meant and the soldier and his buddies quickly made the inspector feel cheap, by accusing him of taking advantage of me, as they put it. How was I supposed to know that monkeys needed tickets to ride the trains?

By late afternoon, the train passed into a desert of white sand, the wind stirring up a storm, while hundreds of beggarly Hindus stood by the rails to grab onto the train as it passed slowly through the desert. It was not more than a few miles further when we came alongside the muddy Ganges River. Once again, the train came to a halt and everyone jumped off as fast as they could and began the quarter mile scramble to the paddle-wheel ferry boat. I scrambled off with the soldiers, but soon lost them in the crowd. Coolies carrying bags, footlockers and other gear were trotting along behind their customers to the boat. I stood hemmed in by bony bodies, wondering if I would get picked up for not having a ticket, when one of the ship's officers beckoned for me to come up to the first class deck, as only fitting for a white man in India.

As I climbed the stairs, Chin ran along the railing. The man who had beckoned to me was none other than the Captain. He did not ask me to produce any credentials; he was only interested in learning what a white man was riding in the third class compartment for. I told him that I was not very familiar with the class system, for I had only been in the country a few days.

The whistle blew and the steamboat paddles churned the water as the boat headed down the broad Ganges. The water level was very low, and the narrow navigable channel was full of sticks. In monsoon time, the river floods the land for miles on either side of its banks. Several miles downstream the ferry pulled up to a dock and the coolies on the dock made a mad scramble to get a hold of all the baggage. People were shoving, elbowing and punching their way to the gangplank so they could get to the awaiting train before all the space was taken. I waited my turn and filed in behind the coolies. As I walked down the narrow springing gangplank, I noticed that there were ticket takers standing at the end of the gangplank collecting ferry tickets. The heavily laden porters did not have to pay I noticed, for they had just boarded the ferry to retrieve luggage. I placed my backpack atop my head with Chin on my shoulder and advanced toward the collectors. Luckily the sun was down and it was just dark enough so that I passed by the ticket takers without trouble. They had mistaken me for a lowly Moslem porter.

The awaiting train had not yet arrived, and all those who had fought so desperately to get off the ferry first were now waiting along with the rest of us. I met my soldier friends again, and they told me to place my gear with theirs for safekeeping. It was a nice feeling to be able to trust them in a land where life is so cheap, and thievery and corruption are common practice. One can hardly condemn the miserable masses for their crimes, for I realized that if I were one of them I would not hesitate to steal- or even to kill- if I were starving. I could not stand the gnawing of my stomach any longer and began to look around to see what the various peddlers were selling. I spent a few minutes sampling numerous bits of food, and at last I found one that tasted quite delicious. It was a ball of spiced curry rice covered in pastry, about the size of a plum. I bought three of them and gulped them down. I chased around and found the same vendor again and bought more, and stuffing myself like a pig, dashing to the water barrel between purchases to wet the hot spices. Before the train arrived I had eaten the vendor out of his stock.

I learned that we were in the province of West Bengal and would be in Calcutta sometime the following morning. One more night to spend on the train of misery. What a relief it would be to get to Calcutta, where I hoped to be able to line up some sort of lift to West Pakistan. At least I would meet some foreigners, and be able to speak English again. All through the night natives who tried to crowd into our compartment bothered us. Fights broke out a couple of times between the soldiers and the civilians. They treated old women with no more respect than the scrawny men. The soldiers always won, even though we were outnumbered; they fought as a team.

It promised to be a hot muggy day as the sun showed itself early the next morning. Towns and villages were getting larger and closer together as we neared Calcutta, and then ran together completely, forming the suburbs of this vast city, the largest in India, with a population of millions, perhaps many of them homeless beggars. I had often heard Calcutta referred to as "Earth's anus" and I was soon to find out why. The train slowed as it entered the city limits, and I could see locals bathing in filthy ponds of stagnant water near the tracks.

Chapter 25:

Calcutta: Overwhelmed by Humanity

I ARRIVED AT the Howrah terminal on March 15, 1957. We piled out and headed for the gates. My soldier comrades surrounded me and therefore when the ticket taker asked for mine, the soldiers pushed me though the exit like I was one of them. We said farewell in the station. The troops were going to their homes on leave.

I walked through the massively crowded station to the exterior where I was immediately besieged with beggars and rickshaw drivers who wanted to drum up business. Scores of homeless were sleeping on the sidewalk in front of the station. I crossed over the busy Hoogly River crammed with boats of every description. A young Hindu directed me to which streetcar I needed to take to the center of the city. As soon as the conductor saw Chin, he shoved us out the door. I hid Chin inside my jacket, behind the Nagga handbag, and boarded the next streetcar. I did not know where I was going except that I wanted to get to the center of the city, where I planned to check with foreign import and export firms to see if I might catch a ride west in one of their cargo trucks.

Most of the buildings near the river were made of red brick. The sidewalks are narrow and cluttered with garbage. When the streetcar came to a large, well-tended park surrounded by prominent looking buildings, I followed my instincts and disembarked. An Englishman out for an early morning stroll informed me that I could find cheap lodging at the Salvation

Army which was just a few blocks away, right off Chowringhee, the town's main thoroughfare. Holy cows were mulling in the streets, creating traffic jams. More beggars, young and old, approached me for handouts, many of them too weak to move their bodies from the hot pavement. People would step over them rather than walk around. I found the Salvation Army hidden behind one of the red brick walls. Rhesus monkeys were sunning themselves and picking through each other's hair on the windowsills of the neighboring buildings. They were fierce looking with their sharp teeth and chattered loudly when they noticed Chin, who screamed in fear of his larger brethren.

The inside of the Salvation Army was old-fashioned and plain, but the cleanest establishment I had seen in India so far. A neatly dressed, barefooted servant took me to the woman who was in charge of the establishment, a tiny, middle-aged English woman. She was pleasant, yet very businesslike. She was running a home for paying guests, not the poor. The charge was ten rupees a day with Western meals, a steep price, but when I saw the food that was being served to the other guests, I could not refuse. I signed the register and joined two men at a table for breakfast. The waiter brought us eggs, toast, fruit juice and coffee, even water that was fit to drink. Chin was not allowed in the building, so I tied him up outside.

One of the guests, a middle-aged journalist, was rushing through his breakfast, excited about his next assignment, which was to commence immediately after breakfast. He would be taking off for Pakistan to write about the war between two tribes in that area. He felt like a real "bushman" as he proudly displayed his camping equipment, all of which was shining new. It was his first experience at roughing it, but he assured me he would not go into the area of turmoil itself, but gather his material from a nearby town. Another chap at the table was a fair-dinkum Australian, about my age, named Bruce. He was affiliated with the YMCA in Australia, but was traveling by plane to Kessel, Germany, for the international "Y" rally. He had stopped off in Calcutta to check in on this place, and was leaving the next day for Germany. When I told him I had just come from sunny Australia myself, the conversation shifted to Sydney. I told him one of his countrymen by the alias of Alf Rockcliffe had relieved me of thirty-five dollars in Sydney just before I had started my trip. Of all the coincidences, Bruce had worked with Alf's brother through the "Y", and Bruce informed me that Alf was now spending six months at Long Bay, which is Sydney's formidable jail. It made me feel better that he had not gotten off scot-free.

Bruce informed me that I would not be able to check with any firms today, even though a work day, because it was a national holiday. I decided to scout the firms in advance so that when they did open, I'd know right where to go. I walked around in circles trying to locate the Afghan Embassy and the Persian Embassy for the directions I had obtained were far from accurate. I was walking down Chowringhee when I spied what was obviously an American tourist. A tall, slender, blond- dressed in tight black trousers, sporting a white shirt with broad vertical black stripes, and an expensive camera slung over one shoulder had sauntered past me accompanied by a well-dressed Hindu. We smiled at each other as we passed, for it seemed wonderful to see people with whom I had more in common. I was not surprised when he came running back to ask me if I was an American.

When I told him how I happened to be in the city, he squealed with delight. He introduced himself as Ray Kidd, an American singer. I recalled seeing his picture in the paper back in Digboi, "RAY KIDD, SINGING HIS WAY AROUND THE WORLD". He asked if it would be possible for us to get together later in the day, so I told him to meet me at the Salvation Army at noon. I was a little embarrassed to so bluntly say where I was staying, especially when he was probably living in some posh hotel.

I met Ray Kidd in the otherwise empty lounge for lunch.

"Till," he said. "I won't beat round the bush... I'm queer. I want to make a deal with you."

"Well, what is it?" I asked, a bit shocked by his frankness.

"From what you've told me of your travels, you haven't had much night life. How would you like to be my guest at Firpos tonight? It is one of the swankiest nightclubs in Calcutta. I have to sing there. I will foot the bill for the feast and drinks. All I want you to do is spend the night with me afterwards. We can have the whole upstairs of the Firpos mansion to ourselves. The rest of the troupes are living on the first floor. Gosh, I hope you're not mad at me for asking."

"No, I'm not mad. At least you're honest."

"Well, how about it then? Is it a deal?" he asked eagerly.

I must admit it would be a pleasure to spend the evening with Europeans in a night club, to eat a fine meal, watch a show, and have a few drinks in an air conditioned bar. After what I have been through the last few months, it would be great, but as for spending the night with him, or any other man, that is something I could not do. I may be poor, sick, hard up and desperate, but there is a limit to what I will do. I had met all kinds of people during my travels, and do not condemn nor condone other peoples' behavior. I'm able to live with my conscience most of the time. "Thanks for the offer, but I'd better get in and eat before it's too late," I said politely, closing the subject.

Ray accepted my refusal with a shrug of his shoulders. "We can be friends, Till, have it your way, then, and you are still invited to Firpos. Here's the address of the Firpos mansion, meet me there at 6, if there is anything you need in the way of clothing, I have it for you."

As soon as Ray left I went into the dining room for lunch. I felt sick inside, knowing that a guy with his talent, and money could do most anything in life, yet he was hardly able to live by himself, in fact seemed lonely. I went up to the room I was sharing with Bruce and unpacked my dress clothes for the first time in three months. They were a mess, musty and crumpled. I borrowed the housekeeper's iron and straightened and hung them out on the roof to air. I took my worn low shoes out to get them dyed from brown to black. Several shoeshine boys hounded me and I bargained with them until one of them offered to dye them for a rupee, probably still double the going rate.

Finally cleaned and attired as well as I could manage, I took off for a night of entertainment at Firpos where Ray and his troupe were stating at the invitation of the night club owner. A starving Hindu was squatting by the sewer across the street, picking up rice kernels from the slimy gutter and moving his thin arm to his mouth with each grain. Scores of rickshaw drivers asked me if I wanted a girl. I walked down Chowringhee to the gate where the guard let me through. Ray and the other entertainers were in the hallway, just about ready to leave. There were Kitty, and Bob Anderson, the famous dance team, and the combination MC and comedian Al, a stocky Englishman. Ray ran up and procured a white shirt and a black tie for me, which I quickly donned and we piled into a large taxi and were off.

The Firpos Nightclub was air-conditioned and the beer deliciously cool. We moved into the ballroom dining room where the five of us sat at one table and feasted on chicken, fish, champagne, and local specialties. The elegant, stately room was crowded with hundreds of foreigners decked in fine evening dress. A young English businessman named Regi joined our table for the remainder of the evening. He seemed fascinated by my travels, and asked me to be his guest for the night. I told him that I had already obtained accommodations at the Salvation Army, where upon he tried to persuade me to spend the night at his expense adding he would gladly pay the Salvation Army bill. Drinks flowed like a river. Ray did not act too kindly with Regi, for he could not bear the thought of me spending the night away from him. I was only too glad to remain with the Andersons who invited me to join them at the Golden Slipper club, which remained open till four in the morning. I was a real popular guy that evening. Ray finally gave up on me about midnight and left in a disheartened mood. Ed, the Andersons, Regi and I remained in Firpos until closing time, somehow in the surge of exiting night clubbers I lost track of the Andersons who had invited me to join them at the Golden Slipper. I hoped into a rickshaw and told the driver to take me to the place. After much backtracking he finally pulled up in front of the Golden Slipper club. The street was dimly lit. I banged on the front door but the guard would not let me in. I protested, telling him that the Andersons had invited me, but he said the place was now closed to additional customers for it was too late.

I walked out to the dark street, where a Hindu was reliving himself into the gutter. I asked him where Chowringhee was, but he just looked at me, and said nothing. Three other figures advanced toward me from around the corner, one of them pulling a rickshaw. I asked them how to get to Chowringhee, but they had other things on their mind. As I was well dressed they probably took me to be a well-to-do foreign business man. They hovered around me like greedy vultures, their eyes deep set. As they shoved me around I felt a bony hand near my wallet pocket. Despite my alcohol-infused brain, my adrenal glands functioned superbly. Flinging out my arms with all the force I could muster the two on either side of me staggered back.

"Ahhh, you filthy bastards, just let me get my hands on you," I bellowed. The thug to my rear grabbed his rickshaw and darted down the street behind the others. I took after them, and within a short distance, caught hold of the racing rickshaw. I flipped it over on its side much to the surprise of its owner who continued to run down the street. For once in India, I felt I was in the right, so I flipped the buggy upright and decided to take it to the police. I grabbed hold of the drawbars and jogged down the alley pushing the rickshaw backwards so that I could keep an eye on my assailants should they return. It must have been about close to dawn by now, the dark, dirty narrow streets empty and quiet except for an occasional cow, or sleeping beggar.

I turned my head to find that all three men were chasing me. I raced on, turning up one dark alley after another in an attempt to shake my pursuers. I could see streetlights about a quarter of a mile down the road. The rickshaw pushed easily once it had momentum. As I neared the lights, the three were gaining on me. With a final adrenalin-fueled burst of speed, I raced to the lighted intersection. Suddenly, a wheel on the rickshaw caught in a pothole and catapulted out of my hands, landing on end, crushing in the canvas canopy. The wheels were still spinning as I swung from the draw poles trying to create leverage to right the buggy. My three followers were now surrounding me, as was a fourth man who had witnessed the accident from the corner of Chowringhee. He was dressed in western clothes, had a light complexion, and spoke both English and Hindustani well.

I explained to the newcomer what had happened. "You are within your rights, but you had better forget the matter. You would not stand a chance in a court in this city," he said in a sympathetic tone. Before I had a chance to consider his advice, a militaristic policeman marched up, swinging his Billy-club. He spoke no English, but his Billy-club spoke volumes and we were on the way to the police station within seconds. The man who had told me to forget the incident had vanished. I tucked in my shirt and straightened my tie to look my best before the official who would undoubtedly tend to us at the station house.

The sidewalk in front had been torn up to lay a new sewer pipe so that we had to climb over mounds of mud to enter the building. The policeman herded us into the front room. The night clerk in charge of the front desk retreated to another room to fetch a heavy set Hindu in pajamas who stumbled into the room, rubbing his eyes. The policeman who had "arrested" us jabbered to the man in pajamas. He was in a foul mood when he asked me what had happened. I told him that the three men had tried to rob me, and that I had taken their rickshaw. He blurted out a command to his able bodied henchmen who spared no time or effort in beating the three Hindus with his club. They held up their arms to shield themselves in vain, for the cop clubbed them about their bodies, and lastly on their legs causing them to collapse in a heap on the floor. As they tried to get up he continued to beat them. I could stand the brutality no longer and jumped in between, trying to protect the three Hindus. The magistrate called the clubber off, and I told him the men had been punished enough. He wanted to lock them up, but he took my advice and let them go. The sun was about to rise as I walked out of the station and retraced my steps back to Chowringhee and the Salvation Army where I took a much-needed rest.

I checked with a number of British firms in vain, looking for a lift to Delhi or points to the North West. In desperation I went down to the Hoogly River to see about getting a hop on a ship to Europe. Just about every Hindu was covered with reddish dye for it was the Holi Festival of Colors. People were throwing it on each other in powder form as well as smearing it on their bodies. Even the holy cows were spotted with flaming red color! On the way back to the hotel I passed scores of Hindus getting their ears cleaned out from men on the sidewalks, who used cotton covered sticks to poke around with. A woman passed me carrying a large basket of cow dung on top of her head, piled four feet high. Three Tibetans dressed in rags were causing quite a stir by selling stones of doubtful value from their cigar box showcase. Much of Calcutta is cluttered with makeshift homes on the sidewalks, streets lined with homeless, miserable starving people.

I packed my bags upon returning to the hostel so that I would be able to get an early start out of Calcutta in the morning. I had breakfast, paid my bill, and walked back to Firpo's mansion to return Ray's shirt and tie that I had borrowed. The gate man let me through and I spoke with Ray's servant on the second floor who was preparing his breakfast to be served in bed.

"Oh, Thill, I thought you had abandoned me!" Ray screamed with delight when the servant showed me to his room. "What on earth happened to you, why didn't you come over yesterday?"

"I ran into a bit of trouble after I left Firpos-ended up with a rickshaw at a police station."

"What a relief, I thought you had spent the night with Regi," sighed Ray.

"I'm leaving for Delhi today, so here's your shirt and tie."

"Thill, I know you are headed west, how would you like to work for me, I have engagements in Rangoon, Singapore, and Japan which will keep me going for several months, how would you like to be my secretary, and traveling companion, you won't have to travel in rags, I will see to it that you live in style."

"You're wasting your time, Ray, barking up the wrong tree."

"But Thill, I'm desperate!"

As I was getting up to leave, a teenage Hindu ran into the room, dressed in tight fitting pants and a sweatshirt. His hair was done up in D.A. style (Duck Tail). Throwing out his arms, he dropped the package he was carrying as the two embraced. His nails were manicured, his eyelashes coated with mascara, and his eyebrows were plucked into sculpted perfection.

"Ray!"

"Gigi, what are you doing in Calcutta? I thought your mother would not let you leave Bombay."

"Oh, Ray, I missed you so, I told mother I was serious about you, and she let me come, but daddy is very angry." Gigi glanced jealously at me. "You told me you needed me Ray- you *are* happy to see me, aren't you?" he said with great doubt in his voice.

"Of course I'm glad to see you, Gigi."

I shook my head and walked out, wondering what the world was coming to. Time to fetch Chin and my backpack. I took a bus to the outskirts of the city, but not before dealing with the conductor's wrath about the monkey. It was a relief to be leaving Calcutta.

Chapter 26.

Riding the Rails to the Iranian Border

THE COUNTRYSIDE ONCE again was a welcome relief from the crowded sea of humanity left behind in the city. The warm sun enlivened me, and the fresh wind blowing through my clothing provided a natural air conditioner. The roadsides were lined with natives walking under heavy loads who looked up in astonishment when they saw a white man riding on the back of a truck. It is just not proper in India. The truck carried us about twenty miles and came to a halt in a small village. The style of huts was a variation on the typical bamboos I'd seen so much of: these were also covered with mud. The setting sun silhouetted hundreds of coolies as they carried baskets of clay in an endless procession to a grinder where it would eventually be made into bricks. The backlit coolies moved so gracefully in synchronicity, along the top of the mountain of earth and back again into the pit, which was over fifty feet deep and a quarter mile square. It had all been excavated by hand labor through the centuries. Man can indeed move mountains if he works long enough.

Despite my earlier luck, hitching rides in India was nearly hopeless, so I crossed over to the train station. Many trains arrived and departed but none of them were going very far, or at least not to any city that I had heard of such as Lucknow or Delhi. It was past midnight when I decided I was taking the next train regardless of its destination. To my surprise it was a military troop train and reserved. None of the hundreds of impoverished civilians boarded it. In desperation I waited until the train started to move out and then ran along beside it, opened a door and climbed into the small compartment at the end of one of the troop carriages.

It was a tiny cubicle with no more floor space than in an American car. There was a small luggage rack, as long as a card table top and half as wide, very close to the ceiling. I climbed into it with much effort and turned my face to the wall so that if any inspectors came aboard they would only see khaki clothing and presume I was a soldier. My legs swung off one end from the knees down. I was miserable, but it was better than stretching out on the floor to be caught by an inspector during the night.

In the morning, I jumped off the train at the next station. I could not complain; the train had covered a couple hundred miles during the night. However, I had no alternative but to walk directly past the gate guard, for the exit from the station was via an overhead walk, and a high mesh wire fence caged in all surrounding area. I strolled up to the guard and attempted to walk past him, but he stopped me.

"Where is your ticket?"

"I gave it to the conductor."

"What do you mean, you gave it to the conductor; don't you know that you must surrender your tickets when you get off the train? What did the conductor look like?"

"He was dressed in a tan shirt and pants, dark skinned, black haired and skinny. He came into the compartment last night while I was asleep and when he woke me up, I handed him my ticket," I lied. The description of the man was accurate, but of course, I had not given him any ticket.

"The man you gave your ticket to was not a conductor. They are dressed in black- you should know that. You will have to buy another ticket now," he said, pointing into the station.

"But sir, how was I to know the man was not a conductor? I do not speak Hindustani so when he held out his hand I gave him my ticket, how am I to know what your regulations are? I have only been in your country a few days." Chin was getting restless under my coat and I was desperate to get through the gate before he poked his head out.

"Perhaps you are telling the truth, you may proceed, but we shall see you again."

I walked out of the gate and walked slowly across the overhead causeway until I was out of his sight, wanting to break into a run, but not doing so for it would indicate my guilt. I wondered what he had meant by his statement that he would see me again. Turning onto the busy main road I passed slowly in front of the street vendors in hopes of finding something edible. An elderly man was cutting up old tires and converting them into sandals. I bargained with him, but he wanted too much. Dozens of Hindus crowded around to watch me, blocking off the road to traffic. I moved on slowly, hungry and exhausted from a poor nights sleep. Everyone stared, or followed, for a short distance. Dogs would bark, and police would check me every time I turned around.

Chin and I were wet with sweat as we plodded along the dusty road, past buildings plastered with drying patties of cow dung. I was stopped in my tracks by a horse that lay in the road on its side, dying under the penetrating sun, his mouth frothy, his eyes and body sores black with hungry flies, too weak to raise his tail to scare them off. He rolled trying to get up, only to fall back on his side. The Indians would not put the dying beast out of his misery for it was against their religion.

We walked on for several miles until Chin collapsed from the heat. A crowd of Hindus gathered around, accusing me of treating Chin cruelly by making him carry his own weight. I was nearly out of my mind from the heat myself, and lay down beside the monk under a tree. Chin and I drank from my canteen, and after a long rest we continued.

Sometime during the afternoon we got a lift in a truck to the holy city of Benares situated on the Ganges. Heavily laden camels were strutting along led by their masters. They alone did not seem to be affected by the heat. We moved on to the outskirts of town where truck after truck passed us, none offering us a lift. My boots were heavy and hot, and my pack felt as if it were filled with lead. I became feverish and unable to think clearly.

Across the road was a sandal shop. I trudged over and tried to bargain with the man to give me a pair of sandals for my heavy leather boots. Monetarily, my boots were worth a lot more, but he would not swap; sandals which are much cooler than shoes and he would be unlikely to travel to any place requiring boots. The salesman walked awkwardly due to his left leg being afflicted with elephantitis. It was rather unsettling; indeed his limb resembled an elephant's leg and foot in size.

At this point, I gave up the idea of hitchhiking in India and trudged back into town to the train station where I fell asleep on the platform. I dared not hop a train during daylight with the numerous inspectors patrolling. Sometime after darkness I bought a ticket for the next village, which was but a few miles away.

When the train pulled in I joined the fighting crowd of hopeful passengers by wedging into a carriage. All the benches were taken, as were the luggage racks. The isles were jammed with filthy, smelly locals, the women in their stained saris, and the men dressed in their dhotis, which resembled billowing diapers. I counted thirty-two people all jammed into the little compartment.

But I was ready to collapse from weariness and there was a section of floor space just before the unoccupied toilet's door. I lay down on my back and propped my feet against the windowsill of the compartment door with my torso in front of it. The natives stared at me in awe, as if I was an untouchable. I felt like one lying in one's own filth, but I was too beat to care. People spat red juice from the pans (betel) on my clothing. Their feet dripped with urine onto my coat as they made an endless procession over my body to the toilet. When they argued and pushed among themselves for more space, they would kick my sides with their bare feet.

I had managed to fall asleep, but I was rudely awakened sometime later by a heavy blow to my chest. The train was at a station and natives were being pushed in through the door window. Before I could get up fourteen bastardly crusty, scrawny young men came hurtling in through the window, feet first, landing on my chest. It was like counting sheep in a dream, yet these sheep were human and their filthy, cracked feet pounded into my prone body, the undersides of their dhotis dirtier than a babies dirty diapers. Once they climbed off my body, I worked myself to a standing position. The compartment was now so crowded that I could only get one foot on the floor for support. Those already in the car began shoving each other and shouting, complaining about the latest infiltration of passengers.

I could take the bodies pressing against me no longer, so packed that our faces were hitting each other, even when they coughed and spat. The stench of humanity was nauseating. Only those in the luggage racks were at all comfortable by comparison. The passengers were all so poor, undernourished and ragged; they resembled inmates of a concentration camp. Many of them looked as if they were on their last legs. How they put up with such conditions daily was beyond me; in my mind, death would be a relief to many of them.

I crawled out the window at the next stop, leaving my bags and cameras in the carriage. They did not seem important anymore. I put Chin in his cloth sack and climbed on to the adjacent carriage which was second class, a significant step up from the cattle car of third. It was relatively empty, but even more striking in contrast was that the people in this second class carriage were all heavy set, healthy looking specimens. None of them were sick or undernourished; they looked more like over-fed market-ready hogs. Their dhotis were pure white, and fresh. They looked smug and complacent. It was a great shock to think that in the adjoining car rode the poverty stricken, the unbearably poor outcasts of life, living more primitive than their own domestic animals. The carriage was twice as large, more elaborately appointed, and relatively clean. Reclining locals, and their wives took all the benches. A few of them stared at me as I stood in the doorway, wondering where I would bed down. The luggage racks were full of baggage and I was not bold enough to remove any of it, nor did any of the reclining Hindus move over to give me a seat.

I lay down in the aisle on the floor, and shoved Chin's bag under a bench so that the curious passengers would not get suspicious if Chin's bag started hopping around. Next to the bag was an elaborate gold vase containing rose-scented toilet water. Apparently it belonged to the wealthy looking woman who lay on the bench above it, dressed in an expensive sari. An inspector stepped into the car accompanied by a soldier; I pretended to be asleep when they pointed at me, which I could just barely see through the slits of my eyelids. They spoke in English and I was sure they would check for my ticket, which I had not purchased, but one of them said that I was an American, as if that meant I was certainly financially able to purchase a ticket, and they walked out. I was beginning to feel like I was a cat with more than nine lives, having slipped so many close calls.

The train chugged out of the station, I felt very uncomfortable. I was dressed as a tramp in comparison to the other passengers who nudged each other and stared at me. To make matters worse, Chin's bag started to hop around from under the bench into the aisle. I shoved it back many times, but it kept coming out again. The passengers were bewildered. Next, the toilet water vase rolled over. The woman was furious. I quickly stuffed Chin under my shirt and pretended to be asleep. I knew that I must get back to the 3rd class compartment before dawn to stand less chance of being detected. Except for the jarring of the floor as the train rattled over the unsmooth rails, I slept soundly.

Just outside Agra, an inspector entered the third class car moments after I had sneaked back. He did not check anyone else's ticket, but came directly to me.

"Why are you not riding 1st Class?"

"I prefer to ride 3rd Class."

"Is that your langur (monkey)?"

"Yeah."

"May I see his ticket?"

"Whose ticket?"

"The langur's ticket!"

"He did not get a ticket."

"You mean to say that you did not purchase a ticket for the langur?"

"Nobody told me monkeys needed tickets to ride 3rd Class."

"This is unusual. I think you are going to be in trouble- you had better come with me," he commanded. I followed him out of the carriage with chin on my shoulder and we entered a special car.

"Please take a seat. Would you care for tea?" he asked in a friendly tone. He called out to a servant from a cubicle and told him to fetch the tea. I was happy for a moment, thinking that the inspector was not such a bad egg after all. Then the servant returned carrying a silver tray upon which was an ornate pot of tea and two delicate cups. Such service astonished me. I felt like a celebrity as we sipped our tea, the servant clinging to my side.

"Thanks for the tea sir, you are very kind," I said.

"You are welcome, but don't you think you had better pay the man?" I placed a rupee into the servant's outstretched hand expecting change, but it did not come. The servant departed just as the train rattled and squeaked out of the station. The inspector then produced a book of railroad regulations.

"What is your destination?"

"I forgot the name of the place, but let me look at my ticket," I said as I fumbled through my wallet and found the ticket I had purchased in Benares for one stop so that I would not be picked up at the station without a ticket. "I can't pronounce the word, but maybe you will be able to," I said, handing the ticket to him.

"This is your ticket?" he asked, bewildered.

"Yes, is something wrong?" I asked naively.

"Why didn't you get off the train when you came to MANDUADIH?"

"The train hasn't arrived there yet," I answered, as if indignant.

"Manduadih is more than two hundred miles from here, the train would have reached there less than an hour after you boarded in Benares. This ticket is worthless. You will have to pay me the difference. You will have to buy a ticket for your langur as well."

"But sir, I did not know the train had reached Manduadih. I wanted to get off there. I must have fallen asleep by mistake. I had no idea Manduadi was so near Benares."

"I am sorry, but the regulations say that you must pay. Here, read them yourself." He handed me the book of regulations, opening it to the page concerning ticketless passengers.

"Your langur should have been in a cage in the baggage car. You will have to pay double for having him in the passenger carriage, and because the langur has no ticket, you must pay the penalty having an animal in the passenger compartment- which is double the fare. Since your ticket is no good, I will have to charge you twice the normal 3rd class rate," he said as he began to figure out what it would come to on paper. My heart was racing, but it was as much from anger as from fear of what I would do to get out of this one.

"I will pay you the normal rate for the monkey and I- to the next stop- where I will get off. But I will not pay you any more than the normal fare. How was I to know that monkeys needed tickets, or where Manduadih was? I have never been in your country before. It was up to the man that sold me the original ticket to tell me about tickets for monkeys."

"But I must obey the regulations, you saw them yourself."

"Yes, I saw the regulations, but you must make exceptions!"

"If we made exceptions, there would be no need to have regulations. You must pay nineteen rupees for the langur's ticket. I am still working out your fare." He calculated on his abacus and handed me the bill.

"Nineteen rupees for the monkey! He only cost me fifteen rupees to buy in the first place. I won't pay it! You can keep the monkey. You treat me as if I deliberately tried to sneak the monkey and myself on the train," which was the truth, but I exercising the power of indignation.

"You do not wish to pay me."

"I won't pay you beyond the normal fare."

"Perhaps the railway police in Delhi will change your attitude."

"But I don't want to go to Delhi- it is out of my way. I want to get off at the next station."

Four hours later I was escorted off the train by two inspectors straight into the Delhi Railway Police Headquarters. The inspector handed a sheet detailing my offenses to the desk sergeant.

"What seems to be the matter?" he asked, looking directly at me.

"Why am I being charged such an exorbitant fare? They treat me as a criminal." The sergeant spoke with the two inspectors in Hindustani dialect, thought a moment, and turned to me.

"Please follow me. This is most unusual. The Chief of Police will need to see you." I was led into another office there I was confronted with a pleasant, intelligent looking official. First I told him my version of what had happened, and then the man who booked me told his story and produced the bill for the combined fares of the monkey and me as proof.

"I sympathize with you Mr. Wallace, but now that the bill has been written up, you will have to pay nineteen rupees for the monkey, and eleven rupees for your fare."

"You mean that it is going to cost me nearly twice as much for the monkey as myself?"

"Under such circumstances, yes."

"Did you know that there were forty-five people in my compartment, and only benches for sixteen? The rest of us had to stand all night. I paid for a seat and I did not get one, and now you want to charge me double my fare, and four times for the monkey? I should send your government a bill for the misery I went through last night. It would probably have been more comfortable riding in the animal car."

"I realize our 3rd class compartments are rather crowded, but the fact is, you owe us thirty rupees."

"Sir, I am not blaming you, but I don't think it is fair. I will go to jail before I pay such an outrageous amount."

With that, he picked up the phone, and I was sent to the second floor to another official. They were stumped. This official called another official, maybe even Nehru himself, and I was volleyed back and forth for an hour. Now that I was booked, someone would have to pay thirty rupees. The bill could not be cancelled: someone had to account for it.

"Will you pay half the bill?" he asked.

"Yes, sir."

"That will be fifteen rupees."

"All I have is a traveler's check for ten dollars. Is there a bank near here where I can cash it?"

"Yes, the inspector will go with you so you will not get lost. We will hold your baggage until you pay the bill."

The inspector and I went to the nearest bank, but I knew beforehand the bank would not cash my check without me producing a currency declaration form on which to enter the transaction-and I had skipped that step when entering the country.

The inspector looked worried, for fear that he would have to pay the bill if I did not.

I knew the American Express could not cash the money either unless I produced the form. To act as if I were earnestly trying to cash the check, I called American Express on the bank's phone. The answer was a resounding "No". The inspector could not believe it, and so I let him hear the direct answer over the phone.

"I'm sorry, but there does not seem to be anyplace where I can cash my money legally," I said, mighty thankful for the technical difficulty.

"Come, one of my friends is a money changer. He will cash the check for us," he said, without conviction. We went out of the bank, turned up a side street and into narrow alley where we entered an oriental rug shop. The inspector had a word with the proprietor in his tongue. The proprietor got out his abacus and did some figuring. He reached in a box and counted out 40 rupees. On the black market my ten dollar check should bring 50 rupees at least, so I refused to accept it.

"I do not have the currency declaration form, therefore I cannot legally change money in India."

"But I will have to pay your fare if you don't," lamented the inspector.

"You told me yourself how important regulations are, you would not want me to make an exception would you?'

"Who would know that you changed your money illegally?"

"When I go through customs and immigration at the border they will check me. When they find that I have no declaration form they will contact Nampong where I entered India to see that the foreign currency I brought into the country is equal to the amount that I take out of the country. If I am short, they will accuse me of black market exchanging. You don't want me to go to jail do you?" Had he known the truth, that I had never received a declaration form in the first place at Nampong, he would have had an open and shut case. But this little secret I kept to myself. It was my only salvation.

Reluctantly, he followed me back to the railway station,

down-hearted at being foiled. I gloated to myself at this little non-existent tool that had the official baffled. The only way I could pay for the train ticket was to officially break another regulation. I did not hesitate to let it be known.

The chief official threatened to call the American Embassy and report me for getting a free lift on the train but they could not prove that I had intently sneaked aboard. In addition, I could tell the Embassy that the Indian officials tried to get me to cash my money illegally. The chief official was perplexed: he could not destroy the bill, nor could he call the American Embassy, nor could he jail me if I had the currency, but was unable to cash it. All during the questioning Chin had been growling at the various officials from his perch on my shoulder. They were careful to keep out of his reach. Although he was nearly harmless, he could bluff a large viscous dog into running for cover.

"We will let you go, Mr. Wallace, on the condition that you cash your check and pay your debt before you leave Delhi. Just to make sure you do not forget to pay, we will keep your personal belongings in our custody. If you should come back tonight when I am not here your baggage will be in the night officer's office. I will notify him that you are to receive your baggage when you pay us fifteen rupees," said the chief official.

"Do you want to keep the monkey as well?" I asked sarcastically.

"No! Take him with you! Get him out of here!"

Chin and I left the train station and headed for town with less than a dime in cash between us. Most of the afternoon had been lost double-talking with the police. A crowd of beggars was gathered together in the square in front of the station. It looked as if it were old home week, a macabre reunion of sorts. They all had one thing in common: legs as large as elephants from the disease.

We walked along the narrow alleys of Old Delhi until it opened to a busy broad street. Three well-dressed businessmen in western clothes were drinking cokes at a table on the sidewalk. Lying in front of them in blazing sun lay a human being, looking up at them. The most diseased, scrawny thing I had ever seen. Literally thousands of flies were crawling in its eye sockets and mouth, and undoubtedly laying eggs on a fist sized bloody growth that extended from the his abdomen. His feet were like leather, with gaping cracks in the soles from many years work as a beast of burden. The skin on his head was tighter than a drum. This person was yet alive for he moaned and his leg twitched. I was surprised that city officials had not removed him from the busy intersection, but instead had posted a traffic cop to direct the vehicles around him. I was somewhat surprised that no one had bothered to cover him: his torso was nude except for a handkerchief rag that someone had placed over the upper thigh region. Yet I was also *not* surprised for this was India and the human being was being treated as any other animal. Life is cheap, so miserably cheap that I wondered what it was all about. To what extent do we care about the calamities of others? If this were to be the end, was it not worth the struggle? As I walked away from the dying man, I felt like a hypocrite among hypocrites. I could have given him what little money I possessed to make his last days more pleasant, yet I needed it or I would become a beggar and thief myself.

I found someone who told me how to find the American Embassy, so I continued on through Old Delhi into New Delhi, the modern planned city of parks and broad boulevards with traffic circles in place of the old fashioned stop signs at intersections. It was a long walk, and very tiring in the hot sun. I passed many beautiful embassy estates and finally came to the American Embassy with its spacious beautiful lawn and gardens. A shiny black Cadillac was parked on the circular drive before the main entrance. I tied Chin to the entrance of the estate and walked up the drive where I was nearly turned away by the door attendant who was impeccably dressed in a dark uniform. He smiled and opened the door when I produced my passport. He had probably mistaken me for a homeless Pakistani like so many Hindus before him. I entered the modern, well-appointed building, furnished with fine office furniture and exotic hand-woven carpets. It was divinely cool inside, my footsteps echoing on marble floors. I asked the desk clerk if it would be possible to change a traveler's check for Indian money. He called in one of the employees, an American who introduced himself as Sam Marlan, a young friendly chap. He asked me to accompany him to his office where he checked my passport and then gave me the official rate of exchange in Indian rupees for the ten dollars.

Sam was extremely interested in my trip, having spent some time in Burma himself. He asked me about the Chinese building of troops on the northeastern frontier of Burma. They had gotten all kinds of reports but none of them had been confirmed. I was shocked to learn that our government had no better knowledge of the area than to have to rely on me for confirmation. I asked Sam if he knew anything about getting maps or visas of Pakistan and Afghanistan and also if he knew of any economical way to get there. He called a friend on the phone who had flown down from Lahore in Pakistan, in hopes of finding me a flight back. Unfortunately the plane was loaded to capacity. He advised me not to go through Afghanistan because the last American to do that had not been heard of since. It was silly reasoning, because people can get lost most anyplace for any number of reasons. I told Sam that I had run into much trouble with police in India, and not a single day had passed that I had not run up against the law in one form or another.

Sam advised me to see the American Ambassador, Mr. McDougal.

A few minutes later I was standing on the carpet in front of the omnipotent ambassador. He was an elderly man who looked somewhat like Dulles, with part of a finger was missing. He looked up through his spectacles and asked, "What is it?"

"Sir, my visa for India expired the day before I got into this country, neither I nor the border officials were aware of it at the time, but since then I have been detained by police at least once a day, sometimes three times a day. Is there any way I can get it renewed?"

"Let me see your passport. My God, lad, how did you ever get this far?!"

"It hasn't been easy, sir."

"There is nothing we can do: if you apply for a renewal they will throw you in jail. You got yourself into this mess. It's too late for you to come crying to me."
"What about leaving India? Am I apt to be apprehended at the border?"

"How you ever got this far is beyond me. But since you have, I believe you can do most anything. You had better just keep going and hope that your luck holds out." And with that dismissal, he lowered his eyes back into his paperwork.

"Thank you, sir."

Chin was waiting for me at the gate where I had left him, facing hundreds of large angry black birds flocked around the tree making passes at him, like strafing planes coming into attack, like a scene out of Hitchcock's "Birds". He was screeching with fear as I swooped him up to rescue him. It was too late in the day to file for visas for Afghanistan or Persia, so I wandered around looking for the Y.M.C.A. After many false leads I found it, but too late for the evening meal and there were no vacant beds. However, I noticed on the bulletin board that Bruce, the Australian bloke I had met at the Salvation Army in Calcutta was due here in the evening to give a talk on the functions of the Australian "Y".

Bruce was surprised to see me when he showed up to give the lecture to the students who made the "Y" their home. The main function of the "Y' in Australia was to give youth something to do in their surplus of idle time. This lessened the number of delinquents who found illegal ways of having fun by channeling their energy through a civic-minded organization. The Asian students listened to Bruce with skepticism that bordering on disbelief. On this continent, it's not a matter of creating projects for the idle since the vast majority of Asians are too busy sustaining bare bones existence. Almost no one had spare time, and those who did were not likely to have the energy to partake of outside activities due to a physical handicap or old age.

The next day I found the Persian Embassy to be closed. I found the Afghanistan Embassy also closed, but a caretaker informed me that a visa for Afghanistan would cost me ten dollars. Both embassies were honoring holidays in their homelands. I could not afford the Afghan visa. It would mean that I would have to go hundreds of miles out of my way through southern Persia, and then head north, rather than go almost due west from Lahore in Pakistan to Tehran.

Taking stock of my financial reserves, I found that I had a five dollar bill American and nearly ten dollars in rupees. I would not get very far on it, so reluctantly I wrote to my friends in Australia to have them forward the $140 that I had left with them for my fares across the Atlantic- if I got that far. I told them to send it to Tehran, Persia explaining to them that I would be stuck there until it arrived. There was also the possibility that I would be unable to get to Tehran to collect it, with the meager fifteen dollars I had left. I would just have to be more resourceful from here on in if I ever wanted to see America again.

Fortunately I already had a visa for Pakistan, which I had gotten in Sydney and was still valid. Once I crossed the border at least I would not be officially regarded as a man without a country. I couldn't leave Delhi in daylight because I had to retrieve my gear from the police which I couldn't do until I paid what I owed. My only hope was to get my bags from the night officer who had never seen me, and hop on a northbound train immediately thereafter. As darkness came, so did rain, and wind. It was a torrent, coming down as if from a break in a dike. The windows clattered, doors slammed and within minutes an inch of water covered the ground. I waited for the downpour to let up, but instead the street turned to a stream. I raced out of the building with Chin under my shirt looking for a rickshaw or taxi, or some means of getting into Old Delhi before the train departed. I ran to a busy intersection through ankle deep water, but all the taxis were full, rushing people to shelter, and many of them could not even forge the streets because of the increasing depth of water.

I finally found a motor scooter taxi that was available. The driver did not want to risk the drive to Old Delhi: reports had come in that the main roads were flooded and impassable. I pleaded with him and he agreed to try, but made no promise about getting to the station before train time. Coming to over a foot of water on the main street, stalled busses and cars surrounding us blocked us in. Luckily the scooter was more maneuverable than the stranded vehicles and we were able to backtrack and race on toward Old Delhi. The minutes ticked by until passing the train's scheduled departure. I dashed into the station to find that the train to Amaristar on the border had not arrived yet, the tracks had been flooded and it would be half hour late. I bought a ticket to the next town, so that I could get onto the platform.

Stuffing Chin under my shirt, I walked through the gate onto the platform and made sure it was the right one. The night policeman sat behind a desk near the door to the railway police office where my luggage was being held. I waited for the train to pull into the station, and then strode into the security police office like I belonged there, right past the officer. I picked up my bags and put on my trench coat, all of which were at the far end of the room. The officer jumped up as I walked toward the door. Whipping out my passport, I flashed it before him. He placed his hand on my arm, which I knocked away, surprising him. He looked at the passport and pointed to the words "R.F.D.2, Ontario, New York".

"Name?"

"Yeah, name!"

He picked up the telephone.

"I can't wait, my train is leaving for Calcutta!"

I ran out the door, my heart pounding. I left for Amaristar about one minute later on the northbound train. I was thankful this would be my last ride on a train in India. If I hung around much longer, they would have my picture posted at all the railway stations in the country. I tossed my gear into a luggage rack and climbed in beside it for a peaceful night's rest.

Late the next morning, the train pulled into Amaristar, the end of the line. I hung around on the platform until the ticket taker had collected the other passengers' tickets and walked unnoticed through the gate to freedom. It was eight miles to the border town of Wagha on the Attari road. I converted my rupees into Pakistani currency using a money changer for a poor exchange rate, but had no alternative. Chin and I, along with eleven natives crowded into an aged station wagon and headed for the border.

Half an hour later, I was standing before the Indian border authorities. They could not understand why I had not been issued a currency declaration form upon my entry into their country, but their reasoning was that if I had gotten this far without winding up in jail, then I must be within my rights. To make conversation, I asked one of the officials if any vehicles crossing the border today were headed for Europe.

"A car passed through this morning bound for London," he said nonchalantly.

"For London!?"

"Yes, London."

"Where is he headed? Do you know? Do you?"

"He said that he would spend the night in Lahore, at the main hotel."

"Can you give me his name, the type of car and his license number?"

"We are not supposed to give out such information. Why do you want to know all these things?"

"I need to contact him. I must go to Europe with him."

The official got out the registration book and opened it to the page where the London bound car was listed. I hastily jotted down the following facts: Occupant A.T. Rajah, Nationality Malayan, Make of Vehicle Triumph T-R-2, 2-seater, Color Red, Model 1956. I had no idea what TR-2 looked like, but cars being so rare in this part of the world- with the exception of large cities- I would certainly pounce on the first red car I came across. I gushed thanks to the Indian official and hurried up the road to the Pakistani customs and immigration station, praying that I was soon to find what I hoped would be my last ride out of Asia.

Chapter 27:

Pakistan & Chasing Rajah

UPON LEARNING THAT I was an American, the Pakistani border official invited me into his earthen-floored hut. He liked my beard, akin to his fellow bearded countrymen. His colleagues did not look in my bags, but gave me a hard time over Chin. Technically I was not allowed to take Chin into the country, but the officer made a concession and allowed the monk to continue.

I hustled up the road to where a bus headed for Lahore was parked, but missed it by a few seconds when it pulled out with a load of passengers from India. I thought I had missed my only chance for the day but a local man assured me that another bus would be along shortly. The only other traffic on the road consisted of natives passing by on donkeys.

This time, the driver did not charge for the monkey. I felt as if the Pakistani people were a friendlier group than the Hindustanis. The bus was crowded with veiled women, their entire bodies covered except their hands, legs hidden by ankle length pantaloons, and hooded shawls with only small veiled peepholes for them to see. Many of the men were carrying huge smoking pipes, two and a half feet long with a large pot at the base. One of them spoke English and told me how to find the main hotel in Lahore where I hoped to find A.T.Rajah.

The hotel was elegant and imposing, with beautiful botanical grounds. I felt very much out of place as I walked up the drive past vacationing Europeans sitting in the gardens sipping their drinks. I was dressed in dirty khakis and of course carrying my trusty backpack, a far cry from the handsome designer luggage lined up under the awning. I looked around for a red car to no avail. I left Chin outside tied to my shabby pack and entered into the lobby. My hopes of getting a lift with Rajah dwindled as the clerk informed me that no such man had booked into the hotel. At first I thought he was merely trying to protect his guests from being bothered by such a person as I appeared to be. Clothes indeed make the man, and in my case they had not only betrayed me, but also broken me. I demanded to see the guest book to make sure the clerk was not lying. He was not. I was beginning to feel a rising panic about missing Rajah before he left, and ran into town to register with the police as the border officials had warned me to do. They authorized me to travel through their district, but could give me no advice on the whereabouts of Rajah. I noticed a road sign: *London 6,900 miles*. If only I could find Rajah! Of course there was no guarantee that he would give me a lift even if I did find him, but he was my only hope. I spent all afternoon looking around Lahore for the evasive red car.

Early that evening, a western dressed Pakistani man approached me. He was a well-built, handsome dark native in his twenties. I asked him if he had seen a red car that afternoon, possibly headed for London. As life would have it, not only had he seen the car, but also he had spoken with its driver, A.T.Rajah. He worked in the local automobile club where Rajah had stopped for information and introduced himself as "Nathan". He was pleased to meet a Christian, as he was one himself, but life was hard in the Moslem country of Pakistan. He, too, wanted to see the world, but the Moslem authorities would not even grant him a passport because of his unorthodox religion.

I strained to glean every bit of information Nathan could share about Rajah. According to him, Rajah was in a great hurry to get to London. He had been driving from Madras in southern India as fast as road conditions would allow. He was headed for Quetta, about eight hundred miles away. There was only one road that led to Quetta, but there was no way I could catch him even if I did get a lift in another vehicle, which was highly improbable. Nathan suggested that I take a train to Quetta, so I enlightened him on my financial predicament. He told me that it was impossible to sneak on a train and ride undetected for such a distance.

We went to the railway station where I checked on the schedule and fare to Quetta. It would cost thirty-nine rupees and I had only twenty-five, plus a five dollar bill. I decided to gamble on the train even though it would mean that I would land in Quetta with about two dollars to my name. Nathan advised me to keep

Chin concealed, for animals were not allowed to ride for free. To make matters worse, I had to convert my five dollars into rupees before I could purchase a ticket- and the banks were closed. Nathan recognized an old friend with his horse drawn carriage, waiting for business in front of the station. Nathan knew where the American High Commissioner of Pakistan lived, so he talked his friend into giving us a lift in hopes that I would be able to cash my American money with him, at the legal rate of exchange.

Several minutes later the cart drew to a halt before the spacious grounds of the High Commissioner's mansion. Mrs. Fisk, the commissioner's wife, answered the door. She found it hard to believe that I was a fellow countryman, and regardless of my predicament she would not change my money for me. I finally had to resort to changing the dollars into rupees with a street money changer even though the rate was sadly less than official. Nathan kept Chin while I purchased my train ticket so there would be no chance of the ticket master seeing the monkey and charging for him as well.

I took the night train out of Lahore, which was scheduled to reach Quetta thirty hours later, baring any unforeseen delays. The train pulled out of Lahore about midnight and was not as crowded as the trains in India, so I found room in the luggage rack to bed down for the night. I lay awake figuring out how long it would take Rajah to get to Quetta. It looked as if the cards were stacked against me. If Rajah drove as fast, and as many hours as he could, he would be passing through Quetta about noon of the coming day, almost 18 hours before I would arrive.

Chin was tied outside the carriage to the railing of the steps and perched himself on the latrine window. Each time we came to a station, I would move him to the side opposite the station so that the inspectors would not see him. A young local started a conversation with me. He worked for the railroad, at Multan where he was now headed. I asked him if he could send a telegram to Quetta for me. Not only did he agree; there would be no charge because he would use the railway telegraph. I printed the following message on a scrap of paper:

To the Police Commissioner, Quetta:

A.T.Rajah, driving a red Triumph automobile will enter Quetta today. Please contact him. I am an American and must go to London with him. Will arrive tomorrow. Tell him he must wait. Thank you. T. Wallace.

The train chugged along the broad, parched, ancient Indus River Valley, once a vital cradle of civilization. There was nothing but sand, and more sand, except for an occasional brick hut, a few natives and their donkeys and camels. Each time the train stopped at a station, my chances of getting to Quetta on time were decreased. By early morning of the next day, the train passed through the city of Sukkur, and then headed northwest into the Sulaiman Mountains. The air became cooler further up the steep incline into the rugged, bleak mountain range. I could see a camel caravan in the valley far below, which seemed to be moving faster than us. We passed through Sibi where inspectors checked my ticket, but did not notice Chin who was safely hidden outside the opposite side of the carriage.

Late in the morning Quetta came into view with snow covered peaks forming a backdrop, and blossoming fruit orchards, green fields, and huts of mud and grass in the foreground. I readied my gear and Chin so that I could get off the train without delay as soon as it stopped. When it chugged into the newish, clean station, I hopped down and ran into the stationmaster's office. He had received the telegram and phoned the police commissioner to find out the red Triumph had come into the town the previous afternoon, but for all he knew, had already left.

I jogged up the road into town, looking for the red car. I had come this far, expended all my money, and I was desperate to find it. It could not have left without me! I asked several natives if they had seen it but none of them understood me, and just laughed at Chin. Finally a man told me that he had seen the car earlier in the morning up the street at a garage. I ran up the road to what appeared to be a repair shop, but looked more like a junkyard. Inside the gate I could see a small red hardtop sports car. Painted on the roof were the words: *Singapore to London – Overland.* A mechanic was busily working on the motor while two men stood watching. I asked the taller, more distinguished man if it was his car. He shook his head, and the short, dark man next to him spoke up.

"No, the auto belongs to me," he said haughtily with an affected English accent, eyeing me with disdain.

"You must be A.T. Rajah then- I am Thill, did you get my telegram?"

"Yes, I received a telegram, some idiot named Wallace caused me considerable apprehension."

"I'm sorry Rajah, I am Wallace, and I must get to Europe, I've been trying to catch up with you since Lahore."

"How did you know that I was going to London?"

"The Indian border officials told me. They said you are from Malaya. I've just come from there. Could I get a lift with you?"

"I doubt it, I don't even know you, and besides the other seat is taken up with my maps. Where did you get that nasty monkey? You're not planning on taking him along I hope."

"Oh, he's no trouble! I could put him in a box. Here is my passport, I've been studying in Australia and I'm just trying to get back home. I could help you drive, and I've been to Europe before and speak some German so that I might be an asset there."

"How much money do you have?"

"I've only got two American dollars now, but there is one hundred and forty waiting for me in Tehran. I will reimburse you for any expense I incur."

Rajah couldn't stop assessing my attire, dirty ragged backpack, and potentially pesky pet monkey. Clearly this was not part of his big plan and it would take everything, every skill I'd earned, to convince him if it were even possible.

Chapter 28:

The Little Red Triumph That Could

ONLY A CRAZY man would agree to take on a bum hitchhiker- and his monkey- for a thousand mile journey across unknown territory! However, the offer of help crossing the desert ahead alone no doubt caused him pause.

"I must be in London on May 3rd to attend a course in administration at Oxford. Do you have all the necessary visas?"

"I still need one for Persia."

"I am leaving early tomorrow morning without fail. If you have your Persian visa you may go with me; otherwise I will go alone."

I ran over to the Persian attaché's house, even though it was a holiday. I was desperate and did not hesitate to bother him. He was dressed in a black double-breasted suit, and looked at me through thick lensed glasses as he opened the door and invited me inside. He led me into his damp cold office and offered me a dainty Persian cigarette from his case. I told him I would like a visa and handed him my passport. He looked through without comment, holding it upside down. It was evident that he was not too familiar with the phonetic alphabet, although he did speak pidgin English after a fashion. I righted the passport for him and he stamped the visa, valid for fifteen days.

I raced back to the garage with the visa, and my permit to travel with Rajah. I offered him a thousand thanks for allowing me to join him.

He told me that as he had entered Quetta four men ran out to stop him and take him to the police commissioner, where he received my telegram. He had no intentions of waiting for "Wallace", but he had gone off the road the day before and damaged the car to some extent. In India he had hit a holy cow and ran over a goat. Therefore he had to lay over in Quetta to get the car repaired for the next sizeable city was Meshed, over a thousand miles away.

Rajah was not more than five feet tall with a plump body, brown-black skin, jet-black wavy hair, large brown eyes, a sparse trimmed mustache, and a straggly curly beard that was hard to see. The only thing I admired about his physical appearance was his teeth, which were perfect. Blended together, his combination of features formed a babyish-looking adult. Raja was of Hindu parentage, but he had been born and brought up in Malaya as a Christian. He had attended English schools, except for the duration of the war when he studied under the Japanese system, rather than be put into a common work camp. He had been an orphan, was now thirty, and a deputy commissioner of labor in Malaya.

Rajah had planned this trip for the past six months, and worked out every last detail on his planned route. But he learned as I had that the maps were not all accurate, there were no roads in parts of southern Siam, nor any from Bangkok to Rangoon. So he had sailed to Madras, India on a ship with his car, and had set out from there. His command of the English language was superior to mine. He was more a "devout" Christian than I, and yet it was obvious that he was miserably confused, for his customs and beliefs were basically Malayan, and Buddhist.

To start our forthcoming trip together on a friendly note, Rajah invited me to be his guest at Quetta's finest: Hotel Lourdes. It was not much by western standards, but it was clean and the food was good. That afternoon the Christian garage owner had taken me to the local Catholic School, for the Mother Superior Florentine was a fellow American. I had never before spoken to a nun, and felt a bit awkward at first. Mother Florentine was a middle-aged kindly woman. She introduced me to the other nuns all of them Europeans who spoke English. They did not see many outsiders, and seemed awed as they spoke to me. The school kids loved Chin, and one of the sisters from Ireland acted like a mere child in her delight-although she was far from one. Her speech and actions were that of a simple minded child. The Mother Superior was without question the boss in all matters, ecclesiastical or otherwise. One of them had had a birthday recently, and invited me in to finish the remains of the stale cake with instant coffee. The Mother Superior asked me about my trip thus far, and my expectations for the future. She considered me to be courageous, devoted to the betterment of man because of my travel, and insisted I take ten dollars American. I felt like an imposter, and refused to take the money, but she insisted, saying that it was a gift, so I took it.

Returning to the hotel, Rajah showed me the maps of our proposed route. He told me about himself, and how proud he was to have recently been commissioned a 2nd Lieutenant in the reserves of her Majesty's Army. Rajah had never been in the army, but through his superior education and government work he had been thusly appointed. He showed me his swagger stick and criticized our military system for not putting officers on a higher plain by issuing such swagger sticks- and batboys. It was evident that he had done considerable reading on military matters, and he considered himself to be Napoleon II. By his reasoning, he was a gentleman of the highest order, for officers are automatically gentleman. Rajah did not walk; he strutted about with an air of importance and authority. It was evident that we were of different make up but I was not quite expecting the treatment he had in mind.

His superior attitude unveiled itself the first day. Rajah ordered me to carry his bags out to the car before dawn. At first I did not want to aggravate Rajah in any way. I was so grateful to be getting a lift, when he told me that he did not smoke, I refrained as well. As we raced along the barren valley, Rajah put on his beret, and continually kept looking into the car mirror to preen, and rearrange his hat. He was dressed in fatigue pants, tucked into canvas jungle boots. He considered himself an English gentleman, because he was a reserve officer in the Commonwealth forces. It was ironic that he should consider himself an Englishman for the Aussie's and Canadians, who are closer to the British than the Malayans, are proud to be Aussies and Canadians, rather than to identify themselves with the British.

We were in the district of Baluchistan, famous for its bandits, and lawlessness. The gravel road was strait with level surface, and except for a few missing bridges, was smooth. None of the smaller streams were bridged. The road would suddenly dip where the water flowed over it, causing the car to fly through the air and crash into the opposite side of the dip, scraping the ground.

We purchased more petrol in Dalbandin, scouted around through the huts and found someone who prepared an egg with a chapatti and tea for each of us. By taking turns at the wheel, we covered nearly four hundred miles by dusk. We had our passports stamped for exiting the country at Nok-Kuni by an English speaking official who invited us into his hut for many cups of chi (tea) and sugar. The border was still many miles away but by knowing we were in the clear and going at top speed, we zipped past the soldiers waving us to halt only to find that in a few miles the road ended and a riverbed full of muddy silt took over.

Being an officer and a gentleman, it was not fitting that Rajah should wade through the cold stream to find a suitable course for the car to follow. "Well, what shall we do?" he asked. We could see the border village of Pakistan about five miles distant. Between the village and us was a two mile stretch of mud, streams and no road. In fact, we could not even see where-or if- the road began again on the other side of the washout. I felt like I was explaining something to a teenager.

"We can play it safe and wait here until the river dries up, or we can try to get across. We might make it, and if we don't, the car will be bogged won in the middle of the mess and either we will have to wait for it to dry up, or else the water will rise and wash the car down stream. It's your car, Rajah." This to a man not accustomed to being told bad news.

"Well, don't sit there and do nothing! Get out and find a suitable course for me to driver over."

I got out and waded through the water, checking several routes, and directing Rajah over the most solid one. We would progress about fifty feet each time. The car bogged down continually and we would have to push it out, only to get it stuck again. When darkness came I was still up to my knees in mud and water and then it began to rain. A Persian soldier halted us and directed us to the immigration house made of earth and straw, inside a walled courtyard. They checked our papers, and allowed us to spend the night in a mud hut. The walls were two feet thick, and the interior was damp and chilly. For chow we had C-rations that Rajah had brought along. I laid out my monkey skin mat for a mattress, whereas Rajah had the more civilized comfort of an air mattress. Fortunately, he did not ask me to blow it up.

The downpour had ceased by morning, but in its wake was plenty of water, which stood on the floor of our hut, and filled the courtyard. We had a rough time getting over the muddy rutted trail to the town of Zahedan, a large village. Rajah had the address of a local business man, which he had gotten from the garage man in Quetta, so his first job was to look up this "contact". Apparently a car passes through Zahedan rarely since the whole town turned out to witness our arrival. A local boy read the address and led us through the narrow walled alleys to the residence belonging to Rajah's contact, who was a man of comparative wealth. A high mud wall surrounded his house, and inside the barrier was a pool of water surrounded by fruit trees, and a patch of irrigated lawn. The mud and straw house was a large, two story structure with thick walls. The interior was damp and cool, but exceptionally well-decorated with Persian rugs, and antiques that had been passed down. Dozens of people stopped in during the day to pay a visit, sip tea with sugar and eat delicious little baked tidbits of pastry. Our first concern was to find out which of the two possible routes would be the best to take to Tehran, about a thousand miles away. We could go due north to Meshed near the Russian border and then west to Teheran, or the second route, which was considerably shorter, through Kerman and Isfahan. His words were not encouraging.

"There is seldom much traffic on either route, gentleman, but now both roads are impassable for the first one hundred fifty miles. You have come too early, for it will be many weeks before the washouts have been repaired. Each year when the snow melts, the rivers rise and our roads are washed away. They were built during the war and have not been adequately maintained since."

"What do you mean by impassable? That there is absolutely no hope of getting through?" I asked.

"Yes, I mean just that Mr. Wallace. Unfortunately our country is not rich like yours. People are too poor to afford cars and so roads are not important to them. Donkeys and camels will go where there are no roads at all." He went on to explain that even huge trucks, which transported crude oil to various ports and refineries, cannot get through now using the few existing roads. His advice was to wait in Zahedan to see if it rains, then have the car hauled by truck over the worst roads. "That is the only way you will leave Zahedan, unless you are willing to wait for many weeks until the roads are repaired," he added definitively.

We brought the car into his courtyard to avoid certain plundering by the curious populace if it were left on the street. We were warned that nothing was safe if unguarded because people led such a meager existence. We would have been unable to drive in town anyway: the crowds blocked the streets before us. I had learned long ago not to rely on the advice of others when it comes to saying that something is impassable or impossible. We had already wasted a day "getting advice" and in the meantime, the road conditions got worse. If we drove with caution and did not race into a flooded area, then we should be able to backtrack if conditions did prove to be impossible. Rajah agreed with this theory, so we decided to set out early the next morning.

The beggars in Zahedan were not as numerous as they had been in Calcutta, nor as skinny or deathly looking. However, the raw weather in Zahedan at present was too much for clothing consisting of nothing but rags, and more rags. Many of them wore no shawls, trousers, or jackets, but simply mealy bits of rags that had been sewed together from those articles. Their colors resembled that of a patchwork quilt, a striking contrast to the shabby condition of the garments.

A stocky, assertive youth approached me making all sorts of gestures, and pulled some money out of his pocket. I ended up converting the ten dollars the nun had given me for Persian tomans at a decent rate. Rajah had planned the trip so well that he had sent his money ahead to banks in various countries and carried only travelers' checks, which are worthless unless there are banks where they can be cashed. There are only a couple of banks in all of Persia, and Rajah's money was tied to the Bank Meli, in far off Tehran. We spent the night in a filthy flophouse. Beds were solid mounds of earth shaped like coffins covered with Persian rugs, with a candle as the only source of light. In the morning the cook served us each a bowl of greasy red slop, which Rajah could not stomach.

We got the car out of the courtyard, loaded it and headed north out of town, to attempt the "impossible". While we were fueling up just outside of Zahedan of the edge of the barren dessert, the sky blackened, the wind gained force, and within seconds, sand began to rise in an ever increasing cloud to the west. We watched it move toward us, and suddenly we were blinded and pelted by a dense shower of sand. We slammed down the hood and covered our faces, but could hardly breathe and retreated into the mud hovel with natives. Within fifteen minutes a deluge of rain drove the sandstorm away. Everything was covered with a thick film of red dust. Rajah's hair and beard had turned from black to earthen-colored.

The rain was welcome in comparison to the sand, so we headed north into the empty vast expanse of barren desert, broken only by equally barren, rugged mountains. The road was no more than a trail. We crept along in second gear, stopping continuously to move rocks and boulders from the road. As we proceeded into the higher country we came to streams and rivers lacking any sort of bridge. Each time I was appointed to wade through the water to check on the depth, a freezing and miserable ordeal. There were no villages, no huts, and no people. Then the road ended altogether having been washed out for miles by floods, which left deeply eroded land in its wake.

Fortunately we had purchased a shovel in Zahedan which came in mighty handily as I began to rebuild the road so we could proceed. We would climb up on the top of a hill and search the desolate terrain to the north for a hint of where the road began. The valley was about ten miles wide with rugged ranges on either side. We knew that the road would run north through the valley, but the question was, where? Many times we would take the smoothest route only to find that we would end up on the bank of a ravine and have to back track. Rocks scrapped on the metal shield protecting the car's underbody, sounding like a bulldozer working in a rock quarry. Even low gear was too fast. The speedometer cable broke, so we had no idea how far we had come by nightfall. We had been on the trail for seventeen hours, and guessing we had covered a hundred fifty miles, but later learned that we had only gone forty miles for an average of less than three miles per hour.

Often during the day the car got hung up on a solid rock, and we would had to use the jack to build a foundation under the wheels so that we could drive forward. Rajah did not care to drive at night for he admittedly had poor vision so I would take over. The clouded sky withheld any light from the heavens, making it inky black everywhere. We had hoped to spend the night in a village but had not seen a single vehicle all day. I hastened our speed, but within a few minutes there was an awful scarping sound and the car lurched to a halt. I got out the flashlight and checked our predicament to find that we were hung up on a rock ledge.

Had the car jack not broken, we would have gotten the off the ledge, but since it did, we would have to think of some other solution. After a few unkind comments from Rajah, I grabbed my sleeping bag and Chin and rolled out on the wet rocky ground. Rajah preferred the comfort of the car for the night. It was not a pleasant thought to be sleeping in the middle of an empty riverbed with streams trickling on either side of us. Earlier that day we had just crossed a small stream, to look back and see a wall of water had filled it to overflowing instantaneously. When we looked for the cause we noticed the heavy rain falling in the mountains to the east, yet not a drop fell on us where we stood.

As I lay down on the cold damp ground I noticed a beam of light to the north. At first it looked like a star, but then bobbed up and down, going out of sight, only to return again a few minutes later. Rajah's first reaction was that of fear thinking it might be a group of bandits signaling. He cursed me for getting the car hung up. We waited for the light to come closer, at times appearing to be miles away, and at others, only a hundred yards away. We listened but could hear nothing but drizzling rain and trickling streams. Then the light vanished, and we gave up thinking that whatever it was had changed course and went to sleep.

I was awakened during the night. I could sense someone was near, and opened my eyes to find the silhouette of a bayonet rifle and a heavily clad man towering next to me. He shouted something at me. I crawled out of the sack and carefully stood up to find that the light came from a truck parked a few feet away. Soldiers surrounded me within seconds. One of them spoke pidgin English, and I explained what had happened. Rajah just about crapped his diapers from fear when one of the soldiers checked inside the car and shook him. I managed to convince the driver to tow us off the rock, which sounded as if guts of the vehicle were being pulled apart from all the scraping. The soldiers hopped into the truck and rolled away, leaving us to spend the remainder of the night in place, rather than to take the chance of getting hung up again.

We had C-ration rice and tea for breakfast. Rajah had a tube of condensed milk, but did not want to share it: being an "English gentleman", he required milk in his tea. I did not particularly care for the taste of milk in tea, but I was more concerned with the nutrient value. Rajah got the car hung up a half dozen times, and then gave up in desperation, so I took over the wheel and drove. The Triumph had surprised me completely. It went through places that I did not think a jeep could go. It was a powerful little car, its main fault being that it had so little ground clearance. A native dressed in burlap with a shawl over his head approached with his camel. He was shivering and indicated that he wanted matches, so we gave him a pack. (back cover photo)

At one point, we found an abandoned fender lying in the sand. We strapped it to our roof because we never knew what we might need next. We had just stopped to take a leak, and Chin was tied to the front bumper to keep him from wandering off. Suddenly, almost out of nowhere appeared a jeep with angry locals gesturing wildly at the fender on our roof and yelling about "Polizei". It took a minute to realize they must have assumed we had stolen it. We thrust the fender back to the ground and tore off as fast as our car would take us. It wasn't until five miles later that I realized with horror and dread that Chin…was still tied to the bumper. I made Rajah go and look first as I couldn't bear the thought of seeing Chin harmed. But there he was, clinging underneath to a shock spring with teeth barred in terror. I promised him right then and there that he would have a banana every day for the rest of his life. He promptly crawled inside my turtleneck where he stayed for days.

The road improved in stretches, but when it got worse, it was really bad. We ran into an area of hailstones that were the size of agates and piled six inches deep. They were so numerous and large, I thought it was rock salt. All afternoon we passed through streams, one of them so deep that that the water washed in over the window and the car started to slide. I jumped out and pushed before the car had a chance to be washed off the roadbed. Sometimes I would wade through streams to check on their depth, as often as ten times to the mile. I was miserably cold, and irritable.

As darkness closed in we passed through a small village, but did not stop. According to the map, Birjend was only an hour's drive, and as it began to rain heavily we wanted to get there before the road got any worse. The road had already turned to gumbo mud, but without rocks so that I could drive as fast as the car would go without worrying about the undercarriage. We were racing through the mud, which caked the windshield. Darkness came accompanied by more rain as we tried to push and dig the car out along the way, water was rising and washing the road out behind the car as we inched forward. The mud was so sticky that it pulled the sole off my dress shoes, which I was wearing while my leather boots dried out.

By crawling around in the mud and water I finally got the car dug out, and with some stones behind the wheels and a good shove we worked our way off the ridge. It was time to admit defeat, turn the car around and head back to the village we had just come through for the night. It was a tiny village, surrounded by a high mud wall, with a few dome shaped mud abodes. The village was in total darkness except for the flicker of a fire on the floor of one of the huts. Rajah was relatively dry, but cursed the road, Persia and me as he stalked into the hut like the Shah himself to complain to the native of his dilemma. I felt like a drowned rat, and hung my pants and shoes on the bumper of the car so that the rain would wash them.

Rajah ordered me to bring his bags into the hut, but I refused. I was getting tired of being his valet; the ride was not worth it, I was doing all the dirty work, and there was no end to it. I put on my dry pants and ate by the fire, while the native poured us tea, and chipped chunks of sugar from a large block of it. Rajah strutted around the dingy cold hut with his swagger stick, and the beret cocked at an angle on his head. He asked the native for some food, but when he got a blank stare for an answer he began to raise his voice, finally shouting at the bewildered native. Through pantomime, I explained to him that we would like to eat. I followed him out to the street, and down the road to a neighboring dark shack. He lit a candle and opened a dusty wooded chest as it if was a treasure cache. Persian bread was all it contained, similar to pancakes, but hard, and about two feet by one foot in size. I counted out ten of them and paid him and returned to the hut to show Rajah my find. He was far from pleased. It was filling, and that was all I cared about at the moment. I warmed up by the fire while Rajah ate but one loaf of bread, and called me a glutton when I continued to stuff myself with the other nine, washing them down with tea and sugar. Rajah parked his car as close to the door of the hut as possible and then emptied it of all his possessions, afraid that the local inhabitants would walk off with them during the night. The Persian bed of clay with a rug for a mattress was large enough to accommodate the four of us. Rajah wanted me to reassure him that we would be safe from bandits. We had learned in Zahedan that two Americans attached to the Persian government had been killed by a mob of armed bandits who were still at large. But that was a long way away and did not seem worth worrying about to me.

The sun shone brightly in the morning, but the air was frigid, quite different from unbearable heat that I had expected to be the normal temperature for Persia. My pants and sho es were not where I left them on the car the night before; apparently someone needed them worse than I did. We left town only to be halted by the washout that had turned us back the night before. Fortunately the water had receded to quite an extent and by hauling earth into the resulting crevasses we managed to get the car through after a considerable delay. Within the next hour we reached Birjand, the only town of any size we would encounter until we got to Meshed, another one hundred fifty miles north. The muffler had fallen off by now, and as we roared into town the crowds started to gather.

We slowed to a crawl to avoid running over the people in the packed streets, dozens, then hundreds of natives had started following us. We parked in front of the military police barracks and walked off to get some chow. Our eggs were cooked in goats grease and tasted strongly of wet goat.

We returned to where we had left the car, but could not get near it: there were easily five hundred and fifty excited Persians crowded around the car. A police officer checked our papers and allowed us to wash at a spring inside the courtyard from a spring that was used to irrigate a decorative garden. The officer was inspecting his police force in ranks as we washed, and issued some orders. They promptly filed out through the archway to the crowd and started to beat them away with their clubs. I had tied Chin to a tree, they had never before seen a monkey and were reluctant to leave. Unfortunately those on the inside of the ring of people could not retreat from the blows of the police due to the rear of the milling crowd pushing so close to get a better look at us, the car, and the monkey.

The police chief would boot a child in the rear end for tossing food to Chin, and then would feed the monkey himself, much to the crowd's displeasure. The crowd began to murmur, and then roar. The police did not want things to get out of hand, and insisted we leave. We got into the car but were so hemmed in by people, we were unable to move. As a last resort, the guards formed around the car and then spread out with fixed bayonets, dispersing the crowds enabling us to roar away.

The road out of Birjand was much better for the most part, except when we hit an unusually deep water hole and the car would conk out. Then we would have to dry the spark plugs before we could get it to run again. We passed camels by the hundreds as they plodded along in their lethargic indifference to life. Eventually, the radiator sprung a leak so we had to stop a couple of times an hour to refill it from the water we carried in two collapsible canvas bags. We refilled the bags with water from a clean spring that flowed down a hillside beside which a woman was squatting in her shabby tent, scraping fat from a white goat skin smeared with blood. A few feet below where we were washing, a scrawny girl was cleaning the matter from the expired goat's intestines, an appalling mess at her feet and on her arms. When she finished, she did not stand up, but hopped away using her hands as feet, a crippled and doubled up creature.

We refilled the water bags and headed north again. The land became dry and we soon ran out of reserve water for the car. Not knowing how far we could get, we headed quickly toward the nearest village on the horizon, intending to refill the water bags. But as we neared the walled town we noticed that it looked a bit strange for some reason. Many of the domed huts were falling apart as if the town had been severely bombed. We learned Persians build a town and when the buildings begin to tumble after many years, they simply move on to greener pastures, rather then rebuild them. The town was a goat village, with not a soul to be found. I raced through the village on foot, looking into vacated huts in hopes of discovering a well, or a least a mud puddle where we could get some water for the radiator with unsatisfactory results.

We drove more slowly after that so the car would not overheat, but it did anyway, and we would stop and wait for it to cool before driving on a few miles when we would wait again. We finally reached a catch basin full of muddy water, filled the radiator and the bags, and continued.

Next came th e drifting sand, and the end of the trail. We headed north by the sun and intermittently found what had once been the road. Every few miles we would run into a sand dune, and plow through it like hitting a snowdrift head on, only the sand did not give way so easily. The car lurched around, the sand blinded us, and the fan sucked it in over the motor and forced it through the floorboards. I was beat from being at the wheel all day and let Rajah take over, determined to reach Meshed before sleeping.

Raja drove like a madman, or a novice.

"Thill, wake up! I think we missed the road!" shouted Raja excitedly. I looked out to find that water was flowing toward us. I got out and surveyed the situation. Instead of fording a river bed, Rajah had mistakenly turned upstream. I pushed him out of the hole, and took over. He had come half a mile from the original road. When I found it, I continued, noticing a dark shadow ahead on the opposite side of the road, which the headlights did not penetrate. I had learned not to drive unless I could see- and slammed on the brakes to stop, but the brakes would not hold. They were set from fording so many streams. When we reached the brink of the shadow, the car bogged to a complete halt.

I got out to see what caused the black hole, and heard rushing water coming from a ten foot drop into a pit. I backed the car away and headed off the road and after much circling around found a place where we were able to ford the stream and head north. We calculated that Meshed could not be far off, and continued to drive even though visibility was nearly void. Rajah did not attempt to drive, for he had as little confidence in his driving at night as I did in him. All night long, our little car cut through rain, fog, and mud, fording streams continuously and eventually winding up through mountains.

Sometime during the darkness I came upon a bus that was stuck in a mud hole. The passengers were mulling around trying to push it out. I gave them a hand, and when the bus got out the passengers pushed us through. For the next couple of hours, the bus driver and I took turns leading the way, while the other would follow the leader's tail lights. It was treacherous, nerve-wracking ordeal, for to miss a curve would mean to drop hundreds of feet into a ravine throughout mountainous area.

When I could take it no longer, half asleep at the wheel, the muddy trail that we had been on for the past three days ended abruptly and we came upon a modern four lane highway. For the first time since we started our journey together, we were able to drive without wondering where the road might be. We headed toward the lights of Meshed shimmering brightly through the rain in the distance.

The city was about as lively as a morgue at two in the morning, and miserably cold and damp. We drove around looking for some sign of life, at last came upon a teashop across from a mosque. We wasted no time in getting in by the fire in the tiny cubicle which was crowded with what appeared to be the riffraff of the city. The other customers stared at the car and us as we drank several cups of tea. Rajah sacked out in the car, and I ended up on a floor made of stone, hard and cold, but dry. A few of strangers pulled back the shirt that covered my face to look at me, but I did not return their glances, too tired to be bothered by them.

The four lane paved highway ended just outside of Meshed and once again we were confronted with washouts. Late in the afternoon we came onto a bus that was lying broadside in the road, on a curve in the mountains. A large truck hauling crude oil was trying to pull it out. The rear of the bus hung precariously over a precipice. No one had been hurt, but all of the passengers were pushing the bus sideways to try to get the bus back on the road. Their team efforts were successful after many attempts and we all pressed forward.

As darkness came we were still a long way from Tehran so we stopped for the night in a small village, surrounded by scores of curious natives as usual, while a police officer checked our papers. The people were so excited that the officer became frightened of the growing mob and suggested we leave his village at once. We were able to assure him that we had encountered much larger mobs, and that regardless of where we stopped, the people would crowd around us.

We walked into a busy little cafe and pointed to tea, rice, and some greens. The proprietor led us to a special cubicle in the rear of the cafe, so we would not disturb the other customers. Candles illuminated the cubicle, and we sat on Persian rugs to eat. Three of the other customers could not resist our presence and came to stare at us as we ate. Chin helped himself to my rice. The natives thought it was funny and motioned for me to unleash Chin. I did so, and within seconds he was out of the room, hopping across tables and the shoulders of other customers, then into the kitchen, into the yogurt bowl, knocking over dishes and out the front door. The restaurant was in an uproar. I dashed down the dimly lit street after the monkey, along with scores of people racing after the evasive monkey. He ran into a tiny grocery shop as the proprietor was bringing in the goods from the sidewalk to close up for the night. Within seconds his little shop was packed with people. Everyone was shouting, "Chin, Chin!" The proprietor did now know what all the excitement was about as we pulled crates and bags out from the wall, crawled under the counter and dashed out of the shop after Chin who had escaped all of us.

By now the police were after the monkey. They could not control the mobs that seemed to be blowing off steam as if they had been suppressed for ages. I finally cornered Chin, and he jumped on my shoulder. The policeman ordered me to chain the monkey and get out of town. I tried to explain that even though Chin was on my shoulder that he was far from being caught for he would not let anyone pick him up. The officer did not understand this, and made a grab for the monk, who sprung to the ground and ran down the street. By now hundreds of people were running up and down the street, swinging sticks in the air as if a revolution was going to break out. I finally caught Chin inside a courtyard. He was as limp as I from the chase and I had no trouble scooping him up. The whole town had been entertained, with the exception of the police who were furious because their authority had been unheeded and they had been powerless to halt the excited crowds. Rajah was highly upset at being forced to leave town because of Chin.

We drove to the next village where we found a hotel of sorts. It was a one room affair, a combination restaurant, kitchen, bedroom, and washroom. Chin was a welcome guest, once again the entertainment for the evening. A beggar ate the scraps which had been given to Chin, further disgusting Rajah who had parked his car on the doorstep and brought all of his belongings inside, including the spare tire. We slept on familiar earthen platforms, not realizing we were silently being invaded by red lice during our sleep. They were uninvited parasites for the next two days, and even Chin was bothered with them. Rajah would not admit that his body could be a host for lice, but from the way he scratched himself it was obvious that he had something.

By noon the next day we reached the outskirts of Tehran and the paved road, which we refereed to as the "propaganda stretch": it was becoming the rule for towns and cities to have a few miles of broad paved roads, so that the average native would think that his whole country had paved roads and hence would feel their taxes were being well spent. We passed many oil refineries, and before long we were in the hustle and bustle of Tehran itself. The amount of traffic, and new automobiles was astounding. It seemed like a false city, like an oasis, for the surrounding country was nearly barren, and the people lived in primitive poverty.

The car was so caked with mud, it was impossible to tell that it was painted red. Our first stop was the Bank Meli, the main bank of Persia. We parked on the street in front of the modern bank, but within seconds curious onlookers blocked off the street. Traffic had come to a halt. Policemen descended upon us and told us to pull up on the sidewalk. But the crowds only increased and blocked the entrance to the bank. Rajah cashed his money and returned to the car but we could not move until the police cordoned off the road and allowed us to proceed. The car was in need of a few minor adjustments, but Rajah was mainly interested in spending the afternoon and night in a gentlemen's lodging. He found a pension operated by a Hungarian woman for ten dollars a day, including board.

The American Embassy was not far away. I walked over to pick up the money that I had requested be sent to me. The hundred forty dollars had arrived, but it was in English pounds, which meant I couldn't sell it on the free market for as much as dollars. It seemed great to have money again, even though it was earmarked for passage fare across the Atlantic. Rajah had taken the car to get it repaired while I shopped around for more Persian and Turkish money at the best rates possible. The only drawback with changing money on the street was that it is highly possible to get obsolete money in exchange for stable currency. I checked with three different money changers to verify all sold the same kind of Turkish money, and I exchanged a few dollars worth. The Turkish Embassy said that it would not be necessary for me to get a visa in advance, that I would be assured one at the border.

I went to the bank Meli and spent two hours haggling with officials to convert part of my English pounds into American greenbacks. I knew I was authorized to do this, but the bank was reluctant to let them go. My friend Hunger was lingering in the wings after so many C-rations and I was finally able to do something about it. After a delicious meal of rice and goat, I bought two pounds of shelled walnuts to be eaten later.

The car fixed, and we left Tehran the following day headed for Tabriz. The propaganda stretch did not last very long, and we were soon back on the dirt road again. The air turned much colder, and by nightfall it was freezing. Ice formed on the puddles and over the rutted road. The radiator froze and the water began to boil. When it reached boiling temperatures, we would stop and let it cool off. We refilled the radiator many times, but it did not work. We pulled up before a small blue mud shelter and ran inside where we were greeted by soldiers huddled around a warm stove. They spoke no English, but understood what was wrong with the car when we pointed to the radiator. They managed to produce a blow torch and I crawled under the car to heat the radiator. The flame was not long enough to heat the radiator through the grill, nor could I get at it properly under the hood, or from under the car. I hailed down one of the drivers of a huge oil transporter who took one look at the situation, mixed oil and gas in a can and dipped a rag covered stick into it. Then directed me to start the car while he lit the torch and shoved it into the grill aperture. The fan sucked the flames through the radiator, the paint caught fire and blistered on the front of the car, but the temperature gauge suddenly went down to normal and we refilled the radiator. We also covered the grill with rags to keep out the cold air. The driver demanded ten tomans, about a dollar, for his services.

We paid him and roared away, but before long we were in the same predicament. We crossed many streams, and had to wade through the frigid water to check on the depth so many times that my feet were numb. The engine got so hot that it lost power. We drained the water from the engine and then carried our gear inside a warm, local hut, where the family had nothing for us to eat. Rajah ate C-rations and I devoured all two pounds of walnut meats, which became sickening as I finished the last of them. For a few cents we were allowed to sleep on musty rags on a clay platform in an unheated, damp cubicle.

When morning rolled around I was in acute agony, doubled up so that my elbows touched my knees. Thinking that it might be a recurrence of the sickness I had had in Burma, I told Rajah that I could not continue. He wanted to leave me- and would have- only he dared not venture forth alone. The man of the hut understood that I was sick and sent for a soldier doctor. Sometime later a raggedy looking, burly young man looking more like a professional wrestler than even a horse doctor, stomped into the hut. He carried no implements to diagnose my ailment. He just dragged me off the earthen bed and stood me on my feet, but my torso was bent over, and I could not straighten up. He stood behind me, grabbed my head with his strong hands, forced my body to straighten out, shoved his knee into my spine and bowed my head backward. I thought my stomach muscles would sn ap. Never again would I eat two pounds of nuts, even though they were inexpensive and filling.

A couple hours later, I was ready to move, but the car was not. We lit another fire by the grill and started the motor. Once the radiator thawed out we filled it with water and headed for Tabriz, the last large city in Persia before we would reach the border of Turkey. The road was so muddy that we had to stop continuously to wash the mud off the windshield so that we could see where were going, not to mention many streams to cross. By night fall we had not covered many miles, and pulled up behind two tank trucks at an inn of sorts standing alone on the high plains. A mud wall about nine feet tall surrounded th e main mud building. We drained the water out of the car, and carried our junk inside. Two truck drivers and the inhabitants of the establishment came out to watch us in the drizzling rain.

Chin's leash came loose, and he climbed up one of the few small trees to jump to the roof of the hotel. The proprietor was after Chin like a bullet, racing up on the truck and jumping onto the wall and domed roof, chasing him around the dome. Chin ran around the whole courtyard with the man was in pursuit, but the undermined wall, weakened from the rain, caved in from his weight. He fell to the ground and raised his arm at the monk, and shouted in anger. We ran through the hut and into the courtyard in time to see Chin sprint from the roof into a fruit tree. The small limb he was on snapped, and Chin fell to the ground but was off again in a flash. Everyone was excited, except Rajah, who was on the verge of tears for he thought we would be kicked out of the place for allowing so much trouble. I finally trapped him in a small hut, behind a crate of liquor bottles, and took him into the hotel.

The little establishment was crowded with tanker truck drivers and everyone was eager to see the monkey. It rather riled Rajah to be ignored whereas it was a relief for me, to be left alone by people. It was snowing outside, and we were warm and entertained.

We headed west early the next morning with Rajah at the helm. I fell asleep in the passenger seat only to be abruptly awakened by him shortly.

"Wake up, I think we are stuck!"

I looked out through bleary eyes to see that we were in deep snow. Rajah had never seen snow until this trip and knew absolutely nothing about driving in it. Surveying the situation, it did not look like a jeep could get through, let alone a Triumph. Huge tank trucks were the only vehicles using the road, and they had made deep ruts, leaving a mound of snow and ice piled in the center of the one lane road. I dug the car out and backed up for two miles where we were able to turn it around. We went into a teashop to warm up and study our maps. We had been told that this was most unusual weather for Persia in April, but it was no consolation to us. It looked like our only solution was to backtrack, and head south for Bagdad, Iraq, hundreds of miles out of the way; no telling when the snow would melt here. There are no such things as snow plows in this part of the world.

Before we had gone the first twenty miles, we came upon a British Land Rover parked on the side of the road. A blonde-headed man was directing a couple of laborers who were repairing a washout.

"What are our chances of getting to Bagdad?" I asked him.

"What do you want to go to Bagdad for?" asked the Englishman.

"The damned road ahead is blocked with snow. We're trying to get to Europe."

"You won't get to Bagdad either. The roads are blocked there, too."

We got out the map and showed him where we had planned to go. From Bagdad, the only road to Europe led through a narrow portion of Syria.

"Even if you got to Bagdad, you would not be allowed to cross that strip of Syria. They don't even allow commercial aircraft to pass over their country. Your best approach, would be to wait here until the snow

melts."

The two laborers were leaning on their shovels watching us. The Persian interpreter was listening to our conversation. The Englishman turned to the interpreter and snapped his orders.

"Tell those two bastardly idiots to stop looking so stupid, and get to work. It is no wonder we can't improve the roads when everyone is so backward."

Rajah wanted no more driving in the snow and insisted I take over. We turned around and headed back into the snow. (see photo 15) The bottom of the car dragged along through the ice and snow. Luckily the wheels were in the mud and got enough traction to push us through after a fashion. It was like riding a bobsled the way the car bounced around in the ruts, ricocheting off the banks on either side of us. Many times the car went out of control and I would have to dig it out while Rajah slept- or pretended to- so that he would not have to get out into the slop and do some manual labor.

Our next obstacle was a roadblock created by a purple, battered, American car- a Kaiser. Of all the places to find a car! I ran up to find a man underneath, and another handing parts to him. Inside were an attractive middle-aged woman, and a huge police dog.

Franc, the younger man, was a husky Frenchman from Paris. The gentleman and his wife were from Belgium. They looked like gypsies, unshaven, muddy, and in shabby clothes, but I am certain I looked a lot worse. Fritz spoke only French and some German, while his wife spoke French and some English. We introduced ourselves, and told each other of our goals. They too, were headed for Europe, but their transmission was not working properly. They fixed it temporarily, and we agreed to follow each other so that we could tow each other out of the snow banks.

The snow kept getting deeper until it was impassable. We backed up to the nearest roadside hut, where we decided we had no choice but to wait for the snow to melt. The hut itself was rapidly disintegrating, but it too, was our only choice: it stood alone with not another hut as far as the eye could see. The landscape was bleak and vacant looking, the sky was overcast, and the cold wind cut through us, numbing our hands. Rajah woke up, surprised that I had linked up with such unkempt looking people. We found our way into the crumbling, dark and musty one room building. Melting snow was dripping through the roof and the earthen floor was soggy with mud.

As my eyes became accustomed to the dark I could see that two of the walls were lined with earthen platforms that served as beds. The only source of heat was a small, unlit wood burning stove that stood in the center of the room. The kitchen area had dirty dishes and clay pots strewn about. In the far corner was a real bed where a woman poked her head out from under a quilt. Her complexion was wan, and her hair matted and disheveled. She threw back the covers, revealing a baby she was nursing, as well as a man, a young boy and a girl. The woman pulled the baby from her and placed it between the others and pulled the quilt over them. She was dressed in filthy pantaloons and a sort of long sleeved dress. She stood up on the bed and shouted at us, then walked over with the grace of a donkey to get a better look. To keep out of the mud she stood on the table. She spoke no English, French, German, Malayan, Chinese, or Hindustani so none of us could converse with her through language. After much charades and haggling we were able to communicate that we wanted to spend the night in her establishment.

We brought all the gear from both cars into the hut, each of us claiming a section of the platform for a bed. Fritz and his wife Hilda tested the western bed which sagged miserably, but after they stashed gear under it, became more comfortable. The witch of the house got her boy out of bed and made him start a fire. For fuel he broke up a wooden crate and stool. Fritz brought in his Coleman lantern so that we would be able to see. The man of the house got up only to be chased out of the building, never to be seen again.

Poor Rajah-his hands were chapped. He had never experienced cold before, and kept looking at his appendages, now red and rough, and asking me if he would ever be the same again. Being a gentleman and all, it was very important that his hands retain their smooth texture. Rajah huddled next to the stove, hardly consoled by my mutual concern that his hands would never be the same.

Meanwhile, Fritz, Franc, and I drained the water from both cars, and then jacked up the Kaiser using mud bricks taken off the back of the hut to use for blocking. It did not hurt the back of the empty hut, which was originally used for animals. A second room in the outbuilding was used for the toilet. Part of the wall between it and the living quarters had crumbled, and whoever said that frozen human dung does not smell has not spent any time with it. It took great dexterity to make my way safely between the piles to find a vacant spot upon which to make my own deposit.

After intense work with cold hands, the three of us removed the gearbox from the car and took it into the hut to work on it.

The little girl was huddling next to the stove for warmth while the young boy was cutting up an old truck tire and tossing pieces into the fire for fuel. The rubber really burned hot, but the smell was overwhelming. Smoke billowed out through the upper portion of the sieve-like stove pipe, filling the room with a dense fog. One their wall was a large propaganda poster of the Shah of Iran (Persia) surrounded by pictures of factories, roads, and farms, which he had brought to Persian life with his modern, progressive government. Below images were several lines of morale boosting slogans.

The witch noticed me staring at the poster and stomped over, clenching her fist and shaking it at the Shah's picture, raising her voice as if swearing at him. She pointed to the broken down stove, leaky roof, muddy floor, and pinched her nose from the smell. She pointed an accusing finger at the Shah's picture and spat on it. I shook my head in sympathy, which was misinterpreted immediately.

She took my arm in what could not be anything but a proposition, pulling me toward her bed. Fritz roared with laughter.

"How about some tea?" I said as I pulled away from her.

"Why, Thill, I am surprised by you! The woman finds you charming and you refuse her," chided Hilda.

We fixed some tea, and mixed some of our rice with the witch's eggs and fed all of us. A tank truck pulled up outside, the driver coming in to spend the night. He seemed surprised to find Europeans in the place, but after eating a few slices of Persian bread washed down with tea, he did not hesitate to crawl into her bed for the night. We went to bed immediately after the evening meal to conserve fuel and kerosene. There was no telling how long we would be stuck here.

The dismal days of cold and damp in miserable conditions all the way around continued. Hilda stayed in bed, as did Rajah until a fire was lit, and tea made which we had for breakfast with bean. Truck drivers ate with us and continued on toward Tehran. Fritz served his wife breakfast in bed, which sickened Rajah. He could not understand how a man could stoop to playing valet for his wife, never mind that he expected such service from everyone around him.

The little baby coughed and cried throughout our stay. It was a wonder any babies survived under such conditions, or would not be crushed when sleeping in a bed with four other people. At one point, the little boy started beating his sister, and when she cried he beat her even more. His mother did not intervene. We were puzzled, and through pantomime she explained to us that she was afraid to reprimand her son for fear that he would retaliate when he was older and kill his mother. It had happened before nearby, and she did not want to take any chances. The dire secrets we would never have known had weather not locked us together so intimately.

Fritz repaired the gearbox as best he could, and Franc and I gave him a hand putting it back in the car. Rajah was becoming apprehensive about continuing on to Europe: if all Europeans were going to be as uncouth as Fritz, Hilda, and Franc seemed to be, why bother? They wanted us to join them and share in the expense, telling us of contacts they had and guarantees that if we accompanied them we would have little trouble with the police in Turkey or Yugoslavia. Rajah was most unhappy when Fritz and I conversed in German, and broke out in laughter, convinced we were conspiring against him. It would not have been a difficult thing to do in such a desolate place.

There was nothing to do but shiver and wait. It was too dark to read, and there was nothing to read anyway. Our feet were soaked and cold from the puddles around the muddy floor about the stove. On the sixth day, we were standing next to it talking when I saw the little boy jerk a stick out of the fire. When he darted back, a ball of flame enveloped his greasy clothes. I pushed Fritz and Rajah aside and chased the boy who was running around the room screaming. None of the others had seen what happened in a split second. I grabbed the boy and squeezed him against me, smothering the flames, which had singed his eyebrows, hair, and blistered his stomach badly. Even his mother was frightened as the boy continued to scream. Hilda plastered the burn with face cream, the cleanest most hygienic thing she could find. It was surprising to find that the boy was not naturally as dark as we had suspected, but in fact was several shades lighter once the layers of dirt were wiped off by the ebullient face cream. We had not seen any of the natives wash since we moved in with them, and warm weather was months away, so there was no hurry.

The second week, the witch tried to seduce me again, this time standing on the bed to sing and dance, motioning me to join her. I tried to deflect her interest toward Franc, and lastly Rajah, but I guess she liked my beard better than theirs. Fortunately she did not have to go long without a man because two tank trucks stopped that evening and their drivers entered our rancid abode to partake of the evening meal. Again the witch had herself a man.

My bed was adjacent to hers, and as Fritz turned out the light she gave me a last, almost pleading glance as if to say "Going once, going twice… gone." We could hardly condemn the old girl for being practical; it was about the only way to insulate her illegitimate family from the cold.

We were all getting restless to be heading west. Our food supplies as well as our host's were running low. The snow was melting, and our only chance was to get through before it snowed again.

Chapter 29:

Rejoining the Civilized World: Impressions from Pakistan through Europe

THE BOTTOM LINE is this: the heart of my 32,000 miles of travel challenges, as well as the most enjoyable, was from Singapore to Calcutta. Once I met Rajah, my trip changed from the exploratory cross-cultural mission it had been to more of a roadless desert-crossing marathon laden wi th mechanical challenges. We had transportation, could drink the water (in Europe), and find safe food and shelter each night, making for far fewer lasting memories. I will share a handful of highlights, 'moments of connection' or 'memories treasured' if you will, for the balance of our journey back to Alaska.

From Pakistan we went into Iran and traveled just south of the Afghan border. We were able to cross into Iran in Zahedan, a border town with little traffic. The only way to buy gas was in five gallon cans, which we poured directly into the tank. It was approximately six hundred miles of dirt road from Zahedan to Mashad, with a stop in Birjand along the way. We would drive up the nearest hill or rise and search for the illusive road. Often times there was no road at all, and we would just have to wing it by guessing the best route. The impoverished natives who spotted us would signal us to stop because they were looking for matches to start their fires. They were that poor. Sadly, we had no matches to give them.

For the most part, Chin was an asset providing a lovely entrée to strangers, and a comforting travel companion on so many lonely stretches. He required very little food and was the absolute best insect catcher in the world, just snatching mosquitoes from the air with his deft little hands, and eating them. But a few times he stepped over the line, and caused me some real angst. I usually had to hide him inside my shirt if I wanted to eat indoors. Once, while having dinner at a restaurant in Turkey next to a group of Russians, all of sudden a small monkey hand reached out and grabbed the forkful of food go ing to my mouth. So I had to expose the monkey and suffer the consequences of bringing an animal into an eating establishment resulting in immediate expulsion to the street.

That was nothing compared to the near heart attack I had in Germany when he *disappeared.* It was nighttime and Raj ah had gone off to find a nice hotel room. I as per usual, paid twenty-five cents for a dive of a room and smuggled Chin under my clothes, sneaking under a sign that said no animals were allowed. Each bedroom area wasn't much bigger than a bathroom stall and the bottom and top were open, just like a bathroom stall. I went to sleep with Chin tucked safely inside it with me, where he slept well. In the morning I went to the rest room and wrapped him in the sleeping bag so he could not easily get out just in case he woke up to find me missing. Unbeknownst to me, when I was in the bathroom he sneaked up the stairs- and out the door! When I got back I was surprised to find that Chin was nowhere to be found. I had vivid memories of his escapades in Singapore where he went into someone else's room and destroyed their belongings, food, film, and cigarettes so I was feeling the urgency of finding him immediately.

In desperation, I went to ask the clerk if he had seen a monkey, but he said they didn't allow animals in there. I hated to admit I had an animal because the sign said no animals and I'd broken the rules. But his memory came back to him and he said, "Gee, come to think of it, a few minutes ago, some kids up on the sidewalk were playing with a monkey." He had seen a man come along who talked to them and then walked off. I figured, my God, maybe the man bought Chin or something. I feared I'd never see him again and I really felt bad, as I had been traveling with Chin for six months now and wanted to get him to America.

The only thing I could think of was to put an ad in the local Munich newspaper stating I'd lost my monkey and describing Chin and where I'd lost him, listing a reward for any information.

I was feeling completely down-hearted and figured I'd never see him again.

Unbelievably, a man who had my monkey finally called. Not only did he have him, but he also begged me to come and get him! He was a professor and had bought the monkey for about four dollars from the children in the street and wanted to get rid of him right away. So I took a streetcar to his apartment and of course Chin was running loose and raising hell, busting china, climbing on the curtains, and the man couldn't catch him. I finally caught him and then the professor wanted me to reimburse him for his investment of four dollars, but I didn't have the money. I held my ground that I was doing him a favor by getting him out of there. It's hard to admit how much emotion I felt having that rascal back up on my shoulder, and it would be the last time we would be separated where I did not know his whereabouts.

Istanbul, Turkey is where east meets west. As we approached, we crossed a very long bridge over the straights of Bosporus. The blue tiled giant mosque has become iconic since my time there-marking the city so majestically. Turkey is mountainous, not so much jagged peaks, but rolling mountains and farmland being cultivated by oxen. Roads continued to be a challenge; we never knew whether the road would go through or disappear into a dead end. There was virtually no additional travel, except for an occasional beat up bus with broken windows.

The military had a strong presence, especially near Erzurum where the dark-attired people were especially interested in our little red car.

As we passed through Erzurum we saw nothing but military for many, many miles. Rajah was quickly back to treating me like his batboy, which was fine, always staying separately in higher end housing. One night, I met an American solider who was in the Air Force and we ended up at a big and fancy embassy or some type. There was a large crowd dressed in tuxedos. I'm not sure what the party or celebration was all about and the details from the night are hazy, as I had quite a few complimentary drinks, but this much I remember: I ended up with a German woman in my room. When I went to leave in the morning, I checked my back pocket for my wallet and realized it was missing. I went back in to the room, and could see that the girl had taken my wallet because it on the counter in the bathroom so I grabbed it and ran out of the house. I remember a doorman dressed in a tux as well trying to stop me from running out of the room with a wallet in my hand. I pushed him aside and ran like hell before anyone could come out and get me. I don't remember what I did with Chin, and I don't remember where Rajah was- and I don't remember how I got in there in the first place, other than meeting a G.I., who was stationed there in the air force. I must have met up with Rajah again and we got out of Istanbul. So much for alcohol, a lesson now permanently imprinted in my brain.

We were in Thessalonika, Greece a few days later. Interesting to me is that what I remember is that the Greeks were eating butter shipped from America under a "Feed the World" program and there were cases of butter that had been donated by the US Government, as it was only eight years after WWII. It was bothersome to me because even though by most standards, I was brought up in a well off household, we were taught to be frugal and we were eating Oleo at home, and here in Greece they were eating U.S. butter-and they were eating it for free.

Also critical in what would become my future upon return to Alaska is that Rajah and I met some people that had a roofing tile business making roofing tiles- by hand. It was interesting to me because my brother Art and I had plans to grow a similar operation in Alaska where we would be making cement blocks- by hand. It was a man and his wife alone who were making all these tiles by hand. All the houses in this region used these roof tiles to fend off the elements. We spent the night with these people before we headed further North, and I was able to study their methods, and would eventually draw upon this and other observations I had made throughout my travels to grow what would become a very successful business, Klondike Concrete, in Chugiak, Alaska.

After Thessalonika we headed through Yugoslavia and went through a small town named Titogard (which in current day is called Podgorica), named after Tito, who was an important, brave Yugoslav fighter during WWII. He was a Yugoslav revolutionary and during WWII was the leader of the Partisans, and led a most effective resistance movement in occupied Europe. This is where Rajah and I splurged, well *I* splurged, Rajah always had money, by eating in a restaurant that had a real floor in it, for the first time in a couple of months. It was a big hotel with a cafe and we went in the evening for dinner. At that time in Yugoslavia, the lights were electric but they were only as bright as candles.

We were the only ones in this ornate, opulent restaurant except for one college age male. He spoke English and asked Rajah where we were from and Rajah immediately said, "America." I was surprised to hear him say that because even *I* often told people I was from Canada to avoid possible conflict due to residual feelings about the war. The guy immediately queried if it was North or South? When we told him North America, he told us that you could talk about anything at all, except politics. Apparently politics was a very touchy subject in this part of the world if you were from North America. I didn't realize until much later that there had been a lot of violent conflict there. The U.N. was there, keeping the peace. Everyone thought it was safe. However, a chilling fact reminded us all that was an illusion: seven hundred males from the opposition had recently been brought to a rural area and slaughtered, all seven hundred of them, right in front of the U.N. troops.

THE ROADS TO Belgrade were terrible. Besides being cobblestone to begin with, they full of bombed out holes from the war. It was bumpy as hell, a constant physically jarring reminder of recent invasions and attacks. As we went through Graz and stopped for a beer, I tied the monkey to a street sign out in front of the beer hall. Graz is not a gigantic city but a decent sized town. I ducked in for a quick beer and came out came out to find soldiers walking away, one of them with Chin on his shoulder. He was already a block away and I ran to catch up with them and asked the soldier where he was going and he said he was just taking the monkey. I told him that it was my monkey and luckily- convinced him. The reason he took it, he said, was that the news had reported a monkey had "escaped from the zoo". That was his alibi anyway; never mind that the monkey was tied up when he took him. Fortunately I didn't have to fight to get Chin back, and I learned my lesson to not tie him up in public.

By now, Rajah and I had traveled together for six weeks, and it had come time to part ways once we arrived in Munich. There was simply no more reason that my "service" was needed, especially since we rarely ate or slept in the same places anyway. We had crossed a major, road less desert together, and weathered some pretty miserable conditions during transit. Despite our many tense times and very different world views, I was grateful that I had arrived safely, and hopeful that the feeling was mutual, even if not expressed. It was an amicable separation.

I had to smuggle the monkey on an airplane from Munich to Berlin where I was determined to try to find my former army troop. There, I sequestered Chin in a bombed out, abandoned building while I went to search for them at the Army base. I found the barracks where my unit allegedly was stationed, but then got the official song and dance. Military relations were bad enough and everything was top secret so the military guards did not even admit that they were there. As much as I tried, evoking every tactic I'd learned along my journey, I never did find them. I hope they will know I gave it my most sincere efforts and I pray they all survived any deployments.

Since I was so close to the border, I could not resist sneaking across into East Berlin. I was curious and wanted to go just for the hell of it. The way I achieved entry was on an underground train at night. It was legal to get in, but illegal to get out. I got off in a city unknown to me and was careful to avoid drawing attention in any way. I boarded a streetcar, trying to be as inconspicuous as possible. Soon a drunken German came and sat next to me- the last thing I needed! He started to interrogate me, but all I could speak was rudimentary German. Still I was able to figure out from the questions he was asking that the streetcar driver knew I was an American. I didn't want to get in any trouble so I got off the streetcar at the next stop, disappearing into the crowds.

I had to walk a hell of ways until I found a restaurant on the left hand side of the road. It was a busy place and I tried to be as invisible as possible, planting myself amongst a bunch of filled tables. But as soon as I sat down, I noticed diners immediately vacated the tables around me: it was obvious I was not one of them. When the waiter came, I asked for a menu in my broken German. He asked me a question about the menu and I replied "etwas zu essen"-something to eat. By that time I figured I had better get the hell out of there, and I left without eating. This was before the Berlin Wall and I still didn't know if I could cross the border back to the American sector (West Germany), or not. I was highly anxious but found luck was once again on my side due to the late night and distracted ticket taker on the east side.

As I came near the Danish border, I spent the night with Chin in a partially harvested cornfield on the side of the road hidden out of sight from traffic. I still had the monkey skin hide to sleep on: it had been my mattress for the entire trip. Cornfields are nice places to stay hidden and the continual rustle of the leaves is akin to sleeping by an ocean. It was a relief to have no worries about insects or snakes this far north and I slept well.

The next day I got a ride in a yellow Volkswagen Bug. I put my pack in the car and learned the driver was going into Denmark, so I was able to cross the border with him. He went into the Customs house to answer questions and a border guard came out to the car questioning me, asking about any animals, food, or contraband. I was a filthy figure with my jacket stained from the monkey crapping on my shoulder for the past five months. I said, "What do I look like, somebody that would have something like that?" He started going through my pack, which was behind the driver's seat, as there wasn't much room in the Bug. He saw the monkey fur pelt sticking out, which gave him reason to question me. It was kind of comical as he was searching through the monkey skin, and right next to it was a real live monkey rolled up in a sleeping bag, under the seat just inches away.

In Copenhagen at a train station, I had to secure Chin in a storage locker where I'd continually stop to feed bananas, bread, and water to him. I was not allowed take him with me very many places in "civilization". It strikes me as ironic that the higher up in the economic chain, the less humanity shared with animals. And to me Chin was practically my child. To tie him or leave him behind was always troubling, but I was determined to get him home to Alaska.

Once, when I was walking down the street I got on a streetcar and a little boy walked up to me and said, "Mommy, Mommy, here's Daddy- I found him!" It was embarrassing, but gave me a sobering pause to consider yet another side effect of war. How many children lost their fathers in the war, and how many others were the products of U.S. servicemen who simply left once the war was over? In Denmark alone, estimates range from six to eight thousand left behind during WWII. The precise number of "War Children" will probably never be known due to the shame, or fears of retribution for the perception of "corroborating with the enemy" that is imposed on the mothers left behind to raise these children on their own. Or equally troubling, these children, often of mixed heritage in Asian countries, are abandoned, or left to be raised in orphanages.

Serendipitously, I ran into a top reporter for the oldest newspaper in the world, the Berlingske Tidende in Denmark. His name was Paul Westphall, which was coincidental to me because we lived on Westfall Avenue near Rochester, New York for years when I was growing up. He was responsible for an article about me after spotting me walking down the street with Chin. I don't know what I looked like at the time- if I had my Naga sword across my chest or not- but it couldn't have been pretty. I spent the night at his house enjoying dinner with him and his beautiful daughter. He also took me on an unforgettable night tour to the Tivoli Gardens, right in the heart of the city.

The main reason I wanted to go to Copenhagen was to see my old friend, Doris Marx, who was there. When we parted in Australia, she was headed to Europe to continue her studies in textile design. As much as I still cared for her, she seemed rather surprised to see me, probably having given up on the idea. Doris wanted to introduce me to her parents who had traveled to visit her in Australia after my departure on the world's largest Swedish luxury liner. Now I learned her mother had suffered a tragedy on their way back. Apparently she had been asleep when the ship held a safety drill, and awoke to the ship's doors closing before she was able to get out. When she tried to stop the doors, her hand was caught, amputating four fingers and her entire palm.

Her parents were lovely people, with plush accommodations. I remember large, soft pillows. The linens on the guest bed were also top of the line. You notice things like that when you've been sleeping on dirt floors and in cornfields on a monkey pelt for six months. It was a day or two before my flight home, and I had the personal guilt of knowing that while I luxuriated, mooning over Doris, Chin was waiting for me in a storage locker. If only I'd known then that she would eventually visit me in Alaska in 1959, I might have been able to feel less heartbroken as I left.

I was able to fly this time because of an insurance policy my grandfather had gotten me, which I cashed in, for the trip home. I went to a major airline to get a ticket with the monkey inside my black turtleneck sweater, which I often wore to keep warm and hide him. I should have known better; the ticket seller took one look at me and knew something was up. "What about your monkey?" she asked.

I said, "Do I look like someone that would have a monkey?" It was that very morning the article in the Berlingske about me, with a good sized picture of me and Chin, had come out. She refused to sell me a ticket because she knew I had a monkey and I had to figure out another plan because I was not leaving him behind, not after all we'd been through. I ended up shipping Chin on VIA airlines from London to New York for a grand total of forty dollars. The cheapest way for *me* to fly was on Icelandic airways via Reykjavik.

Our first stop was supposed to have been Oslo, but the airplane had problems and landed in Stavanger. It's a beautiful village and the airlines bought us a meal in a real interesting local place as compensation. After Stavanger, we flew straight to Iceland. The plane was a two engine DC3. Sitting across from me on the plane was man with a guitar who was constantly playing a song about 'Maryann and the shifting sands'. He played relentlessly, but softly. They brought a meal to each of us and I noticed how sloppily he ate, even though well-dressed in a white suit. He barely used utensils, instead stuffing most of the food into his mouth with his bare hands. I thought somebody who was that well-dressed would have been taught good manners, so I wondered how he could eat like that in public. After dinner, I reached out to him and learned about the song, about Maryann, and why it meant so much to him: his seven year-old daughter was killed in a house fire and he had been badly burned on his hands and arms, trying to save her. His clumsy table manners were because of the deformities in his limbs resulting from that fire. Once again, I was humbly reminded that you could never judge someone without walking in his or her shoes. To this day I cannot hear that song without remembering his life of pain. "Down by the sea shore, sifting sands, down by the sea shore, Maryanne."

Chapter 30:

Coming Home: Re-entry Blues and Recovery

BY THE TIME I made it to New York, I had fifty cents to my name. I wondered how the hell I could go to find Chin with no money for ground transportation. Somehow I managed by walking and bumming rides, including a fast escape from a bus for which I did not pay. Once reunited with Chin, I wanted to get to my parents' place near Rochester, which was three hundred fifty miles away. My only option was to hitchhike. When I finally made it to them after three days on the road, I was so sick, weak and tired that they barely recognized me.

I spent a good month at my parents' house recovering. I had some tropical disease that they never did properly diagnose. I had yellow jaundice, Sprue (an intestinal disorder like Celiac disease), and later I learned that I had malaria, which was not a surprise given how many millions of mosquitoes had feasted on me over the course of my travels. Eventually I recovered from all of these, but it took a good, long while.

While in the process of patiently recuperating, I figured one of the best things to keep my adventuresome spirits aloft was to try to go across Lake Ontario from Canada in a fifteen-foot boat at the tail end of a hurricane. The object was to get our deceased family doctor's boat back to America. His son asked me if I would go with him, and I was helpless to resist the challenge. Chin wanted to go, too, as he had become leery of any type of separation from me after his lonely trans-Atlantic flight. We drove more than one hundred miles to the west end of the lake and spent the night in their cabin. Their wooden boat, a fifteen-footer, hadn't been in the water since the previous summer.

It was roughly sixty miles to cross, and unbeknownst to us, even big freighters weren't running because of the storm's wake. We took off in rough water and after several hours and thirty-five miles out on the lake; we could no longer see land. The boat leaked like a sieve, and we had waves coming over the top. I was wearing a field jacket with Chin tucked snuggly inside. We were exhausted and the water was waist deep in the boat. Our food was floating back and forth. We were so tired of bailing water from the boat that we were almost ready to welcome drowning just to be done with it all. We got the bright idea that maybe another ship would see us at night because we had a couple of flashlights. We could see a ship off in the distance but we were hidden because the waves were so big. Then our engine quit running and the sail's cables to the mast became disabled. The doctor's son hung the uninflated rubber raft from the mast as a distress signal.

In what must have been at least my ninth life by this time, a giant ship changed course way out in the lake and headed right towards us. We thought they might run us over. It was a British Petroleum America ship and there fifty sailors lined up on the deck taking pictures of us. I thought for sure they were going to just take our pictures and leave. I was sure they were going to let us drown; I couldn't imagine a big ship coming out of their way. Indeed they started to depart much to our collective woe. But they were just angling to approach us from a different direction. The scary part was being tied up to a three hundred foot ship as it rose up in the waves and came crashing down. We climbed aboard, while one of the sailors retrieved what they could find from our little boat.

When I got up on the ship, I took Chin out of the inside of my sweater and those guys couldn't believe I had a monkey with me. Someone made a joke that we were out on the middle of Lake Ontario "monkeying around". They tied our boat to the rear of the ship and towed us into port in Kingston. Unknown to us, the ship had radioed the U.S. Coast Guard, who called our parents and said we had been sited- but they didn't think they could save us. Thanks to this premature evaluation, our poor mothers were left with the impression we had drowned. Eventually we called our moms who came to Kingston and picked us up. We went into a restaurant and had a hamburger. It was quite simply the best meal I ever had, as I never thought I'd be eating again.

After finally recovering enough to travel again, my brother Art endowed me with a 1951 Hudson and my cousin Chappy donated eleven tires for the unpaved journey across Canada to Alaska.

You can rest assured we used every damn one of them.

Epilogue

Reflections on Global Travel

I WROTE THIS manuscript from memory while recovering at my parents' house in Upstate New York upon my return. I had not kept a journal while traveling for a number of reasons including bearing the weight of yet another object, lack of writing utensils, and severe weather often soaking my entire backpack. When looking back on the trip there were so many decisions, thousands of decisions and I was just a naïve twenty-five year-old guy. My journey became one of doing the impossible, of doing anything necessary to survive. I had been brought up with so much confidence, I never questioned my ambition to take a westerly route all the way back to Alaska. In some ways, that was the beauty of it all. I was so ignorant; I was fearless and open to everything. I had hoped to work my way around the world but quickly learned that wages were so low in undeveloped countries I would never make enough to pay for travel. The truth is I lost over twenty-five pounds and was very weak for most of the time because I would not offend people by refusing their offerings of food, even when it was unsanitary or unappealing as sheep's blood. It was vital to my survival that I was not perceived as a threat or superior to the people upon whom I relied throughout my journey- but that philosophy also almost killed me.

When I left my hometown, I was so brainwashed all I wanted to do was fight the communists. I had no idea of all the other struggles facing people around the world. I had no idea Malaya was under guerrilla attack, or that the KSOB was there, or why. A map of the world shows many countries and borders, but these are all imposed by leaders with separate agendas. The every day common man does not realize any benefits from drawing borders around pieces of land. In my travels, I found very few people who had the time or resources to go more than a few miles from home due to fear of the known. Most natives did not dare to venture far from their communities their entire lives. The majority of the world's population- I'd say ninety-nine percent- is so busy feeding, clothing and sheltering his own family, he has no time for wars. It's ludicrous to me that so many lives are lost and resources squandered in the pursuit of intangible power, and excessive material possessions. Given all the beauty and abundance of our planet, can't we all get along?

My motivation in the beginning of my travels was to be a sort of 'goodwill ambassador' for my country. I had read *The Ugly American* and didn't want the world to see us as portrayed in that book. I loved my 'supremely advanced' country so deeply; I felt a need to set the world right in their perceptions of us. I believed we did not come from a "mean place" or were a country that would knowingly do wrong to others. Instead, we took in the poor and downtrodden from all over the world and gave them a chance at a shared dream. While I learned that we are not necessarily without fault in our international actions, I also learned to have a compassion for all the world's peoples and I have come to the conclusion there are many "right" ways to live. I viewed us as equal beings no matter what fortune- or lack of fortune-bestowed upon us due to luck or place of birth. The villagers near Nakam with only three eggs among them did not hesitate to feed me. The poorest people in Burma laughed the most often. I was not judged for being dirty or having no money to pay for so much that was freely given. Instead, I was welcomed as a traveler, revered for the courage I was exhibiting by leaving my comfort zone and breaking bread with them, gratefully. That is a lesson about humanity I will take to my grave: wealth is a relative perception and we have much to learn from the hearts and cultures of others.

I admit I was not a good correspondent. I sent only one letter to my parents- which caused them untold anxiety, and have not maintained contact with anyone since the trip. Rajah did correspond with my parents which helped relieve their anxiety, and continued to do so for a few years after the trip. They knew that I may not have survived the trip if it were not for him, but I held a bad taste from his treatment of me. I only heard from Rajah indirectly when a religious zealot who knew him passed through Anchorage and asked to meet with me. What I took away from that meeting was that Rajah might have joined some type of religious cult. For all his bravado, he was still very much searching for meaning internally.

The only map I had for the entire trip was a world map. It was a sacred thing as it was the only thing I had to go on but gave a big picture more than any specific direction; there were no roads on it. By the end of the trip it had big holes in the seams because I had unfolded it and folded it so many times.

On the whole, I spoke little English in my travels. People have to communicate and so that left me to use pidgin English, or ridiculous charades that made my look like a fool. I think Americans in general live in a type of accommodation of other languages and culture, but lack a genuine inquisitiveness, which would serve them well in travel. I'm all for getting to know our neighbors: they are never as bad as we've been told. We need to lose the high school mentality of having invincible rivals and get back to being open, receptive and tolerant. My advice to travelers is to learn as much as possible in advance of going to a new country. A little understanding and appreciation will go far in connecting with your hosts. Eat and dress according to their customs. The only time I was ever almost robbed was the only time I wore my suit. I also suggest that you go while young, before you have the attachments of work and family: old enough, but not too old. Learn to travel as slowly as possible. I could have easily spent an entire week in each place I spent only a day. It is the only way to see the minutia of differences; even *within* a single culture there is so much to learn.

I'm hoping I've made the world a little better place having been here. I know Chin had a bit of adjusting from his jungle lifestyle to the years he spent with us in Alaska afterward, losing a good bit of his eighteen inch tail to frostbite one bad winter. But I am ever grateful for his companionship and his 'bridge' to so many people as we moved among strangers. Children, music and animals all share a common language.

I like to believe I have influenced others to travel. (see photo 16) I love the concept of 'broad horizons'. My second cousin took a 'round the world trip' years after I came back, and ended up marrying a girl in Argentina. Travel for *extended* experiences. I have taken my children traveling throughout our country and Mexico by RV for months at a time. I encourage young people to get out there and see the world, helping whenever you can. When I did this trip I wasn't trying to 'get anything' out of it; I was simply trying to get home. So much in the world has changed including much more ease with the physical aspects of travel; more roads, types of transport and frequent air travel. However, with ISIS, Ebola, and the growing threats of global terrorism, I can't imagine doing the same trip now.

As for me, my own heart was finally filled when I met Ella, my wife of fifty-five years, a young Swiss girl (see photo) riding her bike across Canada and up the Alaska Highway with two girlfriends. I was immediately won over by her kindred adventurous spirit, damn near making a fool of myself chasing her all over Alaska, looking for the white hankie she would tie on the bushes near their campsites. It was for her that we created a homestead on the side of a mountain overlooking the grandest of all our country has to offer, from the sparkling waters of Cook Inlet to the continent's most majestic mountain, Denali (formerly known as Mount McKinley). As we felt growing up on our farm in childhood, it finally dawned on me that there was no place else I needed to go. Being here is like living in a national park. We have spent our lives living where most people only dream of vacationing. It is from this vantage point that I count the blessings of a life well-lived. (see photo 17)

I find it interesting to be this close to the end of the road, and to realize how much time I wasted. I hope others who read this will be inspired to use their time to see our amazing world, and to do as much good as possible while on earth. I'm saddened to see how importance of the pursuit of money, and the holding onto it, has taken over so many lives. People have always told me that I should "write a book" about my travels so I leave you my story, but I'd much rather just live it all over again, every step of the way. I shall take my final sleep with visions of cattle wandering aimlessly around the streets of India and elephants moving teak logs through rivers in Malaya, the fairyland of shining ice on the jungle greenery viewed through my frosty breath in Kyaukme, and my fellow man wearing colorful patchworks of rags in India, wearing shoes made from burlap sacks and shreds of tires, and their millions of toiling, busy hands of so many skin colors shaping abodes and crafts of daily living, while chattering away in dozens of languages I do not understand but which still soothe me. Above all else, I will feel the comfort of a thousand small gestures of kindness, completely outnumbering a handful of moments of vague fear that only pushed me to become a stronger, more purposeful human being.

Like I said in the very beginning, I'm one lucky guy.

Photos

1. My Nagga machete carried for most of my trip after trading for an army surplus knife.

2. My infamous near death experience during paratrooper training.

3. Venice, 1954 on a weekend pass from base.

4. The pack I bought in Australia and carried around the world.

5. Crossing the Nullabor Desert with Aussie mates over the Christmas holidays.

6. Ed Rice, and the lovely Doris Marx and friend on our ship between Hawaii and Australia.

7. Visiting with the locals in transit near Fiji.

8. Parade in Burma, celebrating a religious festival unknown to me.

9. Flanked by headhunters in Burma, as well as translators.

10. Official paperwork necessary to take Chin across borders.

11. From the pages of the Singapore Tiger newspaper.

12. Chin Peng

13. Myo and Khin's overladen truck which allowed me to earn my ride on the Stillwell Road using my mechanical skills

14. My ride with leaking barrels of gas on the Stillwell Road.

15. Rajah's car at higher altitude somewhere before the Pakistan border toward the end of our journey in the red triumph.

16. My Swiss miss, Ella, whom I was proud to marry and share life in Alaska for 55 years.

17. At my 50th reunion where my classmates were most interested in hearing about my travels.

18. In 2010 before my illness took hold.

The other images are of just two of the kind families who took me in along the way and for whom I was eternally grateful.